VISIONS OF CREATIVITY
IN EARLY CHILDHOOD

Connecting Theory, Practice and Reflection

JOY LUBAWY

AMERICAN EDITION

Redleaf Press®
www.redleafpress.org
800-423-8309

Published by Redleaf Press
10 Yorkton Court
St. Paul, MN 55117
www.redleafpress.org

Redleaf Press edition 2010
First published in 2009 by Pademelon Press, 7/3 Packard Avenue,
Castle Hill, New South Wales, 2154, Australia; www.pademelonpress.com.au.

Cover design by Jim Handrigan
Cover illustration by Claire Schipke
Interior design by tania edwards design
Chapter opening spreads and top photo on page 122 by Jim Handrigan
Printed in Canada
17 16 15 14 13 12 11 10   1 2 3 4 5 6 7 8

Excerpts from *Eight Ways of Knowing: Teaching for Multiple Intelligences* by David Lazear, copyright ©
1999 by David Lazear, were published by Hawker Brownlow Education.

"If You Go Down to the Woods" by Edward Gill first appeared in the October 2005 edition of *The Ecologist,*
© 2005 by *The Ecologist.* Excerpts reprinted by permission of *The Ecologist;* www.theecologist.org.

"Life's Rainbow" by Sheila Banani was originally published in *When I Am an Old Woman I Shall Wear
Purple,* copyright © 1987 by Sheila Banani. Poem reprinted by permission of Sheila Banani.

"Music Promotes Motor Skills," "Importance of Outdoor Play," and "Fostering a Love for Nature" were
originally published in *ExchangeEveryDay,* copyright © 2005, 2006, and 2007 by *Child Care Exchange.*
Excerpts reprinted by permission of *Child Care Exchange.*

"No Way, The Hundred Is There" by Loris Malaguzzi, translated by Lella Gandini, was originally published in the Catalogue of the Exhibition "The Hundred Languages of Children," copyright © 1996 by
Preschools and Infant-Toddler Centers—Istituzione of the Municipality of Reggio Emilia, Italy. Excerpts
reprinted by permission of Reggio Children.

Untitled poem on page 233 by Patricia Cameron-Hill and Shayne Yates was originally published in *You
Won't Die Laughing,* copyright © 2000 by Patricia Cameron-Hill and Shayne Yates. Poem reprinted by
permission of Shayne Yates and Patricia Cameron-Hill.

"When the Currawongs Come Down" by Ernie Constance and Slim Dusty, performed by Slim Dusty, was
originally recorded on *Stories I Wanted to Tell,* copyright © 1986 by Slim Dusty Enterprises Pty. Limited.
Lyrics reprinted by permission of Slim Dusty Enterprises Pty. Limited.

Library of Congress Cataloging-in-Publication Data
Lubawy, Joy.
  Visions of creativity in early childhood : connecting theory, practice, and reflection / Joy Lubawy.—
Redleaf press ed.
      p. cm.
  Includes bibliographical references and index.
  ISBN 978-1-60554-038-2 (alk. paper)
  1. Early childhood development. 2. Creative ability in children. 3. Arts—Study and teaching (Early
childhood) 4. Education, Preschool. I. Title.
  LB1139.5.A78L84 2010
  370.15'7—dc22
                              2010013538

Printed on acid-free paper

For Yvonne Winer, more than 30 years mentor and friend

Acknowledgments

First, I would like to thank my partner, Peter Law, who suggested this book, encouraged my creative thoughts on long car trips and supported my development of the structure for the book. Peter has been a constant support—reading the manuscript, asking questions, making suggestions and helping with corrections. He has been the Information Technology specialist and support person I so often needed.

Second, I would like to thank my friend, Daphne, who has shared many hours in the swimming pool with me as I talked about my aspirations for each chapter, listened as I explained the insights and awareness that were developing about each topic and, finally, read each chapter with enthusiastic and valuable feedback.

Thanks also to Sue, Barbara, Monique, Trish, Kathy, Tracy, Mary and Kristy whose enthusiasm and encouragement of any project I have been involved in has been much appreciated. I would also like to thank The Braggers (an email support group for anyone working with young children) for their ideas and support.

Thanks to Rodney and Carmel Kenner from Pademelon Press for giving Australian educators a voice!

Last, but certainly not least, thanks to the children who have shared their lives with me, who have trusted and talked with me and shown me what they know and think about. I cherish their stories in my memory.

Foreword

In my first year of teaching, the principal of my school helpfully presented me with a "creative craft" book for young children. Eager to impress, I dutifully devised a program using this and other "crafts for young children" books as the cornerstone. The program relied heavily on crepe paper, cellophane and teacher-made cardboard templates. What followed was a year of just surviving really. But, in my second year, I began to realize that I was doing little more than keeping the children busy.

It became obvious to me that, despite the title of the book I'd been given, this work wasn't creative. In fact, these so-called creative crafts actually *stifled* creativity—both mine and the children's. Nor was it education. Tracing around a ladybug template did no more to teach a child about ladybugs than did tracing around a triangle. I could see that the children were doing none of the thinking, yet shouldn't thinking be a central tenet of education? This realization set me on a voyage of discovery. It led me to books by Piaget, Erikson, Dewey, Freire, Gardner and Bruner, among others. It took me to the writings of Loris Malaguzzi and twice to the city of Reggio Emilia, where the education of its youngest children is taken as seriously as the education of the rest of its children.

And, it took me to a woman named Joy. I first heard of Joy when a colleague breathlessly told me about a wonderful workshop she'd just been to in which the presenter, a practicing early childhood teacher, had talked about enriching the block area with cloths, stones and figurines. This presenter, and her friend named Yvonne, explained how to make tabletop shadow puppet screens for the children to use to tell their own stories. And about all the wonderful ideas she had for using music in the classroom. And there was more. Of course, the presenters were Joy Lubawy and Yvonne Winer—Joy's mentor and friend to whom this book is dedicated.

That was ten years ago. Since that time I have had the privilege not only of attending Joy's workshops myself but also of getting to know her as a warm and humorous friend who lives her life with openness, generosity and passion. Joy knows that creative early childhood education has nothing to do with teacher-designed cardboard ladybugs and that it is much more than merely keeping children busy. Rather, Joy knows that a quality approach to early childhood education requires a deep respect for the capabilities and competencies of young children and their families. She knows about the centrality of relationships and the need for a stimulating environment full of interesting, meaningful experiences and interactions. And she knows it requires large amounts of energy and a great deal of reflection, all liberally sprinkled with a dose of fun. In *Visions of Creativity in Early Childhood*, Joy's stories from her many years of experience give us an insight into this complex dance of connections between children, teachers and families within the context of the physical, social, emotional and cultural environment.

In this book, Joy's stories bring this dance alive. Her vignettes provide practical insights that make real the richness, complexity and possibilities for early childhood education. The warmth and wisdom of her stories illustrate how educators can bring together many ideas such as those of multiple intelligences, emergent curriculum, Reggio Emilia, developmentally appropriate practice, the project approach and student-centered learning. The result is a meaningful and authentic approach to early childhood education.

In her workshops Joy speaks of the power of the narrative, that we are all storytellers and throughout history important facts and ideas have been transmitted generation to generation via the story. Joy brings her love of narrative to this book. An eloquent and engaging writer, she is a storyteller herself who listens patiently and appreciatively to the stories of the children she obviously knows so well. The real-life experiences she shares with us encourage us to listen more reflectively and to risk being close to the children we work with.

Joy's own journey as an educator mirrors my own—and that of many of our colleagues, who will no doubt read this book, nodding as they read—as it recognizes the changes and challenges that have been so much a part of our professional lives. Joy's openness to new ideas means that she has been at the leading edge of change for some time in Australia.

This book is candid, a warts-and-all, taking-risks kind of book. Joy reveals her inner thinking, her mistakes, her wonderings and her awe in the presence of a young child. It is a book for all teachers of young children, experienced or inexperienced. How much different my first year of teaching might have been had the principal been able to give me a copy of *Visions of Creativity in Early Childhood*. Now it will be a wonderful resource to support and inspire my work.

Jane Merewether
BA, BEd (ECE), Early Childhood Teacher, St. Mary's Primary School, Bunbury WA

Contents

CHAPTER 3
Exploring Kinaesthetic Dimensions   67

CHAPTER 4
Exploring Mathematical and Logical Dimensions   93

Introduction

This book emerged during conversations with my partner, Peter Law, as we traveled in the car. I have been presenting in-service sessions for people who work in the childcare and education industry for many years, and the questions most often asked were about curriculum design, documentation, creativity and imagination, how to manage stress, and how to bring all the ideas together in an achievable way.

My own fascination with Howard Gardner's theory of multiple intelligences began with a series of workshops with Dr. Julia Atkin. I began to see the theory as structure for our reflections about creativity and enchantment in young lives and not just as a method of making sure we catered to all children in every part of the curriculum in some sort of check-the-boxes method. Thus began the journey, physically and metaphorically, to bring these ideas together in a book that would be useful to practitioners, students and academics.

I have watched with interest the swings and roundabouts that the early childhood sector has enjoyed and endured over the last 30 years, while being constantly reminded by Dr. Yvonne Winer of the history and philosophy that stretch back a hundred years or more. Dr. Winer helped me find my philosophical and educational roots and to measure each new influence against what we already knew. So, I have watched—and at times participated in—the rise and fall of objectives and outcomes, developmentally appropriate practice, teacher-directed activity-based programs, the struggle for acknowledgment of play as something intrinsically essential, the influence of Head Start and, in most recent years, the wave of influence from Loris Malaguzzi and the educators from Reggio Emilia in Italy. I have considered the zone of proximal development from Vygotsky and created my own understanding of what he meant. I have thought about the scaffolding theory from Bruner and realized it originated from the physical help we give a constructing child and that it altered to become the metaphorical and philosophical approach we understand. These educators (and others) bring me to where I am today and the message I want to share with the reader about a core belief in the intelligence, integrity and ability of the young child and our role as a more knowledgeable and experienced learning partner—a facilitator and guide, a helper, helping the child reach forward to grasp the next exciting possibility and assisting wherever necessary in the preparation for a life's journey.

I wonder if we can call this approach a *connective* curriculum, meaning the way we bring together a variety of theories and influences alongside our own research and experience. I hesitate to use *integrated*, because this has other special education connotations and *holistic* or *child-centered/focused* seems to have had its day somehow (though it is still with many of us). *Connective* is more than all of these things because it brings together the philosophy, theories and practice alongside the development of a strong curriculum. It's not just about child development; instead it's about children discovering, theorizing, experiencing, and learning. It's about telling the learning story, and from this the development story will also become evident. It's the child's learning that takes the center stage. Let's bring these ideas together. Let's connect!

Welcome to the journey.

The Author

Joy Lubawy grew up on a sheep and wheat farm in Eastern Australia, enjoying a free and natural environment. As a young adult she first chose a career in nursing and then later, as a parent of two young daughters, began studies in 1974 leading to a career educating young children aged three to five years. Time passed—her daughters now have children of their own—but Joy's passion for young children's learning still burns brightly.

Joy was a teacher at Kurrajong School, Wagga Wagga, for children with additional needs for almost two years and then the teaching director at Charles Sturt University Campus preschools for 24 of the next 26 years, followed by a short time at Kingfisher preschool before her retirement from the classroom. She has been a distance educator with Charles Sturt University for 15 years and is the co-author of a highly successful book (with Pademelon Press, Australia), *Building Walls of Wombats,* as well as a new publication (with Gryphon House, USA), *Preschool Math.* She is also co-singer/songwriter on two CDs of songs and stories for young children, titled *Wombats in the Belfry* and *Play, Dance, Sing with Young Children.* Joy has also self-published *From Observation to Reflection: A Practitioner's Guide to Programme Planning and Documentation* and, more recently, *Pancakes and Red Buckets: Creating an Emergent Curriculum with Children Ages Birth to Five Years*.

Joy is passionate about the emergent curriculum and has been on a journey of discovery about the ideas coming from Reggio Emilia. She also has a long-term fascination for Howard Gardner's theory of multiple intelligences and its implications in the lives of young children. Joy is interested and experienced in most of the curriculum areas, especially the arts (painting, drawing, clay, music, dance and drama), as well as early literacy and storytelling, science and math.

She is interested in the ideas that emerge from the NSW Curriculum Framework. Joy encourages reflection about what we do as well as presenting hands-on experiences for adults working with young children. She is entertaining and at times blunt!

Her approach is from the classroom, and she uses stories and pictures to illustrate ideas and challenges.

Joy's career—within the classroom of the three- to five-year-old child, her experiences as an author, part-time academic and presenter of workshops on the topics of imagination, creativity and multiple intelligences over several years—has given her a depth of practical understanding that enriches this book. She writes from the heart with passion, insight and practical experience.

She is acknowledged as a leader in the field and travels extensively, presenting seminars challenging educators about authentic child-focused programs, the importance of imagination, and how this is made visible in documentation and planning. Joy lives in Wagga Wagga, New South Wales, where she runs a consulting business with her partner, Peter. Joy would love to hear from you and can be contacted through her Web site, www.jnpconsulting.com.au.

EXPLORING VISUAL AND AESTHETIC DIMENSIONS

*Before words, language, abstract reasoning,
cognitive patterning, and conceptual thinking were images.
The human brain naturally thinks in images.*

David Lazear

What do we mean?

When we close our eyes but can still see the candle's flame; or are a great distance from the ones we love and can still see them in our mind's eye; when we ride a train in our memory and imagination while reading a story to the children . . . we are exercising our visual and aesthetic dimensions.

It's not only the ability to see and see clearly that we are talking about. It is the ability to remember what we see, to categorize and to represent in other ways, as well as the ability to respond to and present environments or ourselves in aesthetically pleasing ways.

The provision of an uncluttered yet visually and aesthetically stimulating space for young children is a good place to begin. Each one of us has an individual sense of what is aesthetically pleasing depending on our personalities and perhaps the experiences we had as a child. For one person a pleasing place can be plain, with white or light colors dominating, or with items made from natural materials that give a sense of space and culture. For another it can mean warm rich colors and large flourishes of accented materials or paintings. But somewhere there will be the common elements of order, beauty and light.

A young child's experiences of aesthetics will begin at home and continue in our centers. Therefore what we do and how we present environments and materials will matter. It will matter that the soft flowing purple fabric spills out onto the table toward the beautiful orange shell, or that collage materials are sorted into clear or white containers, ready for a child to choose from, or even that the pastels are invitingly settled onto wooden platters. Take another look at that light-colored tabletop we hope children will draw at. How can the children see where the paper begins and ends when the paper is the same color as the tabletop? Is that why the children are not drawing? Cover the table with brown paper or a fine cloth, hold the cloth down with elastic threaded into a small hem around the edge (and pulled tight) and see what happens.

One morning Sarah arrives with an armful of yellow and purple dahlias. We set a blue vase in the middle of the table on a small wooden roti board that raises the vase above the surface of the table. At first the children and I choose pencils to represent what we see, then pastels on new sheets of paper, encouraging each other to make bold strokes. Amy comments, "I can see all the purple ones. That's why I am doing purple." In another part of the room near the easels, Joshua finds some small sponges and begins to dab purple and yellow. From where I sit, I can see he is responding to the vase of flowers on the table. Before the day is over other children use a variety of collage and other materials to create two- and three-dimensional representations of the vase of flowers. The focus is the simple display of the dahlias in a way that honored Sarah, who brought them, and the natural beauty of the flowers. The children create the rest.

Howard Gardner (1991) and Loris Malaguzzi (1998) remind us that before children learn to write they use graphic languages to explain their knowledge, wonders and ideas to help themselves develop logical sequences in their theories. We'll return to this idea in future chapters.

Leonard spreads long blocks on the floor, piling them on top of each other to create a pattern; it's a kind of spiral, I think to myself. "It's a spider's web," he tells me. He is using his graphic language; he is recording like any scientist what he has seen in the garden. An adult visitor seeing him with clipboard and pen, magnifying glass in hand and looking closely at a leaf-curling spider hiding in one of the bushes is told, "I'm doing research."

"That's the hospital," Connor tells us. He has used blocks and roadways to create a city with several other children. Houses are added to the playscape and then a much taller building. He has been to the hospital recently to visit a sick relative. We notice the number of roundabouts in the road design and realize he is very knowledgeable about the hospital's location! When we pause to listen and reflect, we quite often find that children are informed about a great many things, sometimes surprisingly so!

In recent years five young men were tragically killed at a railroad crossing nearby. I see Max building a train track and adding some of the roadways we recently bought. David stands watching and then collects some "fence" pieces from the block cupboard and adds them beside the track where the road crosses it.

David drives some cars along the road, and Max a train along the track. "Ding, ding, ding, ding, ding," says David and lowers the fence across the road to stop the cars. He has placed a pedestrian close by, whom he also brings to a stop.

After the train leaves, he lifts the barrier, and the car and pedestrian cross safely.

I comment to him about his great idea. "You don't want to drive into a train, or you end up dead," he told me.

I almost miss the significance of the line drawn down the middle of the grandfather's chest one morning, until I think for just a couple of extra moments and remember that Catherine's grandfather recently had coronary bypass surgery. Sometimes in our fast-paced lives we find it difficult to wait and listen just that extra moment or two. Congratulate yourself on those times you manage it; it's worth acknowledging.

Stories and examples from the classroom

Sinead brings two large wild green orangelike objects, round and hard with a lumpy surface, to the preschool. Her mother sent them in a small wooden box lined with purple silk and a small pink rose—an invitation, I realize, for the children to investigate the aesthetics and reality of the inedible fruit. I am eager to make the most of her invitation. I place the fruit and flower on a wooden fruit stand and make sure the watercolors (in small glasses with fine brushes) are the best colors available. I add some pastels in case they are needed and some black pens. The white paper against the white-topped table is not appealing, so we quickly cut some small pieces of litho paper, turn them rough side up and frame them on light brown

Adrian paints from still life.

Jack attends to the detail in his painting.

card stock. Now we have an invitation. In the final chapter we will examine some of the headings we can use in documentation and program planning. "Invitation" is one of these headings.

Isabella and Josephine talk about how to draw the flowers.

The next day we find some large purple flowers from the garden and the last of the summer's hydrangeas and place them in a vase. This time the paper is framed by light purple and pink card stock.

When we encourage children to use their graphic languages, we assist their learning. Children draw to learn rather than learn to draw. When children draw, or paint, or make a model, they look carefully for the details, they notice what they might have previously overlooked, and they engage with the object in question. Similarly, adults will find that when they take on the challenge of a 750-piece puzzle while on holidays, their visual acuity and attention to detail will be significantly improved.

Jack appreciates the invitation and returns the next day to represent the flowers.

Implications

It is *easy* to say the process is more important than the product. It is *easy* to say the children's ideas will be valued and expanded. It is *easy* for us to say we recognize the child as an individual, yet it seems so hard to do. Here are some ideas that might encourage you.

USE THE SPONTANEOUS MOMENT

Over the last few years we have encouraged educators to be mindful and aware and to plan what they will offer to the young children, often in response to an observation from the day or week before. It has become a requirement in many situations that this plan or program be written into a formal document displayed for families to inspect. However, what we also encourage educators to do is to use spontaneous moments, those moments when a child comments on or shows us an object or asks a question about it. The moment can arise from an object a family has brought to share, a weather event that is currently happening, some birds that have landed in the tree, a butterfly that is visiting. These are significant moments; they hold the promise of creativity, and they are possibly the beginning of an interesting learning journey. We need to remind each other to value and use these moments, writing them into our formal program in a space we leave vacant for just such a purpose.

A chance encounter with debris from the hickory tree on the brick paving means that, instead of sweeping up the mess, we provide some magnifying glasses, clip-

boards and pens to "draw what we see." This is a very new experience; the children know they can draw people, and so many of the children draw people, even though they can't actually see them in the glass. This causes Sue (a work colleague) and I to reflect and consider what to do next.

We are able to return to the same situation the following day, but this time we provide paper with a large black circle drawn on it. The same clipboards and pens are available. We observe the children really focusing on what they can see inside the perimeter of the magnifying glasses. One child even draws the lines between the bricks, and another takes the large freestanding magnifying glass to where other children have drawn with chalk and records what she observes there. Of course, many children also notice the tiny hickory nuts and wispy sweet-smelling flowers we have intended them to focus on. We have encouraged the children to see.

CONCENTRATE ON ORDER, BEAUTY AND LIGHT

A wonderful range of paper, pens, pastels, watercolors, thick paint, thick and thin brushes, glitter, glue, boxes and fabric pieces are a great place to begin, but unless supplies are presented in ways that invite exploration, or in ways that encourage children to see and find materials, we are not really providing for the development of creative potential. When you go shopping in the supermarket and are assailed by the disorganized arrangement of the products and the advertising, you know how easy it is to come home with a can of crushed tomatoes instead of a can of pureed! It must be like that for the children sometimes. They see this and reach for it, but their hand picks up something else, or they just can't see for the clutter.

Kirrily (a colleague) tells me that she arranged the crayons and pastels into their color "families" in some small upright containers and suddenly noticed how the children began to explore color.

I cover a table with a thick black velvet cloth underneath some tiny easels (made using book or plate stands) with onionskin paper attached to a black covered clipboard with small clip. We add a plate with small glasses and fine brushes for watercolors for each easel/child space on top. We notice how readily the children are drawn to the area and how they concentrate on their work, returning again and again to the experience. The richness of the cloth, the contrast of the white paper against the clipboard and table covering, the thrill of using beautiful glasses to hold the colors and the richness of the magenta and the company of friends is irresistible!

We find containers for the playdough and present the equipment we think the children will need or they have suggested they would like in small baskets on a shelf nearby. The table is left empty; the children respond to the space, bringing the dough, cellophane, matchsticks and hickory nuts that they need to the table so they can express an idea. Like a blank canvas, it was an open invitation for children to enjoy and create. If we keep this image of a blank canvas alive, we can more easily move toward a more open-ended and creative environment.

RECOGNIZE THE IMPORTANCE OF INTERACTIONS

I will write about what Lilian Katz (1998) tells us about interacting with children—our conversations instead of directions—in other chapters, but it's very important in this context as well. Here is a story to illustrate this point.

Jay scribbles a couple of lines on the page. Last week he started to draw a person when Sue was with him and coached him, but today on his own, he has taken a shortcut. The adult returns and comments, "Where are the eyes?" He adds some to his scribble. "A nose?" He adds that. "A nice big smiling mouth?" He is into the swing by now and adds this and then some hair, arms, legs and even ears. He is so delighted, and yet without the adult prompting, asking questions, making some suggestions, taking notice and challenging, he would have settled for the quick scribble. The adult is vitally important, being careful not to overstep the mark and defeat the child but always asking about the representation. "Is it a sunny day? I can't see from your drawing" or "What is your family doing? Oh, watching the soccer? Well I can't tell that yet—perhaps some goal posts would help me see what your drawing is about. That's better. Is it raining or a sunny day? Are you hot or is everyone wearing a hat?"

In our efforts not to get in the way of the child's creativity, I believe we have stepped too far back. We get in the way of creativity when we take over, when it's our idea and our model and the children are asked to recreate our model, but we don't get in the way when we ask the right questions or make the best comments. We don't always get it right, but we will with practice.

USE BOOKS AND TALK ABOUT ILLUSTRATORS

We have the most incredible range of picture books currently available. Artists create wonderful pieces of art. Each illustrator has a particular style, the large brushstrokes of some, the fine pencil lines of others, the use of tissue paper or stiff papers by another and natural materials by another. The children will become aware of this with your help. Share your insights and listen for theirs.

"Here is another book by Eric Carle. I wonder if this one will have a sun or moon in it. Shall we look before we read the story, or will we let it sneak up on us as a surprise?"

"Look at the way the artist makes it look like this cup is shining. He put a tiny dab of white here on the green, and it makes it look like it's shining."

"See how the artist lets us look through the tree at the sky. I wonder if we can see the sky through the trees outside. Let's go outside and look."

"Wow, look at this sun. Many artists paint the sun and they all do different things. Let's find a few in our favorite books and see what they do. Is this one hotter, do you think? She has used a lot of red and orange."

LOOK AND LOOK AGAIN

Place interesting objects or illustrations from favorite and recently read books or prints of a famous painting close to the easel. Some children will use them, and others will not. The ones who do will attend to the detail of the large shell, noticing how the orange color curls around inside and the edge is rough with grooves. They will notice how the train goes behind the hill to emerge on the other side in their favorite book, and they will enjoy the work of Claude Monet and his bridges, ponds and water lilies. Draw attention to a child's work, gather a few interested children to look and encourage or ask if you can use the painting at the next group meeting time to share with the other children some good ideas.

DISPLAY WORK

Try to take photographs of children working on something special. Include the context and display the work as well as the process. When the children painted the wild green oranges, for instance, we laminated their work and placed photographs of them doing the paintings nearby. The children comment on the photographs, and they encourage the children to visit the ideas again.

Natalie sits at lunchtime next to her painting (recently hung) of some sunflowers. She glances around and comments, "Clever, aren't I?"

CREATING CONNECTIONS

"Joy," says Gary. "Can you get down on your hands and knees for me?"

I am happy to oblige. We find an open and carpeted area. I am curious though to know what is on his mind. He carries a clipboard, black pen and paper.

When I ask him, he replies, "I am learning to draw elephants." I think to myself, "Well he chose the best person for a model." I ask for more information.

"I want to see if I can see four legs or two when you look from here . . . and here," he tells me. Now that makes sense. We have recently enjoyed a book titled Daisy Drew an Elephant, *and he is thinking about this story and the many different ways elephants were illustrated. Several children in the group enjoying the story had noticed that in some drawings you could see only two legs and sometimes three or even four. I felt much better when Sue asked me what Gary and I were doing! I wondered if she would understand that Gary was making connections.*

So often (we hope) it's the children who make the connections. Children are not constrained by boxlike thinking. The connections the children make are the most significant because the learner's connections are about learning, not about how to write down what the intention of the adult is. Try to reflect the connections the children are making in your documentation—more about this in the final chapter.

Anthony throws a big blue cloth around himself and over his head. I make the connection that it reminds me of Arabic dress and give him a book I brought from the library called The World of Allah. *"You might like to look at this," I suggest.*

He does. He shares more cloth with several other boys, and soon they are building what they see in the book's pictures. Wonderful buildings emerge in the Arabic style complete with onion-domed roofs.

"It's the Egyptian king's castle," James tells me.

I have not mentioned Egypt; that is his connection. "It's like The King, the Mice and the Cheese *(a favorite story by Nancy and Eric Gurney)," adds Anthony. More connections! The children are able to make connections when our environments are open-ended and rich in materials, equipment, conversations and experiences.*

The connections that the more knowledgeable and experienced adult makes are a valuable contribution to the learning community. Share your connections with the children; just don't let them be the *only* connections happening.

Space, aesthetics and materials

We all need our own personal space to move in freely and safely, enough materials for us to use without having to wait and push into a crowd. We so easily provide environments that are like last-minute holiday shopping, push and shove, rising tempers and temperatures, loud voices and frustrated people. No one, including small children, can concentrate on visual and aesthetic dimensions when under this sort of stress.

Children need more than two easels available, with space so they can walk around and see what other children are doing. They also need more than the standard primary plus one secondary color (usually green) if they are to represent their ideas and knowledge about themselves and the world they live in.

Melinda asks Daphne (a volunteer at the center) for some gray paint. "One jar with light gray, please, one with dark gray and another with a sort of in-the-middle gray." Daphne mixes the colors with her, and they talk about how much black and how much white will achieve the right shade. Melinda returns to her work. She is painting shortly after September 11, and her painting shows the plane crashing into a tall tower, fire coming out and windows with faces of people, a pile of debris forming around the base of the tower, pieces of paper floating from windows and a small flower rising from the ashes. She needed the particular shades of gray to show the building, the smoke, debris and the windows.

Children need sufficient paper to have several attempts at drawing, painting or collage. They will thrive when given lovely soft pastels in a variety of colors.

"Oh look," says William when we open a new large box of colors. "There are five greens." He has spent the first months of the year coloring entire pages red, yellow, and green or blue with pastels held on the side. He truly knows about color; it's been his fascination. Now he is exploring the shades and tints available.

Other materials lend themselves to the development of aesthetic awareness. Clay (terra-cotta or white, clay mixed with paper to form paper-clay and clays with added texture known as grog) is a familiar material in many early childhood programs. A table covered with a couple of layers of colored (olive green works beautifully) burlap held in place with a large piece of elastic will invite children to participate. The traditional method of providing a small lump of clay with a thumb hole pushed in (so it can be filled with water and kept soft between uses) seems to me to suggest to children that there are only a few options available—to make pots, cups and saucers or perhaps nests for birds. Instead, see how it works when you add a small clay pot with some chunks of soft clay, or pieces torn leaflike ready to use. Cover the pot with a damp cloth to keep the clay moist and inviting and you will have provided an open-ended and more desirable environment to discover the wonders of the material. Natural materials such as shells, bark, leaves, twigs, hickory nuts and pebbles (for younger children, larger pebbles) or discarded items such as buttons or pieces of cloth will encourage exploration into avenues you may never have thought possible.

Good old-fashioned playdough can be made into more than biscuits and muffins, and scissors will find a new life as well with a little additional effort.

The playdough is made available on a table near a light table and a sunny window.

Some transparent circles (placed in a basket so the children can access them to use on the light table with cellophane and other transparent materials) soon find themselves being transformed into a dog outside its kennel on the nearby window.

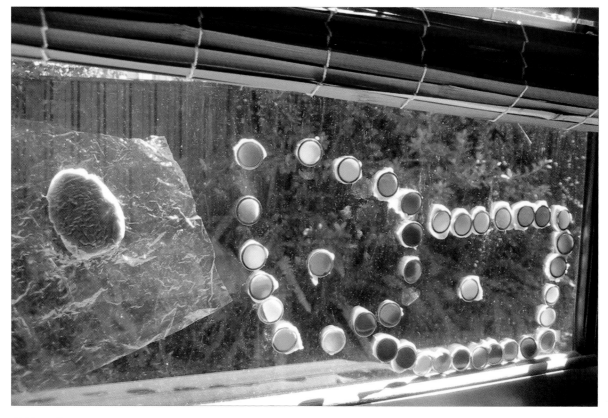

Children often use familiar materials in new and exciting ways.

Stencils, coloring-in and green caterpillars

Consider, if you will, the next few stories.

Christina is painting a holiday tree. There has been some discussion over morning snack about how many different types of holiday trees there are in shops downtown or put up and decorated in homes. We have asked the children to paint some of their ideas about what they have seen or how they would like a holiday tree to look.

This is in direct contrast to the adult model—where an outline is drawn onto the page and given to children to decorate and cover with color. I have to admit I used the adult model, even before the holidays, before I began to think about individuality. I think Loris Malaguzzi might have been right when he suggested that we first have to change what is inside ourselves, what we believe. When we start to think differently, then our practice changes. We cannot simply alter our practice without altering the underlying belief system.

He says in an interview with Lella Gandini (1998, p. 58):

It is important for pedagogy not to be the prisoner of too much certainty, but instead to be aware of both the relativity of its power and the difficulties of transplanting its ideals into practice.

Be patient; change will come. It simply takes time, exposure to new ideas, encouragement from trusted peers and mentors, continued reading and conversations with colleagues and a safe space to experiment with new ideas.

Christina paints a beautiful tree complete with an embellished top.

Her friend Harry is nearby, and when he is finished he steps back to look at his own work and also at Christina's. "Wow, I really like yours Chrissie. I think I might paint another one and make it just like yours," he comments. He hangs up his first attempt and gets paper ready for the next one. Christina looks a little perplexed. I ask her what's wrong. "Joy, you can't do that can you? You can't make something exactly the same as someone else!" I ask her if she minds him using her ideas. "No, sharing ideas is okay." Then she smiles and holds her fingers out in front to make a point. "Then again, you'd never get it exactly the same, would you, because we are different people." She's happy, and so is Harry. He uses her ideas as much as he can; however, when he comes to the embellished top of the tree, he seems a bit confused and makes a shape. I ask him about the top of the tree. "I don't know what it is. Christina has one on hers." "No way is his shape similar," I think to myself. "It's unidentifiable."

I tell him, "Christina put an angel on top of hers." "Oh," he says. Now he understands, but he is happy to leave his painting as is.

Individuals.

We tread a fine line. We are often tempted to draw a butterfly shape, copy it and provide it for the children to cut, paint or color inside the lines and then hang up to brighten the room. It will brighten the room, no doubt, and many of the children will enjoy the opportunity to do some good old coloring-in. In actual fact no great harm is done when we provide such an experience, as long as that is not the only experience we offer, and we can provide materials that we have negotiated with children or have thought may be useful in response to a story about butterflies. Alternatively, when we have observed some in the garden, we might encourage the children to show us their ideas about butterflies. Then we are reflecting the image of the child as an individual. It's a subtle shift, but when we find the courage to try it, we can be so greatly astounded by the creativity of the children. It's worth a try.

Recently, after a professional development session focusing on being authentic with children and other challenges from the NSW Curriculum Framework, the director of a small center nestled in the Kosciusko foothills area held a parent evening to share ideas she had for the direction the center would take. She gave an example of egg-carton caterpillars and assured parents that, after considering the implications of the idea of authenticity, they would no longer be part of the program. Later, a parent talked quietly to her. "How will my son ever learn what a caterpillar looks like?" The parent was a teacher from the local primary school, and we could understand where she was coming from. Her experience has been quite different from the journey early child-hood professionals have been on for quite some time now. It doesn't, however, mean we have to follow suit—our challenge is to provide authentic and creative options, even if the child enjoys them for only a year or so. The children will revisit these notions of authenticity and creativity at various stages of their schooling and future adult lives, and my dream is that we can suggest an appreciation of them in their early years!

My friend replied gently, "From observing real ones in the garden as they visit our flowers, and from photographs of them. He will create and represent his impression of them using whatever he chooses."

I must admit, I wondered just what the caterpillar made with six bumps, painted green and with pipe-cleaner legs would turn into. How easily we can slip into old habits.

Responding to children's interests

Whenever possible try to use ideas that have come from the children. Let their interests guide your choice of objects to stimulate wonderful graphic representations. Of course, allow contributions by families (encouraging children to bring interesting items they have is an exciting way to stimulate artistic adventures. Even superhero figures can be wonderful to draw when placed on a raised, velvet-covered block or plate on the floor or a table) and feel free to add ideas from your own adventures as well.

A conversation about "hot and cold" one extremely hot February day leads to 9 months of exploration of hot and cold colors, hot and cold (and spicy) foods, melting and freezing, hot (stolen) objects, hot music, the passage of the shadows across the garden and the change of the seasons. Eventually in November the conversation turns to hot rods.

"I wonder what a hot rod would look like?" I ask. Monique (a work colleague) arranges to have one brought by. I have no preconceived notions about what it might look like; I don't really know what a hot rod is except a car, and I certainly don't know what color it might be. It is interesting being in the same situation as many of the children about this. I am not able to influence their predictions. The children talk about their ideas and settle down to put them on paper. By November they are familiar with using pens, clipboards and paper to sketch ideas, predictions and theories, so the task is welcomed.

The children share their predictions.

We observed the different ideas the children had about how the car would look.

The next week, the children enthusiastically greet Richard when he drives the bright red and shiny hot rod in through the gates.

Ally expects the car will be shiny, adding details with glitter paint.

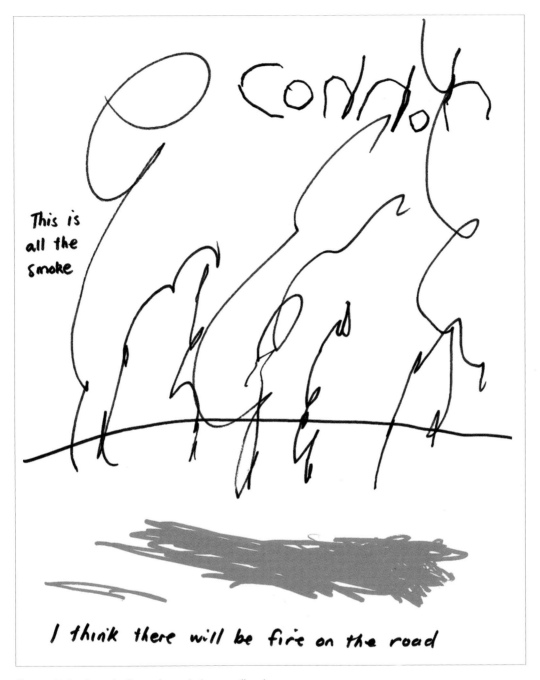

This is all the smoke

Connor

I think there will be fire on the road

Connor thinks about the fire and sounds the car will make.

It was interesting to see how the children's interests and personalities were reflected in their predictions. Each child had very different expectations.

At first, using some traffic cones, the children are prevented from climbing over and through the vehicle, and instead concentrate their attention on the outside of the car. Small stools enable the children to shift from one perspective to another, and clipboards provide them stability to rest their paper on.

The bright red, shiny hot rod poses for a portrait.

The children move around to position themselves at some point that interests them. They look and look again. They observe details and record them in their own documentation of the event. They are drawing to learn!

The children look carefully from every angle.

As the crush of children lessens, a few children remain to look from new angles. Grace arrived at preschool late this morning and is eager to quietly record as much as she can, telling me, "Now one from over here, now one from in there." Richard, the owner of the car, even allows her to sit inside the car!

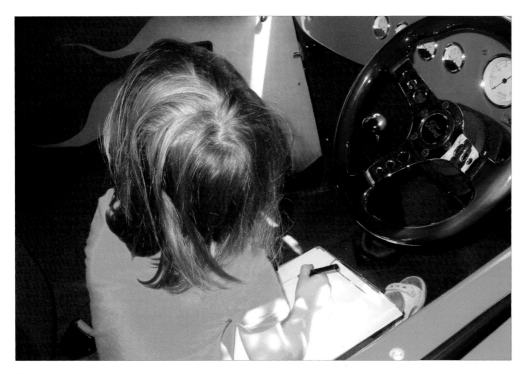

Grace records her observations from many angles.

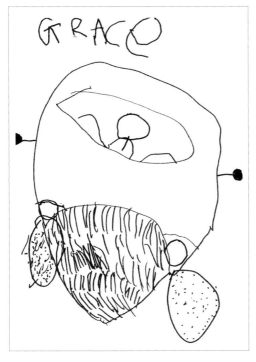

Several children show the difference between their prediction and the reality.

Grace draws the car from in front.

Other children notice fine details and incorporate them into their drawings.

Ally documents her new knowledge about hot rods.

Olivia notices the running boards, the small rearview mirror, the knot-hole in the tree, the way the lights stand up above the hood of the car. She even notices the spigots where air is pumped into the tires.

Being real

I observe Fletcher. He is painting yet another painting filled with stripes. He has been doing striped paintings for weeks now. He even wears striped t-shirts. I take yet another picture to add to his portfolio and I wonder about what he has been doing. Sometime around that time I read Big Rain Coming *(by Katrina Germein and illustrated by Bronwyn Bancroft) in response to the hopeful buildup of some storm clouds. The children are aware of the drought. It's been a long and hot summer, and they too would welcome the relief that rain would bring. The children respond to the rich colors and shapes on the pages that the illustrator has created. We talk about them as well as the story about Old Stephen's prediction of rain.*

Later at the easel I notice Fletcher has added something new to his stripes. Some of them head off at about a 60-degree angle across the page.

"Fletcher," I say quietly. "I can see something new happening in your painting today. The stripes here are wandering across this way."

"Yes," he smiles at me. "I was looking at how Bronwyn painted in that book."

I ask for more information.

He turns the pages of the book and shows me Old Stephen's leg when he rests against the tree.

"The lines go out like this," he tells me.

Then he shows me the lines the branches make above Old Stephen's head.

"And there too."

The illustrator had spoken directly to Fletcher, and his paintings took off in new directions, literally!

I could have said (and I am so relieved that I didn't), "More stripes, Fletcher? Aren't you about tired of them?" Or even worse, "That's nice!"

When the hot rod visited us, I noticed that Fletcher had positioned himself near the front of the car. I was not surprised when he sat near the radiator—it has stripes.

Fletcher sat in front of the radiator and drew what he could see.

The context!

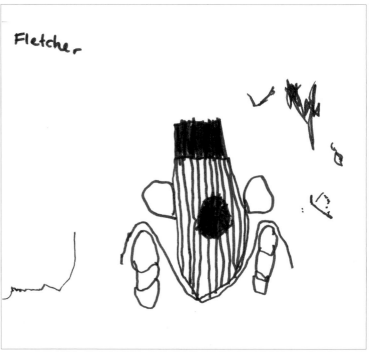

We can see what he is seeing.

Draw and draw again

In Reggio Emilia (I read in *One Hundred Languages of Children*) the children were asked to look at a bike and to talk about what they could see and then to go back inside to draw it. After some time the same small group of children was invited to come back outside with their paper and pencils/crayons/charcoal/pens to draw the bike again, but this time while looking. How often do we return to an object so the children can see it one more time? We so easily forget that that is what an artist will do. An artist will practice every day; yet we draw a couple of times a year and wonder why we don't improve. We try to remember how an elephant looks and then draw it, with often disappointing results. Yet if we were to study elephants closely, sit and watch what they do, how they move, the subtle color variations as light falls on their ears and the lovely soft sweep of the eyelash, then we would draw a much better elephant. We have simply not learned to see.

Lochie tells us he is going fishing on the weekend. We ask him about the boat he will be on. The children ask many questions, and he answers them as well as he can. The adults think up more questions, and he answers them too. Finally, we ask the children to draw what they imagine the boat will look like. The following week Lochie's father brings the boat to the preschool and the children climb on board using the small ladders from the obstacle course.

They examine the boat in detail, ask questions, use their touch and smell, and look carefully. Later, when asked to draw the boat from their new memory, even the children are surprised with the comparisons. I notice later when I print the photographs and look at the drawings that one of the girls had observed and recorded exactly the registration number on the side of the boat. It doesn't have to be boats or hot rods, it can be anything. Try it. It really works.

Making stuff

One of the parents at an information evening says, "The children don't get to make anything anymore." I pause to think about this. It's true many of us have discarded mass-produced projects such as green egg-carton caterpillars, or 25 identical sunflowers to celebrate spring or even the old favorite, a cut-out Humpty Dumpty with a belt around his waist. It is not easy to make these changes, and the first sign of opposition or even a gentle challenge from a parent can put us back to the familiarity of suggestions from the books and magazines we have collected over the years. But (we can ask ourselves) are the children no longer making anything?

I thought about Sarah, who that day had taken a paper circle, added some cellophane strips across the top and scrunched it together in the center of the circle. She cut a small hole in the paper, placed her index finger up and through and turned to me. "Look Joy, it flies; it's a butterfly." Is this not making anything?

I think about Harry, Abby, Georgia and Jack working with boxes on large pieces of cardboard. Ideas and ways to solve problems flowed thickly as the children explored the ways to build houses. Some added a chimney—it had to sit up straight and not fall off. Others added a roof. When it was time to add the fence and garden, Jack had an idea that soon became popular: he used clay to hold the popsicle sticks straight. Abby added flowers and trees into the landscape she created around the house, using clay to hold pieces of greenery collected from the garden. Is this not making anything?

Cultural richness

Go to an imported goods and crafts shop! The smells of the incense and soap and perhaps the latent cooking smells from the homes the artifacts were originally used in crowd your mind along with the colors, shapes, textures and materials available. Along with these shops, there are thrift stores and garage sales. Using these resources, we can purchase culturally rich materials reasonably easily to add to the aesthetic environments we wish to create.

Go to the camping shop and find metal dishes, scrounge some old wooden crates or cuts of timber, some old tires (keep free of spiders, please), a plank and an old rug or cuts of beautiful fabrics. Cut up last year's UNICEF calendar, harass people to share other calendars from here and there, and laminate them—they will last years. Find books at the local bookshop or from specialist retailers that have marvelous illustrations and stories about ordinary people doing ordinary things in extraordinary places. Go to the swap shops and find books about art and artists that have been discarded. The local library may dispose of some of their books each year, and you can purchase them. Hound the bookshops and find out when they are discounting beautiful coffee table books that you know will enrich your environment. Take photographs of bridges and musical instruments, fountains and people, and enlarge them, print and laminate them, and you will soon have your own collection of wonderful things.

Present materials so that the children can see them. Store them down low where children can reach, presented in the most beautiful, simple and effective way you can possibly imagine. Bring items from varying places together, which adds a depth that concentrating on one culture alone does not. Reflect the materials or artifacts in the colors available at the easel or the pastels lying ready for use. Encourage the children to really look at the materials, to feel them, to smell them and to respect them.

Being inclusive

A few years ago, I had a boy with autism in my class. He painted every morning. He painted up to 40 paintings before lunch in the first months he was with us. His paintings covered the entire page with a variety of colors. We always provided colors that would look good on the page together, and his paintings always looked good to us. He was safe painting. From the far side of the easel he could watch everybody. As the year progressed, he painted less and less and played with the other children increasingly. We loved his paintings. Eventually an adult art class asked if they could have some of his collected works to use to mount their line drawings on. His parents agreed, and one such drawing (and a frame painted by this child) found its way to the Vatican. A card addressed simply "Daniel the Artist," carrying the Vatican seal and sent to the preschool said it all.

Karen Miller (1994, personal conversation with Joy Lubawy) says that her idea is to "watch what the child does, and make it legal." She explains that children show us in their actions what interests them, what they are learning to do and what is important, and that we should watch and respond with new ideas that will extend their interests. This will take care of their development.

Our observation of a child as an individual should guide the provision of materials we make, the techniques we use and demonstrate, the equipment we provide and the space and time needed. If we concentrate on the individual, we should not encounter problems being inclusive, as we are thinking about how and what will work best with that particular child. Observation, then, is the key!

Techniques and skills

We often see young children hold a paintbrush as if to drill a hole in the paper, or perhaps stab it instead of holding it in a more orthodox fashion like an artist does. So, why not share your insight about this with the children? Demonstrate how to hold a brush so that it sits back along the space between the thumb and index finger, tell them you can see the end of the brush, and now you will use only the tip of the brush, not push all the bristles onto the paper.

> *"You'll need to dip it into the paint again. See, the brush is getting dry and makes those marks. Dip again—remember to wipe a little so it doesn't drip. That's the way. Yes, use the tip of the brush, just like the artists do."*

Here is a little rhyme that might help:

> *Dip, dip, dip.*
> *Don't let it drip.*
> *Use just the tip.*
> *Great work, that's it!*

When we show children a technique, how to fold and tear paper, or how to start cutting a hole in the middle of the page (fold and cut a little snip to give enough space for the tip of the scissor to reach into) or how to hold pastels and crayons on their side to achieve large sweeping lines or to make a rubbing, we are not interfering with their creativity. Instead, we are showing them the techniques needed to use particular materials.

It is quite okay to show children how to cut a piece of clay from a slab using fishing line stretched between two pegs, how to make a mixture of clay and water (called slip) so that the clay pieces can be stuck together or how to get a drawing to stand up using some cardboard and a small box or cardboard folded at right angles stuck behind. Make suggestions and ask questions. However, when we give children the materials and an idea that have only a couple of possible results, we are interfering with creativity.

A visit to an art gallery to see an exhibition of children's work from China means I have a great new idea about a technique. I show the technique to the children. First I draw with pastels onto some litho paper (shiny side up) what I can see outside the classroom window, talking about the tree, fence and flowers I observe, and then I paint over the picture with edicol dye. While the paper is still wet, I turn it over onto some newspaper to blot off excess, and then turn it back over to see the results. We all gasp because it looks so different.

What amazes me, however, is that NONE of the children drew what I had drawn. They drew about going skiing and being caught in the blizzard, about their families, their houses, pets, cars. We concentrate on the technique. There is a fine line between teaching a technique and making a model to copy.

A fine line

Our role is to help children become aware of what they are seeing, to look and to draw, to look again and to draw some more, not to offer gimmicks and shortcuts that stop children from exploring this dimension.

I can't is an incredibly common statement.

There are a couple of ideas that might work in this situation. To start with, is it reasonable that the children will be able to do what you have suggested, or are you asking something completely beyond their current developmental level? If you are satisfied that they can indeed succeed at the task you have in mind, then talk about how we all have to learn everything. The text might go something like this:

When you were very little you didn't feed yourself. When you tried you put banana in your ear and up your nose and it was so funny, but you tried and tried and now look what you can do.

When you were little you couldn't walk, so you rolled and crawled and held on to the table, and one day you knew how to do it, and look what you can do now: run and jump and you are even learning to hop. Well, drawing an elephant is just like that. We start and it's not so good the first time, but when we try some more we get better.

Where can you start? Do you think the trunk is the place to begin? Yes, I think so too. Look at this picture of an elephant; see the end of the trunk? It does look like a circle sort of shape. I could lend you one of those if you like. I could draw that little bit for you, and I think you could do the rest. You okay if I do that?

Let's look at how the trunk looks; it is long, and look, there is a line this side and a line that side all the way up to here. Do you think you could draw that? I thought you could. Well done.

Now look at those big flappy ears. I can make those shapes with my whole arm; can you? Yes, that's the way. I wonder how we can make that shape on the paper. That looks terrific. Now I can see the elephant coming.

Some eyes next, or do you think the big body should be next? Yes, I was looking at the big bump on top of the elephant's head too; I like the way you put that on—now it's looking seriously good. Legs? How can you add those? I was noticing the little toenails elephants have. They are unusual, aren't they?

I think we'd better show someone else this picture. It's time to really brag about this. You have made an excellent effort and concentrated so long, and you didn't give up even when you thought you couldn't do it.

When adults ARE interested in children drawing, painting or constructing with collage materials, they ARE often present to see children achieving wonderful work. When left alone we often see children who take shortcuts or don't even visit the area. Your role as an adult makes a huge difference. I often hear the comment "The children in my class don't paint much," and I wonder, is the adult ever nearby and talking with the children? Is the adult interested in the process and part of the learning communication that is possible, or is the adult just the person who hangs the painting to dry?

Here are a couple of other suggestions:

- suggest but don't provide models;
- help but don't dominate;
- hold things steady;
- find materials that will help, but don't have a completed object in mind;
- ask questions and encourage, but don't always insist on doing it your way; and
- remember, trying is important.

Aesthetics

We have covered some of this already in this chapter: thinking about order, beauty and light, the individual nature of aesthetic expression and the child's developing sense.

I wonder then what effect we have when we insist that collage be symmetrical or that we can't allow a child to tear a shape and insist she cut it, or worse still we draw the line for her to cut! Perhaps we need to take a close look at our own aesthetic sense and discover its origins.

I fully realize that for many of us, time is a limited commodity. If your center never closes, or closes and opens with the arrival of staff and children, then there is limited time available to keep an orderly appearance, but it's important! Storage units—clearly marked and easily accessible—are essential ingredients. We don't need to have every toy and piece of equipment available all the time on open shelves. We can have SOME of the equipment and materials available and presented so children will notice them. We can add complexity and more materials over time, but we also need to remember to remove materials too.

I sometimes visit rooms where the art display from February is crowded with the more recent work from September, but nothing has been removed; it has just become increasingly cluttered. I can't imagine how an adult can work in an environment where every available ceiling space seems to be occupied with yet another mobile or hoop hanging with 25 identical daffodils and not go crazy. Imagine what effect this is having on the children's developing aesthetic sense. How can they learn to see, to differentiate what is important from the maze and mist of trivia? In an aesthetic sense, less is much more!

I wonder what happens to young children's developing aesthetic sense when they are surrounded with easy-to-clean-and-maintain floors and walls, where there is no texture available, no natural environments or materials, but a steady stream of red, yellow and blue plastic on plain vinyl floors or artificial grass?

Image of the child

THE CHILD IS A SOCIAL BEING

Much of what a child explores, discovers and makes sense of comes from interactions with other children. Any area of an early childhood service provides opportunities for children to work with a friend, talk with them, negotiate desired outcomes and learn to give and take a little.

Two independently capable young artists are finding it a little difficult to settle all the issues, but when we see children working with a common goal it's particularly satisfying. The only unsettled question in this case is who will take the painting home. Eventually Amber does.

Children learn from and influence each other. When we expect to see this happening, we will encounter it and document it. What we expect to see influences what we make visible to others. If this is one of your images of childhood, then document it, and show others this is important.

One child paints a rainbow with several people underneath. Abby, who is close by, likes the idea.

Abby chooses another sheet of paper and makes some alterations to "the ideal person" she and Milla are exploring; the hairstyle changes, and the body changes. Milla is now following Abby's lead at this stage. They wordlessly share ideas and bounce off each other.

Grace and Amber work on a painting together, negotiating the colors and the subject matter.

Abby incorporates a new idea and uses it in her painting.

Socially constructed learning.

The leadership ball is tossed back and forth.

Milla settles on her ideal person for today.

THE CHILD IS AN INDIVIDUAL

It's difficult being an individual sometimes, and it is certainly a challenge to recognize, allow for and encourage individuals in our classrooms.

Recently someone asked me if I was satisfied that I had covered all areas of a child's development in the portfolios. I thought about this. "No, and actually I hope not really. I want the portfolios to reflect the child. Some children are engineers and others are scientists or artists. I would think I may have missed some areas in my endeavor to gather what the child tells me is important about them as an individual."

While part of me accepts that as an adult I *should* collect information about all parts of the child's development, doing so is in conflict with recording what actually is happening. The challenge I suppose is how to record what children are doing authentically, without insisting they carry out tasks for our recording purposes.

Reflections, challenges and wonderings

Alise Shafer (2001) from California, addressing the International Festival of Learning in Fremantle a few years ago, challenged us to think about the child's development of logical (and scientific) thought. She also pushed us out of our all-knowing "teacher" complacency by suggesting that "the child is the physics professor, the exam is Friday, you'd better listen." (You will read about her presentation many times in following chapters. She had an enormous impact on my thinking.) Another part of the Reggio Emilia provocation had begun to fall into place.

Her talk reminded us that children can parrot back to us statements we have given them about why and how, but that they need to build their own understanding over time in ways that mean something to them. Piaget called it a schema, and Lubawy and Jarratt (1999) referred to it as building walls of wombats, or building walls of knowledge about specific things. We knew it, but somehow the true meaning of what we knew became more real.

Alise encouraged us to talk with the children, to ask them what they knew, to allow them to explain what their theories were. We were prepared for some surprises, but when we overcame the obstacle of our own egos and knowledge, we were stunned by what began to happen.

It seems so obvious NOW, but as Malaguzzi (1998b, p. 92) reasoned in an interview with Lella Gandini, young children were not yet able to write their ideas down, and so they had languages other than the spoken word that they used. He says:

> Putting ideas into the form of graphic representation allows the children to understand that their actions can communicate. This is an extraordinary discovery because it helps them realize that in order to communicate, their graphic must be understandable to others. In our view, graphic representation is a tool of communication much simpler and clearer than words.

If children are not yet able to write their ideas, then we should encourage them to draw, paint, collage, build, form with clay or dough, dress up and act a role or any other "language" the children wish to use to express their current thinking. It's a window into a child's mind. If we listen and watch with our hearts as well as our ears and eyes, we will see what is happening and possibly know what children are thinking about.

I am sure then that no child is thinking about how to make a green egg-carton caterpillar with six legs and two antennae made with pipe cleaners. Instead I believe the child is watching the caterpillar eating a yummy green leaf, concentrating on the movement of the jaws as it eats and on how not to get stung or irritated by chemicals the caterpillar may produce. The child may wonder how to keep the caterpillar alive or observe some of the colors that camouflage it. The child may consider where it comes from. A child noticing the flash of brown and orange as a butterfly whizzes past, dodging children and plants as it makes its way to a nearby bush, is not counting the legs and antennae, imagining the three distinct body parts and so on. Instead, the child is watching in wonder as the colors flash and the butterfly maneuvers itself and finally settles.

The children can be armed with clipboards, paper, pens and magnifying glasses to watch and to draw what they see as the leaf-curling spiders carefully emerge and move farther away from the safety of the leaf while the children remain still. Thrilled when a slight movement makes the spider retreat, the children can still see some tiny legs just at the edge of the leaf.

Simon sees a jet's vapor trail in the sky. "I wonder what that is," I ask.

He tells me, "It's the mark the engine makes as it flies through the air."

I plead total ignorance of the topic, and so he says, "Come with me and I'll draw it for you."

He draws the first picture, the jet on the tarmac.

"Where is the white line?" I ask. He gives me one of those looks only a four-year-old can, eyes rolling. "It hasn't left the ground yet. He's just warming the engines."

He draws again, a jet taking off. I ask the same dumb question and get another look!

"The jet is still climbing."

Then, finally, a jet high in the sky with trail of white behind.

"There," he says at last. "The engine is hot, the air is cold, and when the air goes through the engine it turns to steam." Well, now I know too. I had quickly worked out how important it was for him to draw the steps so I could follow his logic. Simon is learning how to think logically and scientifically. His thinking depends on him being able to record what he is considering.

PUTTING IT TOGETHER

I have often heard it said that the whole is greater than the sum of the parts. When we see the connections we can see the entire concept. This helps us make sense of and more easily remember a subject, forming a sound foundation for additional learning. My own experience studying for exams is that when I can step back and see that subject as a whole and can also see where it fits with other subjects, then I am ready to pass that subject. If all the component parts are still individual bits of information, then I know I have a lot of work ahead of me—I have not understood and have not learned the material.

As educators we have been encouraged to think in separated units, themes, subject areas or developmental descriptors. I wonder then how much this has influenced what we do. Do we present our environments as if nothing is connected to anything else, or do we present a sense of the whole, a whole world, a common humanity, a whole child, an entire environment? Art is part of math and science. It contributes to literature and drama and can also express the same emotions that music does. Art is not separate and artists are not separate, so let's see how we can bring all parts to a rich whole.

Connecting dimensions

In this chapter we have looked at the artistic expressions of young children in some detail. We have examined the role we play providing materials and space, allowing time and inviting children to participate using aesthetically pleasing environments. We have considered the importance of order, beauty and light instead of chaos and clutter, and we have thought about talking with children.

We have also considered the development of logical and scientific thought using the wonders of graphic literacy, a pre-writing form of written language. We have looked at children with differing needs being able to participate in individual ways, and at some of the implications we face when documenting these details.

Art (and its associated topics) is not an isolated entity. It is part of who we are as a people. Not one of us lives in an environment totally devoid of aesthetics. Our books and television screens reflect visual and aesthetic dimensions. The shape of our cars, the design of our furniture, the faucets in the bathroom and the shape of windows at the back of a house, the placement of gardens and pots of tulips reflect who we are. Art and visual creativity is not something for just one small part of a classroom; instead it's all over, inside and out. It's on the way to the center and as we close our eyes at night. We need to learn to see—that makes our life richer for the experience and awareness.

Biologists and engineers draw their observations and plans, mathematicians look for order and patterns, scientists look for detail and record their thoughts, musicians record emotions on paper, the dancer and mime artist consider how things will look to an audience and most people like the order of a neatly made bed! It's all part of being a human. We are the connective tissue.

Creating new experiences and ideas

The children are an amazing source of inspiration if we just listen and watch! Talk with them about their ideas and ask them to suggest things they might like.

My eyes were opened to some of the possibilities of playdough when I visited another preschool one afternoon. The staff at this center have been on a journey toward Reggio Emilia–inspired practice for a couple of years, and I wanted to see how it looked from their point of view.

The playdough was stored in small, individual transparent containers on a shelf unit close by to a table left bare. In baskets were the familiar items we often see, rolling pins, cutters, plastic knives and garlic crushers.

The idea was for the children to select a jar of dough, use it and then return it when they had finished. It started me thinking.

I remembered seeing a picture in Curtis and Carter's book *The Art of Awareness*. One of the display panels in the back of the book was about children building connections, making friends with dough.

I shared the pictures in the book with some of the children in my own class the following day. I wondered what ideas they might have about using dough in more creative/active ways. They began to tell me what they would need. How often do we do this? Ask the children what props or materials they might need? If the children are active learners, we probably need to consult with them.

"Turtles and some fish."

"Rocks."

"Twigs and hickory nuts."

"Cellophane."

"What colors?" I ask.

"Blue and red and yellow and green."

We collected the equipment the children suggested. I was literally transfixed as I watched the children exploring ideas and showing me with their graphic language what they knew and were thinking about.

I see Emma push some yellow dough into a round shape and add long pieces around the edge. I think perhaps a spider, or even a person. "It's a sun like Mr. Carle makes," she tells me (Eric Carle). I smile. Then she places a piece of red cellophane over the top. "The sun is setting," she tells me. "Now it's dark." She added blue over the top.

Kenya is also busy: a piece of blue cellophane on the table, yellow dough spread out, some twigs from the garden, polished river rocks scattered here and there, a fish on the blue and small turtles on the dough/twigs. "The little turtles are just hatching and they are going up over the rocks and sticks to the sea. The fish is swimming," she tells me.

Ted spreads dough carefully over a piece of red cellophane, covering the entire surface. As he places two sticks upright in the center, I approach to take a photograph.

"Not finished yet," he tells me. I ask him if I can take pictures of the process. He says yes, "but you'll have to come back." I come back and he has added more sticks in the center. Still not finished. Finally, he calls me, "Finished!" Fish and river stones surround the sticks. I wonder about his ideas and I ask him. "It's the dam. It's all dry, and the fish are waiting for the rain to come." We've had drought for several years, and the dams nearby are almost empty. I ask his mother about it—they have been to look at the dams recently. They've been a big item on the news and in the newspaper as well.

The stories speak volumes.

TAKING CARE OF YOURSELF

A colleague (thanks Amy) told me about using Curtis and Carter's *Designs for Living and Learning* in her classroom. Instead of her fussing and getting frustrated trying to achieve some of the delightful environments she saw before her, she gave the children some "stickies" and suggested they use them to show her which pages they liked best. Hundreds of stickies later, the children were finished. She then opened the book at some random pages over a series of months and placed the book where families could see the pictures. She asked the families and other members of the local community to think about materials they might have that they could lend or give the center so that the children could create some of the environments themselves. She supported the children as they arranged environments, collected materials, added new ideas and finally played in their own creations. No stress! We could take a leaf out of her book, couldn't we?

"I'm not at all artistic or creative" is such a common comment from adults.

Christine Stevenson and Ursula Kolbe (1999) suggest that, instead of thinking how to make the best butterfly, caterpillar or Humpty Dumpty, we put our creative focus into sourcing and presenting materials so that they invite the children to participate and leave the creativity to the children. We refocus the lens to consider and nurture the creative.

Some favorite books that might assist you in establishing creative environments to stimulate the visual and aesthetic dimensions are:

Comune di Reggio Emilia, 1996, *Catalogue della mostra. I Cento Linguaggi dei Bambini*, Reggio Children, Reggio Emilia, Italy.

Curtis D and Carter M, 2003, *Designs for Living and Learning: Transforming Early Childhood Environments*, Redleaf Press, St Paul MN.

Edwards C, Gandini L and Forman G, 1998, *The Hundred Languages of Children*, Ablex Publishing, USA.

Kolbe U, 2001, *Rapunzel's Supermarket*, Peppinot Press, Byron Bay.

Kolbe U, 2005, *It's Not a Bird Yet; The Drama of Drawing*, Peppinot Press, Byron Bay.

Smith D and Goldhaber J, 2004, *Poking, Pinching & Pretending*, Redleaf Press, St, Paul, MN.

Just as humus in nature makes growth possible, so elementary music gives to the child powers that cannot otherwise come to fruition. . . . The imagination must be stimulated; and opportunities for emotional development, which contain experience of the ability to feel, and the power to control the expression of that feeling, must also be provided.

Carl Orff

2

EXPLORING MUSICAL AND RHYTHMIC DIMENSIONS

What do we mean?

Try to imagine a culture without music. Not really possible is it? Indeed, the history of music runs through our human story—from the simplicity of a simple drumbeat through to the complexity of a Gregorian chant, the intricacies of Mozart, contemporary synthesized music and the repetitive sonic vibrations of the modern dance night.

David Lazear (1999, p. 105) in *Eight Ways of Knowing: Teaching for Multiple Intelligences* writes of musical intelligence:

> Of all the intellectual capacities, none develops earlier . . . true both in the evolution of the human species and in the development of persons from birth to adulthood.

It appears that a child in the womb responds to the musical tones of the human voice and may even develop some musical capacities. Newborn babies respond and turn toward the sounds of familiar voices—especially their mother's—and, when placed on the chest of the father, are often calmed by the deepness of his voice.

Lyn Zollo, writing of her experiences while pregnant with her young son, Luca (2006, p. 11), shares her ideas on the topic:

> I discovered that Luca was a communicator from within the womb. He liked music, the sound of his dad's Italian singing and waited each night for a massage from Dad before he would go off to sleep, waking when he heard his dad's voice the next morning. Luca didn't cry when he was born, he simply looked up at us wide eyed with curiosity and snuggled into my chest. We had been communicating but just hadn't seen what each other looked like.

We are exposed, perhaps overexposed, to the sounds of music just about everywhere we go—in supermarkets, elevators, our car, our homes, restaurants and even on the street. How often do we pause to really listen, and how early do we learn to screen much of it out?

Many educators are threatened by music, believing it is beyond their ability; others thrive on it, feeling comfortable enough to experiment and explore. My concern is that the variety of quality and interactive music may so easily disappear from the early childhood experience or become merely an ornament in the curriculum instead of a valid way of expressing creativity and intelligence in all areas.

Don Campbell (1983, p. 4) challenges us, saying:

> The question of music as part of leisure, pleasure and entertainment, versus its power as an enabling agent for human learning at large, is now at hand.

Let's continue and discover some of the ways that music can become an essential *connective* ingredient in early childhood programs.

Stories and examples from the classroom

We usually begin the year with a new group of children aged four and going to school the following year. Many of the children have not attended other prior-to-school settings. Some of the children have been exposed to music and rhythm at home and some have not. So the question as always is, where do we begin?

It mostly depends on the age of the child: the smaller the child, the smaller the group or experience should be. For a young baby, music and rhythm is something up close and personal, rocking in an adult's arms and being sung to, a musical windup toy near a cot, a squeaky hammer that makes a sound when hit against something or a favorite toy that responds when the child sits on it. As the child matures the actions become more deliberate, and if we allow time, space and opportunities the child experiments with voice and other sounds to create new music.

The end-of-year rock-n-roll party gathers families and friends for a celebration of a year at preschool. As I watch and listen to the dancing, singing and using of handmade, make-believe and real instruments, I reflect on the year that has made this possible. It was a magical year, filled with challenge and success, and here on this last evening together we celebrate everything we meant to each other.

John plays his handmade guitar for the rock-n-roll medley.

I had started the year in a new center after many years in a very familiar setting. This room is different, the staff and families have a different profile, and the equipment available is different. All these (minor) differences stimulate an awareness within me of the process of encouraging children to become more musically and rhythmically aware. Creativity comes from having sufficient skills and knowledge to create something new, and this is what I hope will happen. But where to begin?

The excitement level is high when everyone arrives each morning—families sharing stories and laughing, younger children crying because they want to stay as well, children who are familiar with the setting and those new to it eagerly exploring together. It can be a bit daunting to some of the children and to me. I notice a few children have retreated to the far end of the room where it is quieter. It looks like a good place to me, so I head that way too. I take my guitar and sit down to softly sing, hoping to gather some children into a group so we can start the day and hoping to claim the space for the children. A flash of inspiration brings to mind an old, old song.

The wheels on the bus go round and round
Round and round, round and round.
The wheels on the bus go round and round
All the way to town.

A few children come and sit nearby. I wonder how I can keep this going.

The people on the bus bounce up and down
Up and down, up and down.
The people on the bus bounce up and down
All the way to town.

A few more children arrive to join the group. The noise level from adults gradually starts to diminish. I am encouraged and challenged. The song is so short and we need a lot of time for the room to settle, that we need it to be much longer.

"A chorus! Yes a chorus. I will use the 'Wheels on the bus' as a chorus. That's a good idea," I think. (It took 26 years of teaching to invent this totally original idea!)

The wheels on the bus go round and round
Round and round, round and round.
The wheels on the bus go round and round
All the way to town.

Mmmm, that seems to be working. Another verse!

The wipers on the bus go swish, swish, swish
Swish, swish, swish, swish, swish, swish.
The wipers on the bus go swish, swish, swish
All the way to town.

Back to the chorus. The song gets longer and longer; it is familiar, it can be gentle and quiet when we want it to be, and yet it generates enough interest for most of the children to gather around the guitar, and the parents decide to either sit down and be quiet or leave us and go about their daily routines. We have reclaimed the space for the children. Safe, nurturing, some quietness and predictability carved with music.

More verses are added, including one invented that morning by one of the children:

The children on the bus pull ugly faces
Ugly faces, ugly faces.
The children on the bus pull ugly faces
All the way to town.

We all laugh! Almost all the children and the staff are finally gathered this morning, ready for what will become the morning meeting time. For 24 years I have been familiar with a routine that gathers children for a group time before morning snack rather than on arrival; I am looking at something new to me. It feels right somehow. We can share stories and events, plan for the day, reflect on yesterday or last week and focus attention on particular upcoming events for the day. I wonder why it has taken me so long to discover this.

I wonder if musical instruments can be added to this newly developing routine. There is a problem with where they are stored, down in a cupboard behind a curtain in sealed containers. I wonder if some nice big baskets from Ghana will work, and when we add these to the environment, we find we have bells, shakers and claves (sticks) available for immediate and easy use. The problem now is which songs to use to encourage the children to learn to use the instruments in a rhythmic and musical way, not just a free-for-all.

Necessity being the mother of invention, I soon go to work inventing:

Get an instrument and play along with me.

(I try to remember a song called "Play your instrument and make a pretty sound" by Ella Jenkins. I know it well and like it, but this morning the tune will not come to me. What we sing is a new invention—we make up our own tune.)

Get an instrument and play along with me, play along with me, play along with me.
Get an instrument and play along with me, and we'll have a really good time.

(I was inspired to add a short chorus—another important ingredient in a good song.)

So, tap your sticks and ring your bells and shake your shakers too.
Shake them too.

(I suggest to the children that only the children holding sticks should play; the others can wait for their instruments to have a turn. It takes a few weeks, but soon the children are listening really closely.)

Tap your sticks and play along with me, play along with me, play along with me.
Tap your sticks and play along with me, and we'll have a really good time.
So, tap your sticks and ring your bells and shake your shakers too.
Shake them too.

(I invite other instruments to join in.)

Ring your bells and play along with me, play along with me, play along with me.
Ring your bells and play along with me, and we'll have a really good time.
Shake your shakers and play along with me, play along with me, play along with me.
Shake your shakers and play along with me, and we'll have a really good time.

(And now the voices . . .)

Use your voice and sing along with me, sing along with me, sing along with me.
Use your voice and sing along with me, and we'll have a really good time.
So, la, la, la, la, la, la, la
La, la, laaaaaaah!

A good morning meeting time needs some other movement too, and soon we are marching to the beat of the big bass drum around the room, in and out of the tables, or joining in another newly invented movement song that generates a lot of laughter.

I also invent a variation to the tune of a well-known movement song, "Johnny works with one hammer." It is such fun, with lots of laughter and children attempting to do the movements. I begin with Johnny and then the inclusive "we." Johnny then becomes the chorus.

Johnny loves jumping, jumping, jumping.
Johnny loves jumping; he could do it all day.

We love twirling, twirling, twirling.
We love twirling; we could do it all day.

Johnny loves jumping, jumping, jumping.
Johnny loves jumping; he could do it all day.
We love bending, bending, bending. We love bending; we could do it all day.
Johnny loves jumping, jumping, jumping.
Johnny loves jumping; he could do it all day.
We love stretching, stretching, stretching. We love stretching; we could do it all day.
We love wriggling, stamping, blinking, clapping.

The elements start coming together—repetition and familiarity (this way the children become confident and participate) and experiences that are long enough to give children time to come to the group. We have singing, movement, and rhythmic awareness happening. The children are eager to join in. The morning meeting time has become mostly music (sometimes a story is added if it is about something that has happened or is about to happen following an interest), and it is joyous, musical, and wonderful.

Cameron, John, Sophie, Georgia and friends make rhythms!

As often happens, one group of children responds to music and rhythm in ways different from another. Some children sing rock-n-roll at the top of their voices and dance or play air guitars. Others create new sounds and rhythms and use music for drama and games. Either way, at the end of the year the children and their families celebrate a musical and rhythmic journey.

(See also chapter 4 for ideas about music/rhythm and developing math.)

Implications

What implications are there for our classrooms? Do we pollute when we have music playing all the time? Are we teaching children to screen out music, to have it like wallpaper, as a background? Instead, how can we include musical delights that challenge? What importance do familiarity and context have? Here is another story. This one illustrates the connection between music, art and literacy.

Jacob brings his painting to me. He wants me to write his story about it for him. I am happy to oblige.

"It's a giant," he tells me.

As I begin to write "Giant," I comment that another word is inside the word giant. *Jacob is a beginning reader, so I know he will respond.*

"It's a.n.t" I show him.

"You mean something as small as an ant is in that big word giant?*" he asks, eyes wide with wonder.*

He takes his painting back to the easel, adds an ant.

I wonder if he'd like to put some speech bubbles into his story, and we look at a few picture books using speech bubbles so he is aware of what this means.

"Yes, write this down . . . the giant is saying Fee, fi, fo fum, I can smell an ant . . . Yum!" "What about the ant?" I ask.

"It's saying, 'I better get out of here fast!'"

Later, when the painting is dry, I ask him if I can use his painting for a game we could share with the children. He is happy for me to do that. I do this and introduce a variation of "Giants and fairies" (that most of us know) so that it becomes "Giants and ants." We first use the low notes on the piano for the giants and the high notes for the ants and divide the group into two. The first half will take the role of giants (who may frighten but not step on ants and are scared of getting bitten so run home when the ants come out), and the second half will take the role of ants (who hide when the giants are out and about).

I wonder if we have a CD we can use. We use some Mozart (from a CD called Baby Mozart) arranged and played (it has wonderful dynamics) so the children can easily distinguish between the heavy steps of the giants and the lighter and quicker steps of the ants. (The actual track used is Piano Sonata in A, K448, 1st movement.) Too often the music we present has been digitally altered to provide the same acoustic level throughout so it can be played in the car. Great for in the car, but it is hopeless for teaching children about musical dynamics. They need loud and soft, fast and slow, lilting and thumping, twinkling and heavy, ordinary 2/4 or 4/4 rhythms or the exotic 7/8 galloping rhythms we find in Arabic music or the 3/4 time of a waltz. They need to hear varying instruments, real ones either live or on CD, and to have time to appreciate the sounds they hear. Children learn to listen if we provide the environments and encouragement, but we can so easily and thoughtlessly teach them to be deaf.

So often we introduce a new song, sing it a few times, expect the children to sing along and learn the words and then add another song. We wonder why they don't join in with us; they do the actions but don't sing. Have we given them the opportunity?

An old song ("The Big Bass Drum") pops into my head, and I add a variation to the morning meeting time. It has taken me several years of teaching to realize we can use a familiar tune and new words. We can make the words up spontaneously when we see the children's reactions, which brings our own creativity and the children's to life.

Oh, we can beat with our feet, and this is how we do it.
Stamp, stamp, stamp, with our feet; and that's the way we do it.
Oh, we can clap with our hands, and this is how we do it.
Clap, clap, clap with our hands; and that's the way we do it.

One morning while visiting a center, I see a little boy named Samuel sitting in a stroller. The other children are taking turns on a small, round trampoline, standing and also holding hands with an adult. I notice Samuel trying to bounce where he sits and suggest he may like a turn on the trampoline. While he sits on the trampoline, I mirror his bouncing movement with some words.

Bouncy, bouncy, bouncy; bouncy bouncy, bouncy. Bouncy, bouncy, bouncy, up and down!

I noticed Samuel's huge smile, and it became part of the song.

Smiley, smiley, smiley; smiley, smiley, smiley. Smiley, smiley, smiley, up and down!

He begins to nod and then to clap, and these actions also become part of the emerging song. In this manner a small boy named Samuel and an adult co-construct a song together. We share it later with the other children in Samuel's group. The children who are able to stand or walk add their suggestions for new verses: wiggle, wiggle bottoms and tappy, tappy feet. I've found that children really sing when they have a chorus, and they use their bodies to make sounds when we encourage them with repetition and fun.

CREATING CONNECTIONS

In other chapters you will note references to musical and rhythmic dimensions. This will be, in part, because of my own particular interests in the topic, but also because I realize that music can be quite a frightening aspect for nonmusical people. You don't have to learn to play an instrument (although it really helps). You can use a tambour (a tambourine without the metal bits) or shakers or other percussion instruments with your voice. If you are concerned about your voice, get some vocal lessons to help you become more confident; sing with confidence anyway and use a CD and other adults to help you. The children will respond to your *intention* if not your ability!

Young children do not yet have experience waiting for a turn if they are the only child in their family and have not attended an early childhood program before. They might not have much experience with waiting even if there are other children in their family; their requests may be answered quickly. In a center, however, sometimes we do have to wait a little while. We can't all crowd into the small space to wash hands before lunch, so we have to wait until it's safe. When we play board games we have to wait until it's our turn to throw the dice again, and we can't move someone else's cards or token. When there are five children playing with the train track, we sometimes have to wait for a turn using the big black engine to pull the cars. We can't ALL be Henny Penny in the dramatization today—that would mean we would have to tell the story 20 times!

Musical instruments can help children learn some of these basic social rules in safe ways: "The instruments have to wait for their turn (we tell the children), so hold them still and listen carefully." The instruments wait their turn; our role is to listen so we can help them. What better way?

Sophie looks scared when it's her turn to be "it" in the game. Jane has tapped her on the head, and she was willing, but right now the task seems so big. How can she get up and run around the circle like the others? "Would you like me to come with you?" asks her friend, who offers a hand to run with her.

Music games provide opportunities to find your courage and to explore your compassion. Jacob's painting sparked a completely new game. Another painting can inspire children to move to music in particular ways.

"When you hear the music play, take your lovely ribbons for a dance. Make them dance above your heads or down on the ground, curling and looping around, making shapes as they go. When the music stops, make a shape on the floor with your ribbon and stay still," the adults instruct the children how to play a new game. (Thank you Yvonne Winer for sharing this Froebel-inspired idea with us.)

"Remember, a cloud is a shape. So is a puddle of water. Your shapes can be anything you like." The teacher hands out shiny satin ribbons in all the colors of the rainbow, and the children respond to the music she offers. When the music stops, the children make shapes on the floor and then walk carefully around them to examine everyone's ideas. They pick up the ribbons when the music begins again and repeat the game, this time adding their ribbon to one another child is holding and considering, do those colors look good together?

Music, games and dances provide opportunities for children to learn to be physically close with safety. They learn to take care of each other and respect one another's personal space. They experience direction changes and follow directions, taking three steps or many depending on the instructions given.

The children hold the outside edge of a small, colorful and purpose-made dancing parachute. It helps them form a circle and to move together in one direction and then turn to move in the opposite direction.

London Bridge is falling down,
Falling down, falling down.
London Bridge is falling down,
My fair lady.

They step into and away from the middle, making the parachute billow up and sink down. (The adult uses the children's suggestions for ways to fix the bridge.)

Fix it up with ice cream,
Ice cream, ice cream.
Fix it up with ice cream,
My fair lady.

And then holding the edges of the parachute, the children turn to walk around the circle again.

London Bridge is falling down,
Falling down, falling down.
London Bridge is falling down,
My fair lady.

Music and rhythm are fun for most children. An experienced and skillful adult can use music to stir them to fever pitch and then bring them down in an instant to lie quietly on the floor with eyes closed in feigned sleep. Adults or children can invent songs and games using a template of familiar ones and some minor tweaking.

Music has a place not only in group times. It can be made available under the lovely shade of a tree with scarves and instruments for children to create stories with and dance for themselves. It can be used when the children relax or rest, focusing the children's attention on the variety of voices and harmonies that humans use. Music is portable, adaptable, and open to creative expression.

The importance of voice

Some of us may be familiar with the stories by comedienne Joyce Grenfell about the typical early childhood teacher and one of her famous pupils. If you are not familiar with Joyce, you will be familiar with the singsong voice many adults use with young children. There is a reason: softer and more musical voices are less threatening to young children—but sometimes do we go a bit overboard? I listen to and almost laugh when I hear the airline attendant give the safety briefing with the forced downward turn to the end of each sentence. We use our voice every day to guide behavior, to praise or redirect or voice our disapproval. A friend (thanks, Sonya) shares this story.

The librarian from the local school comes to the local childcare center to share a book as part of the transition to school program. She brings a very favorite picture book, The Magic Hat, by Mem Fox. The children in the center love this book, and their teacher loves this book. They have read it a hundred times, the teacher thinking of new ways to use her voice to amplify the wonderful words the author has written. The teacher usually almost sings some parts; the children join in, hands going this way and that with the words.

This day, however, the librarian sits, holding the book to face herself, and reads in a monotone voice, "Oh the magic hat, the magic hat, it moves like this, it moves like that."

Simon, sitting near the teacher at the back of the group, lays down, legs in the air in a dead antlike position, and says quietly, "If that's the best they can do, I ain't going."

We don't have to overdo the "voices" when we read a story, as it may overtake the meaning, but do *something* with your voice! I often tell the story of the lessons from Jack, our much-loved pink and gray Australian parrot. He lived with us for a number of years and had many lessons for us. Jack really used his voice to communicate his thoughts and feelings. When disturbed by an unfamiliar sound, he urged us to "*listen!*" If we didn't, we'd get a sharp nip on the ear. He knew we needed to listen so we could stay safe. He was very aware of safety issues; he would hear the small birds in the tree outside alert everyone that a hawk was nearby. If he saw the hawk through the window, he would literally scream "*git*" and fly around the house, calling the emergency number on the phone, "ring-ring, ring-ring," or tell us with great authority, "It's a dog." I have used his ideas when telling many of the stories that are familiar to us, bringing them to life in ways I never thought possible. You may be able to imagine what Hattie the hen really sounded like when she saw the fox (*Hattie and the Fox*, a story by Mem Fox).

Young children develop their singing voices quite early; the ability to sing in tune is a response to opportunities to sing, being sung to, listening to familiar songs and learning to sing along at an early age. It's important that children have these experiences at least before they are five for their vocal range to be developed and to refine the ability to sing in tune. Professor Frazer Mustard, from Canada, told the delegates at the Early Childhood Australia conference in Hobart a few years ago, "That is part of your job, to sing to children."

Let's do it again

Repetition allows the children time to learn the song, find their courage and singing voices, learn to participate or wait, take turns and share space. You do not need a huge repertoire of songs; instead, you need to be able to rearrange the ones you have. For instance, the first week of spring we began with a simple chorus:

Spring is a happy time
Spring is a happy time
Spring is a happy time
Happy, happy spring!

"What are you going to do this weekend?" we ask the children.
"I'm going to the farm to ride motorbikes," Jarrod tells me.

Riding motorbikes on the farm
Riding motorbikes on the farm

Riding motorbikes on the farm
All because it's spring.
Spring is a happy time
Spring is a happy time
Spring is a happy time
Happy, happy spring!

"I am going camping with my family," says Tom.

Camping up by Blowering Dam
Camping up by Blowering Dam
Camping up by Blowering Dam
All because it's spring.

Spring is a happy time
Spring is a happy time
Spring is a happy time
Happy, happy spring!

The song takes shape; children join in the chorus and add new words about their expectations for the weekend. The following week they reflect on the experiences and Jarrod adds about doing doughnuts on the four-wheel bike. (I try not to panic!)

"Doing doughnuts on the quad," we sing for Jarrod.

"Finding eggs under the tent," for Tom.

When children learn they can have power over the words, suggesting and having their suggestions used, imagine what a sensation it is. The key ingredient though is repetition, not novelty! Add new songs or games here and there, but keep returning to the familiar ones. Have five good songs to use with instruments and use them in different combinations. Have another five good marching/jumping/twirling/nodding songs and rotate them. Have five great songs with a chorus and use these. They will provide a sound foundation. Add a few little spicy treats here and there and your musical program will come alive with fun and vitality.

Using instruments with children

Use the songs you know well and are confident with, such as "Punchinello." Here is a suggestion.

What are you made of Punchinello funny fellow?
What are you made of Punchinello little dear?

Your head is made of cheese, Punchinello funny fellow.
Your head is made of cheese, Punchinello little dear.

What are you made of Punchinello funny fellow?
What are you made of Punchinello little dear?

Your eyes are made of peas, Punchinello funny fellow.
Your eyes are made of peas, Punchinello little dear.
Your mouth is made of strawberries, Punchinello funny fellow.
Your mouth is made of strawberries, Punchinello little dear.

You and the children can easily invent parts of the body and suitable foods to add to this song.

Ask the children to hold instruments still and listen to the verse and play in the chorus. They learn to wait for their turn, they become familiar with the beat and they can add suggestions for the verses. It's an ideal song really.

Here is another suggestion. You will be familiar with the old song "She'll Be Coming 'Round the Mountain When She Comes." The version about six white horses is not the only possible version. Ask the children to make suggestions. You can add classification skills at the same time quite easily.

Sing:
She'll be coming 'round the mountain when she comes.
She'll be coming 'round the mountain when she comes.
She'll be coming 'round the mountain,
Coming 'round the mountain,
Coming 'round the mountain when she comes.

Sing and play instruments:
Singing yi-yi-yippee-yippe yi
Singing yi-yi-yippee-yippe yi
Singing yi-yi-yippee, yi-yi, yippee
Singing yi-yi-yippee-yippe yi

She'll be wearing . . . (invite suggestions about clothing)

She'll be eating . . .

She'll be playing . . .

She'll be riding a . . . when she comes.

That's five *different* versions of the song. I was visiting a group of university students recently and used this song. Later, I was astonished when several students commented, "I thought you could only sing about the six white horses."

When the children are familiar with chorus-type songs and can listen and wait for a turn, bring out your favorite stories and add musical instruments for the characters. One, "The Three Billy Goats Gruff," is a suitable candidate. A musical instrument can be chosen to represent the troll, perhaps a drum with a big voice. Another instrument can represent the large billy goat, with two more instruments to represent the middle-sized billy goat and the small billy goat. It works brilliantly to choose stuffed toys to act out the story. Children scream with laughter when a lovely cuddly bear plays the role of the troll. A fat pink pig might be the middle-sized goat, and a fluffy yellow duckling might play the smallest billy goat, and so on. Extend yourself and develop new ideas when you can.

Songs, games, stories, drama and dance

Scared of doing drama? I am not surprised. We see people who do it really well on a video or in a workshop and we feel less than confident. Somehow it doesn't work for us in our center with our children. Over many years of teaching, I have found some less-threatening ways that have worked for me and might for you as well.

START SIMPLE!

I am sitting at the playdough area with a few children in the first weeks of the new year. There are a couple of small holders from the glue stick we often use to paste children's work into their portfolios. There are 10 small holes in the blue tray, suggesting small muffins, and one of the children carefully rolls the dough to fit the space. I start to roll the dough as well and intend to use a song I have written for Preschool Math about "The muffin man," but for some reason the song that comes out instead is "Five tasty buns"!

Five tasty buns in the baker's shop
Round and sweet with sugar on the top
Along came Ashleigh with a penny one day
Bought a tasty bun and took it away.

Ashleigh liked being included in the song. Jack smiles at me. I know he wants to be next.

Four tasty buns in the baker's shop
Round and sweet with sugar on the top
Along came Jack with a penny one day
Bought a tasty bun and took it away.

A little group is forming; soon many children are included in the song. That afternoon, just before families begin to arrive and the children are gathered, I sing it again, this time using my fingers. We can't use everyone's name; there isn't time, so I promise we will return to it later.

The next day I am prepared with some scarves and old pennies from my own small coin collection. "Mmm, we have some pennies in a box we could use and some lovely cloths that would be great icing. I wonder…" I had been thinking the evening before.

We gather the children into a large circle. This is the first time they have done this, and it takes a little organizing, but we finally manage it. I ask five children to be tasty buns. They bunch themselves onto the floor, and I cover them with the small cloths, talking about a chocolate one, a strawberry one, one with hundreds and thousands and so on.

I hand five pennies to five other children and appoint a baker. The game begins. It is such a hit, and everyone wants to play it again and again and the next week and the next!

We are introducing the notion of drama but without trying to do something that is too hard. I was reminded by Alise Shafer speaking at the International Festival of Learning in Fremantle a few years ago how easily we start at step fifteen instead of where the children are. She was talking about young children using clay and paper without the background we assume from an adult perspective, but the idea flows across all areas. Start simply!

A familiar and much-loved story also works well as the starting point for drama. Use a story!

We have been reading The Tale of Peter Rabbit *by Beatrix Potter. I know from experience that this story works wonderfully well for a drama game with music. The children are familiar with the story.*

"If you want to be a rabbit this time, come over here near me. If you'd like to be Mr. McGregor, go over to the window, near Trish," I say.

The children divide into roughly two groups.

I use the piano (I don't really play the piano; I just use it. Keeping your fingers about one note apart works quite well):

Mr. McGregor loved to walk in his garden.

I use the lower notes for some good thumping sounds, like big footsteps.

He counted all the carrots, he counted all the radishes and he counted all the lettuces. "My garden looks very good," he said.
But while Mr. McGregor was sleeping that night, some little rabbits, Peter and his friends, crept under the big gate and right into the garden. They pulled up the radishes, they pulled up the carrots and they nibbled on the lettuces.

Now I use tinkling sounds from the higher notes on the piano.

Then the little rabbits go home with very full tummies to sleep under the old fir tree.

The next morning, Mr. McGregor got out of bed, stretched and looked outside. "Oh, dear!" he said. "Someone has been eating my radishes, and someone has been eating my carrots and, oh, look at the poor lettuces! It must be those little rabbits again!"

I use the lower notes again and invent more footsteps suggesting Mr. McGregor stamping around the garden.

We continue the story for some time: Mr. McGregor planting more carrots, more radishes and more lettuces, the little rabbits coming out each night to scuttle around the garden. When the children are ready, ask them to swap sides so they can be the rabbits or play Mr. McGregor.

The beauty of using a musical instrument to assist (a piano is good, as is a guitar, but so is a tambour, some bells or tapping sticks and your voice) is that if the game gets a little out of hand you can bring it to a stop easily using the instrument. An instrument helps control the situation.

What about dance? It's not as simple as putting on the music and seeing what happens. Doing that we often get chaos, hurt children, or children standing, not sure what to do. Outside under a tree with familiar music and some dancing props, it is much simpler. The children have space to move, and only a few interested and knowledgeable children will join in and they are in control. But if you want to introduce the idea of dance to a large audience, then it's not quite that easy, is it?

USE HOOPS

It takes a few years, but we finally locate some colorful child-sized hoops. They work wonderfully for helping children make a circle. I put the hoops on the floor (you need a large space for this) and the children sit in them. The hoops make excellent seats for a train game—getting on and off at the various stops around the zoo to be elephants or tigers and then sitting back on quickly when the whistle blows. I wonder about using them for dance.

"These hoops are very interesting. You can pretend a lot of things with them," I begin. "If I hold one like this, I can pretend it's a mirror and brush my hair." I model the movement.

"If I hold it like this, I can scoop up some water and water the flowers over there." I suggest another movement. I invite other ideas from the adults and the children in the group, and we practice the movements. A hat on a sunny day, a basket to carry fruit, a suitcase and closing a window are added to the repertoire of ideas.

Finally the music. I choose some tai-chi that fosters slow, deliberate movements. Children who don't want to dance are offered some bells and chime bars to add to the orchestra so they can be involved another way. Beautiful! This music also suggests butterflies emerging from cocoons and spreading their wings. The choices are yours and the children's.

USE A CD OR TAPE

We listen to Lynley Dodd reading (on a tape) Hairy Maclary from Donaldson's Dairy a few times during relaxation. The children love the story and the characters.

I promise that tomorrow we'll play a Hairy Maclary drama game.

Tomorrow arrives!

We once again ask the children to sit in a large circle, as large as they can make. We needed space for the "stage" in the middle. The adults chose the first characters,

Muffin McLay, Bottomly Potts, Schnitzel Von Krumb, Bitser Moloney, Hercules Morse and of course Hairy Maclary and Scarface Claw, the toughest Tom in town!

We make a few suggestions about how the game might go but largely leave the children to work it out and interpret the story themselves. We play it many times, and each time the children listen to and interpret the characters in the story, waiting for their turn. The audience sitting on the side claps and cheers at appropriate times. There are masses of wonderful familiar stories that lend themselves to interpretation with a table covered in cloth (for Foxy Loxy's den in the traditional tales Henny Penny *or* The Mitten*) or other simple props. Keep it simple! A simple chair in the middle of the floor can be ideal for bringing Mem Fox's story* Night Noises *to life. I remember one child becoming one of the most wonderful old dogs, partly asleep and being roused by the sounds outside the house as we read the story.*

The CD player, musical instruments and other devices

It is best if the CD player is close to the action, not out of the way and needing you to leave the area to turn it on and off. My own concern is about music playing all day and the children not learning to listen, as well as adding to the noise levels in the room. It's a personal thing I suppose, but for me it doesn't work. Here are some other suggestions that might make your life easier.

ORGANIZE

Find a safe place to put your CDs and tapes so you can easily find them.

I found it useful to make individual taped copies of stories (previously on one tape) so I could play just that particular story when I needed to. Make a catalog if you need to that shows you where each song or dance can be found so you can find it in a minute.

STORE

Keeping instruments grouped with others that are similar or mixed in large baskets with handles works extremely well. The baskets are light enough to bring to the floor for easy access and sturdy enough to protect the instruments. If the instruments are available for everyday use, we usually use them every day. If they are stored away and hard to get at, we will leave them there; that's human nature. I don't think we need to have the instruments available for children to use all day—I for one can't stand the noise! Take a few out under a shady tree on a blanket with a portable CD player the children can safely use instead.

PROPS

Hoops and pieces of cloth work well. We bought some light muslin/cheesecloth in a large roll and cut it into lengths about as long as a child's wingspan. We hung them on fences and spray painted them with edicol dyes. Later we painted them with glitter glue/paint for added beauty. They made wonderful and enduring butterfly wings. They don't wash, but how often do you need to wash butterfly wings?

DEMONSTRATE

Let's face it: musical instruments are expensive, even the simple ones. Children do not necessarily know how to use them, so a demonstration of how they work and how to take care of them will reap benefits. Supervise and encourage the children to use them carefully, not as weapons against each other. It's like everything else—we show respect for musical instruments by not throwing them around or dropping them where we stand, but by putting them carefully back where they belong.

SPACE

If space for the children to move in easily and safely is an issue, try splitting the group in half. Let one half do the actions and dance or play the game, and the other half add to the orchestra. You can even divide the group into three, with the third group sitting near you as the enthusiastic audience. The children will swap places and have a different turn quite easily with a little direction from you.

PARACHUTE

Colorful, specially made child-sized parachutes are available for a reasonable cost, and they last years and years. They are easily washed, stored and light to carry. How to start?

Circle dances like "Zum Gali Gali" (found on *Jewish Favorites*) or "Here We Go 'Round the Mulberry Bush" or "London Bridge Is Falling Down" (traditional songs) are excellent ways to help the children learn to hold the edge of the parachute and turn to go one direction and then turn to go the opposite way.

Drama games based on a story like *Who Sank the Boat?* (by Pamela Allen) are also good ways to introduce the safe use of the parachute. For instance:

We choose five children to sit in the middle of the parachute. The other children and adults are sitting around the edge, legs crossed, holding the edges quietly, and we begin to tell the story.

Max goes fishing with his friends one day. They go fishing out in the bay. He packs some sandwiches for lunch and takes some drinks. They pack their sunhats and sunblock too.

At first the sea is very quiet, and the friends throw out their lines, and wind them back in, throw out their lines and wind them back in. The fish are not biting. They sit and have their sandwiches and a drink and then settle down to have a nap while the sea gently rocks them to sleep. (We encourage the children at the edge of the parachute to make little waves.)

They don't see it because they are asleep, but a big black cloud appears and the wind starts to blow. The children wake up and look around. The waves are huge. (We encourage the children to make the waves bigger and bigger.)

"We'd better row back home," says Max, and the children row as fast as they can, the waves getting higher and higher, until they are safely back again.

An alternative is a story about the dragon hunt (an alternative to the bear hunt).

We choose a group of children to go on a dragon hunt. They go under the parachute and lie waiting. The story begins like this . . .

One day some children are out looking for the dragon. They walk across the river, through the long grass, and over the rickety bridge. Finally they arrive at the entrance to a cave. They creep in. At first they can feel just a little breeze (the outside children apply a gentle breeze by making the parachute slowly lift up and down), but as they go farther into the cave, the breeze becomes much bigger (the outside children apply a little faster and bigger movement) and finally they feel a huge blast of red hot wind. They are so scared they don't wait to see if it is the dragon. They just run back home! You can imagine the rest.

Cultural richness

Wow, what an opportunity! There are countless songs, dances and pieces of music from all around the world that we can use any day in our centers. Search at Putumayo (www.putumayo.com), ask your local retailers, harass the specialty books and CD suppliers and listen for music that attracts, and then track it down. Many instruments are available from varying cultures as well—find out where to get them and tell others. Combine the music with interesting pieces of cloth and you have a kaleidoscope of culture alive and thriving in your center.

Learn or locate simple songs like "Head and Shoulders, Knees and Toes" in a variety of languages. Ask parents to assist with new words and songs that are familiar to them. Look for music that covers a range of rhythms, not only the 2/4 and 4/4 we usually associate with music for children, but also 3/4 and 7/8. Rock, soul, blues, jazz, country, classical and folk—they all play their own part in bringing the world of music to the children. Set your imagination free, listen to music and imagine how it can be used to enrich the environment and the experiences you offer.

Being inclusive

It can be a challenge to meet the needs of some children; these stories tell ways that it becomes possible with some lateral thinking.

MAKE SPACE AVAILABLE

Katrina is confined to a kind of body-fitting wheelchair. We always find a space for her in the circle for the games. We make a small supporting beanbag so she is at the same level as the other children, and we make sure she is chased as well as chases other children in Duck, Duck Goose. That was the favorite game this year. It is wonderful to see the other children make allowances for her. They chase her really hard, but never quite catch her! Julian (a young athletic man working with her) takes her as fast as he can, her hair streaming behind her. She smiles from ear to ear with excitement, encouraging him to go faster. Other games she remains in the chair and is pushed, faster and faster, screaming with excitement.

BE OBSERVANT

I notice that Dougal (a little boy with Down syndrome) loves jumping songs, especially those with a predictable chorus.

Jump, jump, jump if you feel you want to
Jump, jump, jump if you feel you can
Jump, jump, jump if you feel you want to
Jump, jump, jump if you feel you can.

He positions himself, anticipating the beginning of the jumping chorus to be the first child to jump up each time, a smile from ear to ear.

Imagine how the song "If you're happy and you know it" could be used!

He changed the way I do this song forever!

Following the children's interests

The children are lying on their blankets on the floor for relaxation and imagination time. We often tell made-up stories about two little raindrops and their adventures in the water cycle. Often (or so the story goes) they fall onto the preschool swings and are then carried around in a child's pocket all morning until the sun invites them to come back into the sky and so on. We use a different child's name each time we tell the story, adding some little detail from that child's morning. The children are used to this quiet time and to listening to special music and letting their imagination respond to the sounds.

One day I play a new piece of music I have found, "El condor pasa," better known as "I'd rather be a forest than a tree," made popular by Simon and Garfunkel. It is a version from my home collection played with South American pipes and is particularly haunting. I notice Edward, eyes closed, moving to the music as he lies there. He is smiling, and I suspect may be humming, although I can't hear him.

Later I ask him about his imaginings.

"Well I was thinking about those little turtles in their eggs we read about earlier, and I was imagining them hatching, crawling out of the eggs and trying to get to the

water, but the seagulls were swooping and scaring them." I can hear the seagulls when I think about it. What a great idea.

I share the story with the children, and we have time for a couple of turns with the game before going home that afternoon. This game is repeated at least 50 times before the year ends. The children choose to be turtles or seagulls and to wait for their turn in the music. When the turtles are hatching, the seagulls wait and sharpen their beaks and test their wings. When the seagulls swoop, the turtles huddle together for safety. All turtles eventually get to the ocean with a splash! (Of course.)

Writing music with children

Grace (my granddaughter) is marching around my garden singing:

I'm walking in the garden;
I'm walking round and round.
I'm walking with my granny;
We hardly make a sound.

She is barely three years old, and yet she is inventing variations to a familiar song.

The opportunity arises most days that we have with young children to create new songs. If we model how we can invent songs, we encourage children's creativity.

- About swinging:

Tom's swinging and swinging at preschool today,
Swinging and swinging his worries away.
Feet in the air and then puts them both down,
His face turns to smiles and not to a frown!
(Points to the sky and then to the ground. Also works for a more general situation.)

(Tom has arrived in a bad mood; he has had a fight with his brother over breakfast and is still fuming. We acknowledge his feeling and find a soothing activity to try, complete with his own song.)

- At the playdough area:

Roll and roll and roll the playdough,
Roll it in a ball.
Roll it here and roll it there—
Careful, don't let it fall!

- At the blocks:

Put a block over here
And a block over there.

Put a block over here
And another over there;
A lot of blocks here and there, everywhere.
It's a building sort of day!

• With puzzles:

Searching and searching, what can I find?
I'm looking everywhere, but I don't mind,
'Cause when I am finished and show it to you,
You'll feel happy and I know I will too.

Just open the window in your imagination; stop the "I can't" attitude and have a go!

Learning to listen and discern

If the music we use is designed especially for children, we may find that the makers of the music have seriously underestimated what the children are capable of. Children need to listen to a variety of sounds, tempos and interpretations so that they can discern changes in the mood of the music.

The songs we sing and teach to the children can be quite complex, especially for the older children. They will respond with delight to "The Purple People Eater," "The Yellow Submarine," and even "Rock around the Clock!" They easily learn songs in other languages if given the opportunity to hear them frequently.

The temptation for adults is to keep providing novelty, yet it is with increasing familiarity that children learn. It takes some time to develop what Eisner (1985) describes as "automaticity." He states that children need exposure and opportunities with the same materials, equipment and environments over extended periods of time so that they develop easygoing awareness and control and from this develop their creativity.

Encouraging participation

Here is a short story about participation. Sometimes we have to look with new eyes.

A few years ago there was a little boy in my class. I mean little. He had a condition that prevented him from growing as quickly as other children. He was a bit timid, a tad shy, and so we were very gentle with how we handled him, encouraging him to participate. We didn't think what we were doing was having any effect. However, one day a visitor came from Early Intervention, and she chuckled as she told us he **was** *participating: his little toes were beating the rhythm inside his sandals. Sometimes you have to look a little harder!*

It takes some children a long time to feel secure and confident enough to get up and perform in front of others or even with others. Be patient. They can participate in other ways.

We all do this and we all do that

There is a fun game actually called "We'll All Do This and We'll All Do That!" The first time I ever played it with children I discovered what a wonderful alternative it was to one I knew called "Punchinello." In "Punchinello" a child goes to the middle to model a movement, and then everyone points their finger at the child to ask, "What shall we do?" It seemed a threatening type of movement I suppose, but I had been completely unaware of that until I stumbled upon this version. The children responded in the way I had hoped they might.

Michael is nearing five years of age. All year he has sat and watched the children take a turn. Each time we ask him, he replies very politely, "Not today, thank you."

We wait, perhaps not as patiently as we would like, but we wait. The day following his birthday, he arrives and announces, "I would like first turn in 'Duck, Duck, Goose' today, please. I'm five." He did it!

Pamela and Elayne are twins. They like to sit together in group times, and so far they have not participated in any way that we can observe. At least they are not crying. Today one of them picks up the shaker that is placed near her (we have placed an instrument nearby all year with that hope) and starts to shake it. Her sister uses the bells the following day. Soon they are fully involved, taking turns, running around the edge of the circle, marching with the big bass drum and so on. We just had to wait for their ideal moment.

Find an alternative way a child can participate. We always need an audience or an orchestra; they can become part of that. No, I don't allow children to hide under a table or bang away with blocks while the others are listening and participating, but that is my hang-up—I can't cope with the distraction! You make up your own mind. I will find a way for the child to sit near me and watch or hold something or invent a role that will work with the game instead. I am not talking about group activities with a two-year-old child—I wouldn't put them in a position where I would expect them to participate—but children starting school the next year, yes, I do expect them to attend usually. There are exceptions of course: a child who is still finishing a project can continue to do that as long as we can see him or her from where we are. A child who is feeling sad or unwell can find a special place to be comfortable in. I am not so tolerant of a child who finds pleasure in disrupting the others while they are listening.

Image of the child

THE CHILD IS AN INDIVIDUAL

The twins, a child waiting until he turns five, a tiny child with little toes beating the rhythm or an energetic and confident child—each one makes us consider what it means to be an individual within a group, how we can make a contribution in our own way. Keep an open heart.

THE CHILD IS CREATIVE

Our aim is to encourage children's creativity in the *musical and rhythmic sense* with the use of informal songs and music, exploration of music, invention of new songs or melodies and experimentation with sounds, instruments, dance and drama.

Reflections, challenges and wonderings

What experiences and opportunities or environments we offer depends on the age of the children, the space available, the routine we have in place and the talents available with the adults as well as the interests of the children. For the younger child music is up close and personal, mostly one to one and often combined with feeding, changing or going to sleep. For the older child it can be more formal and in a group situation, as well as some up-close and personal moments, when he is at the play-dough area, doing puzzles, or on the swing.

Drama is the peek-a-boo game we play with a baby, the train game as we deliver food to her open mouth (we hope) and the round and round the garden game we play on her tiny palm. For the older child, it is role playing dress-up, cooking, doing the wash, taking care of the sick and injured or staffing the flower shop. Drama can begin as mime and guessing games and continue to full-scale dramatizations of a familiar story.

Movement with children is an essential ingredient in their learning. The rhythmic beat of music provides opportunities to learn about time intervals that mathematics needs. The classification of ideas for "She'll Be Coming 'round the Mountain" and other similar songs provide opportunities for children to use this understanding in musical ways.

Dancing involves balance and control of the body, and in turn control of the body enables us to sit well so we can concentrate on a task. It helps us hold things well and use them most effectively. So, learning to sway, to clap, to nod or to wink is important to the total development of a child.

Participation generates courage and self-esteem as we overcome some of our innate shyness to share our ideas with others. The child who never participates is missing something really important in her social and emotional development.

"Now kangaroos, when you are jumping remember that you balance using your front legs held like this," the visiting storyteller tells the children.

"When you stop still to listen, your ears will turn this way and that; you might scratch your tummy like this or lick your forearm to make yourself cool. You might even shake a bit if you are frightened," she adds. The children set off to make her story come alive. They jump, arms carefully placed; they stop and listen, turning their ears this way and that. They scratch and lick and wait for instructions from the story. Some are clearly frightened, shaking nervously. She has brought the elements of nature into our classroom.

Drama encourages children to put themselves into the place of another in their imagination. It helps children develop empathy and awareness of others.

Drama helps children explain their ideas. What an incredible and easily overlooked tool.

PUTTING IT TOGETHER

In this chapter we have bounced around like the kangaroos from music to dance and movement to drama, but I hope with some sense of wholeness.

"The arts" in the form of drama, music and movement are essential elements in an early childhood program for a reason. The social skills that children learn when participating together in a group, to tell a story, to respond with movements, to make music or to sing, are important for adult life.

Children learn about math (time and space) using music, drama and movement games.

They have firsthand experiences of being crowded, of being able to move freely, of having to stop suddenly and of taking care of others. It's difficult to draw the demarcation lines, as whatever we talk about always ends up being part of a sense of the whole child.

Connecting dimensions

Glance back over the chapter and see how other dimensions impact the expression of music and movement ideas. We have explored some of the sensory elements, listening to sounds, noticing differences, noticing changes and silence. We have explored the notion of waiting for a turn, sharing space and taking care of each other, of being responsible. We have acknowledged individuals, cultural aspects and unique abilities as well as feelings.

We have looked at ways to help children participate as fully as they can, respecting others and materials and following directions, while having space to invent creatively.

We have taken ideas that have come from the children and found ways to share these ideas with the whole group, acknowledging ownership and encouraging creativity, making it possible for children to share successfully.

Creating new experiences and ideas

Let your imagination run. Sounds so easy, and when you get started you will find it is. I hope that some of the practical and simple examples in this chapter will show you how achievable it is if you have the will to do it.

Just like every other aspect of encouraging the development of young children, we observe closely, we value their stories and ideas, we share and make possible this experience with others, we follow their lead as much as possible and we try to find experiences that they can manage easily but will still stretch them a little.

TAKING CARE OF YOURSELF

Be prepared to make mistakes! A few challenges a day indicate we are trying something new and have moved out of our own comfort zones! Encourage the adults you share space with to think of new ways for children to experience musical and rhythmic dimensions. They might be as nervous as you, so your leadership can accomplish real change. Go to workshops and learn new skills, find someone to teach you basics on a guitar or piano, enroll in singing lessons. Reach out and see what is possible. Each time you develop a new skill and share it with the children, you have enriched the lives of everyone, yourself included, and it will feel good.

Lachlan solves many problems to complete his painting.

Cushions, teddy bears, sleeping bags and books make for interesting tent play.

Here are some useful CDs that might assist you in getting music and rhythmic dimensions started in your playroom:

The Baby Einstein Music Box Orchestra, 2000, *Baby Mozart*, The Baby Einstein Music Company, LLC.

Jenkins E, 1968, *Play Your Instruments and Make a Pretty Sound*, Smithsonian Folkways.

Jewish Traditional et al., 1997, *Jewish Favorites*, Centaur.

My leaps were high: I was flying like a bird, gliding through the open sky. If the music had allowed it, I would have leaped into the air all night. There was no hard work, only sheer joy.

Li Cunxin

3

EXPLORING
KINAESTHETIC
DIMENSIONS

What do we mean?

I have been teaching adults to play guitar. I have a small group of enthusiastic folks who started as absolute beginners—nonmusicians, with just an interest and desire to learn to play. We meet week by week. At first there were large numbers, but gradually the numbers reduced as some zoomed ahead and others didn't. I tried to work out what the problem was. For some, they found it difficult to know exactly where their fingers on their left hand were going. We placed some spots on the neck of the guitar so they could see the shape of the chord, but some still had trouble putting their fingers back in the same space or applying the required amount of pressure on the string. Some found it easy, and because of this they wanted to practice more and they made amazing progress. The people who found it physically difficult didn't get the same satisfaction from practice. It never sounded right, it felt difficult, they didn't develop confidence and they stopped coming to lessons. Perhaps I could start them again one day and we'll go more slowly.

It made me realize, though, how important kinaesthetic memory is. When I dial a familiar phone number, sure, I use the numbers in my head, but my fingers know the pattern. If I really stop to think about the number, I can't dial my friend. When I relax and let my fingers do the remembering, then I am much more likely to get the right number. It's the same with using my cash card: the PIN has a pattern, and my fingers remember the pattern. When I play the guitar my fingers remember the shape of the chords and can return home instantly. When I type I can mostly find the letter I want in a fraction of a second. When I use scissors my fingers remember what to do, and when I drive a car I don't have to think about putting the clutch in and how to let it out while at the same instant applying pressure to the accelerator. The lower part of our brains, the cerebellum, stores memories of movement especially well. It also coordinates balance and posture. I was watching the series *The Human Body* again recently, and it started me thinking in new ways about kinaesthetic memory and movement. The presenter showed us some astronauts learning how to move in low-gravity atmospheres and practicing in a large swimming pool. One of the astronauts explained that when she first started to use a robotic arm, she found it difficult because she was thinking too much, but when she relaxed and just felt the movement, her cerebellum took over. She could move the arm as if it were just an extension of her own body.

I drop the lid from the car polish in the garage. Peter and I look and look for it with no luck. I get down lower and use my hands to help me look. My eyes know to follow my hands, and my attention focuses. There among some leaves curled against the wooden fence, I can see the black lid so clearly. When I just look I may not see what I am looking for, but if I use my feet or hands as well, I can see. I am not very good at doing jigsaw puzzles, and so I have been doing some lately to practice these skills and learn to see better. I find when I move my hands over the pieces on the table I can see where they should go; it's almost as if my hands have eyes as well. I know I am a kinaesthetic learner, but I often surprise myself with how much I rely on my hands or body movement.

As a child, when learning a poem, I would walk the poem, reading aloud and putting the words into the rhythm of my movements. Then I could recall the movement and the words came with it. Dancers tell me that they learn the movements with the music, and later, when they hear the music, they can remember automatically the movement associated. We often use a variety of senses together, and a lot of this action happens in the cerebellum.

Think about a skill you have learned—to crochet, knit, play tennis, ride a bike, pump the swing with your legs, dance, play the piano, embroider, use a sewing machine, cut an onion or swing a bat. Was it difficult at first and then with practice become easier? The more you practiced the easier it became? I think the problem is we don't often practice enough. I watch the young boy across the street practicing golf skills with his father; not with a golf ball but a small plastic ball so his movements become more exact and he can find what is known as the sweet spot when connecting club with ball. That is how to become a great golfer, which is what he'd like to be. Perhaps I will see him playing in the U.S. Open one day. Artists draw and paint every day. They have done so for years, and they have practiced making the connection between what they see and feel and what they can paint, draw or make. We may not ever get to be a great artist or golfer, but we can improve our skills when we practice. So, that's what this chapter is about, helping children practice.

This item came from the *Child Care Exchange*[1] recently:

> What can music do for your physical education program?
>
> In a recent study, 4 to 6 year olds in a music and movement program showed more growth in motor skills than those in a standard physical education program. Evridiki Zachopoulou, Aggeliki Tsapakidou, and Vassiliki Derri placed 50 children in an experimental music and movement program, and 42 in a traditional physical education program. After 8 weeks, the experimental group had improved significantly in both jumping and dynamic balance skills when compared to their peers in the traditional program.

I would imagine that the difference is the fun that music adds to movement. Imagine an adult aerobics class without the exciting music. When we enjoy what we are doing, we want to do it more. It changes the way we perceive time, and it gives us direction and encouragement. Music provides the underlying support of the beat as well, and this in turn stimulates our bodies to respond with more enthusiasm.

Stories and examples from the classroom

I notice that Neville rarely participates in the "art/craft" area of the classroom. I usually find him building with blocks, doing some puzzles or using some construction equipment. One morning we take all the children outside to look at the shadows on the grass. There had been a conversation the day before about shadows and what

---

[1] You can enroll for a daily bulletin from the Child Care Exchange by writing to them at exchangeeveryday@ccie .com and asking to be included.

makes them appear, and if you could see shadows on a cloudy day. I have noticed that the shadows are particularly long in the mornings in our garden and they look pretty wonderful today, so out we go. I hand out clipboards and black pens; the children take little stools to sit on. We talk about what we are trying to observe and how we can put these ideas down on paper with the black pens.

It is the first time I have the chance to observe Neville using art materials. He sits for some time and looks, and then begins to draw some straight lines. I notice his hand shakes, that he holds the pen way too high to have good control, and I realized he may not have much experience with these materials. The challenge is to gently guide and encourage him to practice these skills; they are going to be important for all his life, and I don't want to turn him off.

So, rather than worry about his skills with the shadow drawing, I decide to begin with something he might enjoy and find less threatening. I start with some playdough, getting him into the general area where we can observe other children using brushes, scissors and pens. We play some games, rolling, squeezing, forming characters and items with dough, laughing, singing songs, and adding enjoyment to the task.

When he is more familiar with this area of the room, the next task is to suggest he try some painting or drawing. He is happy to come with me, and if I sit near him and encourage him, he finds the courage to begin. "You can paint the whole page red or yellow or blue or whatever color you like, Neville," I suggest. I know a whole blank page can be daunting to young artists just beginning. As he lifts the brush, I gently suggest he move his hand down the handle, closer to the tip, and that way he can make the brush go wherever he likes. He tries this, and hand still shaking, he begins. Gradually over some weeks he starts to enjoy the new skill, applying a layer of paint to the paper. He likes the idea of a whole page and then gradually branches out to put other colors in patterns and stripes. He starts to hold the brush more firmly and takes control. He explores the relationship between his arm and hand movements and what happens on the paper.

One morning we have a performer visit. Pete the Plumber has been a favorite visitor for many years. Neville laughs all the way through the performance. He loves the silly stuff, enjoying even the subtle humor. Afterward I invite the children to take a clipboard and pens and some paper and to draw something they liked from the show. Neville is one of the first to settle down, and soon I see him grinning at me. He has the self-satisfied look of someone who has just learned something very special.

One of the things I love about Neville is his ability to recognize his own learning. "I drew Droppo," he tells me, hand across his face in surprise, delight and perhaps embarrassment that he has done it. Droppo is a little drop of water that Pete the Plumber has as a friend, in a tiny bottle. Droppo has huge adventures in the water cycle and brings back tales for Pete. (He was on an iceberg once that crashed into a huge ship, and on Kathy Freeman's brow as she crossed the finish line at the Sydney Olympics.) Neville has really entered Pete's imaginary world, and suddenly there it is, a real drawing. He has done what he intended and it worked. What a special moment we share.

Implications

We all know the exhilaration of achieving a new skill after a lot of practice. We know the fear of failure, hands wet and sweaty, butterflies in the tummy, as we approach the new skill. We should not be surprised that we meet some resistance when teaching young children new skills. Yes, some children may be afraid; they might get sweaty palms. They may even get angry with us when we try to push them a little faster than they are comfortable with. Our role, however, is to encourage, to give a gentle shove out of comfort zones and to tempt children into trying new things. If we include fun, laughter, humor, or music, we often can slip in a new skill unnoticed or without undue stress. I believe that our role is to encourage children into exploring new areas and not merely to stand by, allowing them to explore only one aspect of their own development as complete people. The more anxiety before we begin, the greater the reward eventually, so it's worth a bit of a push here and there.

So, when a 4-year-old shows no interest in drawing, painting, cutting, and pasting after six months, I am inclined to take the initiative and entice her into these areas. Perhaps she is already proficient, having done plenty of these activities at home, and we will know this when we observe her. Perhaps she is afraid and will need some support. I remember Lachlan. After six months of playing in the sand and other interesting places outdoors, I enticed him indoors using a "weather excuse" one cold and miserable winter's day. Within a few weeks he almost needed a truck to take home his artistic inventions. He simply needed to be redirected, challenged and supported.

Likewise, if I notice that a child spends the entire day every day just painting, I am inclined to want to tempt him toward block building, some puzzles, adventures in the sandpit or playing games on the grass. Many times it is like opening a window for the child and inviting him into a new wonderland of adventure. The rewards make it worth the effort.

CREATING CONNECTIONS

We often hear about the mind, body and soul connections. Here are some that might interest you.

The importance of the body

As you sit reading this chapter, are you at all aware of your body? Probably not, unless you are uncomfortable (in which case you may not be paying attention to the text).

We go about our usual work and play oblivious of our body's functioning. A good thing too, I might add. If we had to think about taking a breath, we'd die when our attention was diverted elsewhere. If we had to think about walking, we would fall over more often and bump into more obstacles than we do now.

Now are you thinking about your body? I mentioned it, and now your mind is really aware, but what about your feet? What are they doing? Feel them now?

Okay, let's move on.

A teacher from Broken Hill taught me this little rhyme and game a few years ago. It touched my imagination, and I will share it with you. (Thanks, Vicki.)

Reach down, touch your toe, and then bring your hand up to your knee and then your chest and then your head as we sing (tune is "Where Is Thumbkin?"):

> Toe-knee-chest-nut
> Toe-knee-chest-nut

Then to the toe, the knee and the nose as we add,

> Toe-knee-nose

Then it gets a little trickier. Touch your toe, then your knee, then your chest and head, your eye, your heart and then point to someone.

> Toe-knee-chest-nut-nose-eye-love-you

Then back to the toe, knee and nose again for the close.

> Toe-knee-nose
> Toe-knee-nose.

Now how about your feet? Still thinking about them, or was I able to distract you? But I wonder what your shoulders are doing and how they can be so tight and stressed and you didn't realize it?

The body is the link between the external world and our own internal view and experience. It's a complex receptor through which we receive and interpret thousands of pieces of information every second. It's what holds us all in one place, gives us the ability to think, to learn, to do, to practice, to see, hear, touch, feel and taste and keeps us alive, healthy, mobile and independent. It's important, really important. The tricks and skills we learn with it allow us to grow up to ride a bicycle, a scooter, to play games with friends, to swim, play basketball, sew, draw, write and show affection. As we grow older our body's increasing skill level dictates in part our ability to live independently, to take care of others, to work and support ourselves. Just look at a person whose body has been damaged in some way and whose functions are limited and you will soon see what a gift you have with your body, aches and pains and all. Not many of us have a perfect one, but we can totally enjoy the one we have.

Let's do it again

One of the most common challenges adults face is our own inability to put ourselves into young children's shoes. We assume that because we can write so easily, it must be simple to learn. We assume that because we can use scissors, it must be so easy to control them. We assume that because we can jump, hop, skip, climb and transfer weight from one side of the body to another, it just comes naturally.

I was reminded to start at the very beginning at an International Festival of Learning in Fremantle in 2000. Alise Shafer told us about young children learning about clay with their bodies before being expected to "make" something. At her center the adults had placed blocks of clay on plastic sheeting on the floor. The toddlers were invited to push, poke, sit on, slide off, crumble, poke into places, flush down the toilet, and taste the clay. When the adults noticed them starting to squeeze with their hands, to start to roll shapes or scratch its surface with other tools, they figured it was time to put the clay onto the table in small chunks for the children to explore further. What have we traditionally done? Cover a table with canvas or burlap, put small clumps of clay in bowl-shaped pieces on the table and expect the children to make something. The shape we have given them suggests a pot; we are not expecting the children to be making pots, so why do we do this? The children may have never seen clay before, but we expect they will make something. How about we let them explore the texture first? How about some small torn-up pieces in a small terracotta pot (with a damp cloth covering it) so that the irregular shapes will encourage exploration of texture and form? Let's start at the beginning. By now you will have worked out what an influence Alise Shafer had on me!

We bring out beautiful plastic beads in wondrous colors and shapes to begin threading! Why not start with poking a stick through some leaves or pieces of bark—discover the process, the place to start, and not bring the children in at step 15! I realize that sharp sticks can be dangerous, but manage the risks; short sticks and space between children and some directions about taking care should work. Remember that they are young children who may not have had any experience with these materials before, so put them into the context of what they know.

We sit a group of children in a circle (that's a new experience for a start), and we expect them to take turns in front of one another or to participate, just like that! Even with our worldly experiences so far, we find this difficult to do, especially with strangers. The children may not have gathered often before; they all could be strangers. It could matter. Be patient and do things again and again and again and again, because it's in the repeating that the children gain confidence to join in, to sing along, to take a turn, to get up and jump with everyone else. We need to do it again!

Space to move. Being safe and challenged

Too often we have been told to sit still! Our society seems to thrive on separating our minds from our bodies. In his poem "No Way. The Hundred Is There," Loris Malaguzzi reminds us:

> The child has
> a hundred languages
> (and a hundred hundred hundred more)
> but they steal ninety-nine.
> The school and the culture
> **separate the head from the body.**
> They tell the child:
> **to think without hands**
> **to do without head**
> **to listen and not to speak . . .**
> They tell the child:
> to discover the world already there
> and of the hundred
> they steal ninety-nine.

Dr. Julia Atkin (1993), presenting a three-day course on effective teaching, asked us if it matters that we use our fingers to count sometimes. If this helps, are fingers any less important than a calculator? She soon put us in situations where we needed to use all our faculties to solve problems: some used fingers and toes, others drew the solution or wrote it down in some way, but we couldn't just solve the problem in our heads. We need to be put in situations like this fairly often to remember how difficult it can be for a young child.

I had the experience recently, while writing the text for *Teacher Notes* for the CD *Play, Dance, Sing with Young Children*, when I was challenged to write some notes on playing the piano for nonmusicians. There was so much I didn't know and had to call for some technical help, but when I had done my absolute best and gave the draft to a young friend, he observed that I still had not mastered some of the simplest things. I still could not be relied upon to have the line that runs alongside the notes on the music sheet to be on the correct side of the notes, for instance. I had not realized there was a rule to apply, and then when I did, I still didn't always apply it. I was glad of his corrections. The point I am making is that we become used to how something looks (like a piece of written music), but we don't really look at the details. When we have to reproduce it ourselves, we discover there is much to learn. Likewise, when children are learning to write, they are familiar with how writing looks, but when they come to make the marks on the paper, they discover it is not as easy as they first thought. For many adults writing is so automatic, they have forgotten and become frustrated when a young child is mastering these skills.

Too often we have been encouraged to control movements and bring the body into line. I often hear adults referring to a young child's physical activity in negative terms. Yet we can expect a young child to be energetic, moving often and quickly, can't we? As a society we attempt to bring the child into line with the rest of us. We encourage them to move less often and to sit still. We insist that they not touch (when touch is such an important learning tool for a child) or taste or smell. We often take away the very sensory tools that will make experiences richer.

Sometimes we find ourselves in environments that are cramped, too small for the age of the child, regardless of how many children are using the space. These environments may meet a legally required minimum, but the cramped conditions have behavioral consequences. Many of our playrooms are far too small for developing children, and too early they learn to inhibit their actions. In our role as child advocates, we can lobby for changes to regulations so that children do not find their development compromised by the lack of suitable space.

I have observed in recent years an increasing number of centers that provide out-door environments that are uninteresting to a young child, with numerous artificial surfaces and too little nature. Children learn by touching real things. They need to squash a leaf and to smell it, to pull it apart to see what makes a leaf. They need to pick flowers and watch them die, or place them in water and watch them open. They are stimulated by being able to walk barefooted over the roughness of some hickory nuts that have fallen from a huge tree. They like to look under bark and find the small creatures that live there. Children want to marvel at the beauty of a spider's web on a frosty morning, hanging there as if crocheted overnight by fairy grandmothers.

Returning to Malaguzzi's poem once more:

> They tell the child:
> to think without hands
> to do without head
> to listen and not to speak
> to understand without joy
> to love and to marvel
> only at Easter and at Christmas.

If we expect children to participate and dance or move to an idea or with music, then we need to provide them with sufficient space to explore their bodies. How can they enjoy being a butterfly, spreading wings after emerging from a cocoon—light cheesecloth wings made from three feet of cloth, painted with spray bottles of food coloring and liberally doused with glitter glue, held in their hands—if they don't have sufficient room to move?

The children also need safe space to develop, but not so safe that they never take a risk. The risks should be modified a little so they can still explore being up high or on something narrow or slippery. We find out about the world through our bodies gathering sensory information. I believe that children need widely varying safe but adventurous environments.

Using movement games and experiences with children

Human beings generally develop from the head down and out from the center. This means we learn to look and smile, hold our heads steady, reach out and touch things and then walk.

We need to use this knowledge when teaching new skills. If a child is learning a new skill such as tying a shoelace, bring the shoe to the middle of the body. The most difficult placement is on the child's foot; it's too far away and too hard to see. When they have mastered tying, then take the shoe back to the foot. Learning to button or zip up a jacket is the same—take the jacket off and learn to fasten the buttons, toggles, or zippers and then apply this new skill when the jacket is on.

Dr. Pam Schiller in her book *Start Smart!* (1999, p. 55) writes about the importance of cross-lateral (across the body) movements for brain development in the early years:

> Since the left side of the brain controls the right side of the body and the right side of the brain controls the left side of the body, the two sides of the brain are forced to communicate when the legs and arms cross over.

Pam even suggests that adults benefit from keeping their fingers moving and doing cross-lateral things in our everyday life to keep our brain hemispheres communicating. She suggests placing the drink on the left side, reaching across and using the right hand to use the glass, or placing the waste paper bin on the right but using the left hand reaching across to put the trash in or anything else you can think of that encourages you to reach across the midline.

She gives many examples of popular songs and games to play, and it's worth taking a look at her suggestions. In addition to this I have suggested a few games that will also work:

> Can you clap, clap, clap on your lap, lap lap?
> Can you clap up high or behind your back?
> Can you clap on your nose?
> Can you clap on your toes?
> Can you clap on your knees and then say please?

This is a great little game to play before eating. It gives the children many opportunities to practice the movements and suggests they wait for others to gather before they eat.

Pam taught me about the "Doodly-do" or "Waddly Archer" song. It is in her book *Start Smart!* (1999). I made some variations and have included the words and actions here.

Waddly Archer

Please sing with me, a sweet melody
two claps on knees, two in front. Right hand to left knee, left hand to right knee
[repeat these last two beats]

Called the Doodly-do, the doodly-do
Left hand pinch nose and right hand cross to left earlobe or shoulder; right hand
pinch nose and left hand cross to right earlobe or shoulder [repeat]

I like the rest, but the part I like best is the Doodly-do, the doodly-do
two claps on knees, two in front, right hand to left knee, left hand to right knee
[repeat these last two beats]

It's a funny little song, but there isn't much to it
roll hands over each other forward and then backward

All you gotta do is Doodly-do it
wave arms across each other in scissor motion, left hand on top, right hand on top

Doodly-do, doodly-do, doodly-doodly-do
Left hand pinch nose and right hand cross to left earlobe or shoulder; right hand
pinch nose and left hand cross to right earlobe or shoulder [repeat]

Come on and Waddly Archer, Waddly Archer
two claps on knees, two in front. Right hand to left knee, left hand to right knee
[repeat these last two beats]

Doodly-do, doodly-do
Left hand pinch nose and right hand cross to left earlobe or shoulder; right hand
pinch nose and left hand cross to right earlobe or shoulder [repeat]

Waddly Archer, Waddly Archer
Two claps on knees, two in front. Right hand to left knee, left hand to right knee
[repeat these last two beats]

Doodly-do, doodly-do
Left hand pinch nose and right hand cross to left earlobe or shoulder; right hand
pinch nose and left hand cross to right earlobe or shoulder [repeat]

It's a funny little song, but there isn't much to it
roll hands over each other forward and then backward

All you gotta do is Doodly-do it
wave arms across each other in scissor motion, left hand on top, right hand on top

Doodly-do, doodly-do, doodly-doodly-do.
Left hand pinch nose and right hand cross to left earlobe or shoulder; right hand
pinch nose and left hand cross to right earlobe or shoulder [repeat]

Toot-toot. *Clap twice*

It's not so easy for young children (and some adults) to cross over their bodies to do actions like in "Waddly Archer," so practice is needed.

A simple finger play like "Where Is Thumbkin?" can be much too difficult when we ask young children to put their hands behind their backs first. My suggestion is to identify which finger is selected for the song first. Children have enormous difficulty isolating just one finger and holding it up. When they are sure they have the correct finger and know where it is, ask them to squeeze it so their body remembers which one it is when they put it behind their backs (first with one hand and then using two). Then sing the verse of the song and watch how easily they can bring out the right finger and manipulate it in the song.

An old favorite, "Knees Up, Mother Brown," can also be adapted to cross-lateral movements by showing the children how to clap their right knees with their left hands and the left knees with the right hands as they bring their knees to their chests. Children will also find it fun to clap on a partner's hands, crossing over the center line to clap the hand on the opposite side, or clasping hands in the middle to turn round and round.

What does matter is fun! If the children are interested and excited by the game, they are more inclined to participate, and if they participate, they are practicing.

Allow approximations and good attempts; it may take time to learn a new complex movement such as some suggested in this section. Adults, please remember to participate too—adults need to join in and support the children's work.

Use CDs that suggest music and movement, and take the percussion instruments out of the cupboard and place them into the children's hands. Instruments are marvelous things for developing eye-hand and finer-motor control.

Songs, games, stories, drama and dance that support kinaesthetic dimensions

Songs or games that have repeated actions are always popular, as young children enjoy repetition. This song, for instance, is a familiar one for most early childhood professionals, but this has a new twist to encourage great movement possibilities.

Chorus:
Jump, jump, jump if you feel you want to
Jump, jump, jump if you feel you can.
Jump, jump, jump if you feel you want to
Jump, jump, jump if you feel you can.

Nod your head if you feel you want to
Nod your head if you feel you can.
Nod your head if you feel you want to
Nod your head if you feel you can.
Chorus

Tap your foot if you feel you want to
Tap your foot if you feel you can.
Tap your foot if you feel you want to
Tap your foot if you feel you can.
Chorus

Clap your hands if you feel you want to
Clap your hands if you feel you can.
Clap your hands if you feel you want to
Clap your hands if you feel you can.
Chorus

Turn around if you feel you want to . . .
Chorus

Wink one eye if you feel you want to . . .
Chorus

Stamp your feet if you feel you want to . . .
Chorus

Wave good-bye if you feel you want to . . .
Chorus

Be prepared to have fun, and feel free to make up new verses and actions.
Another variation goes like this:

Jump, jump, jump if you feel you want to
Jump, jump, jump if you feel you can.
Jump, jump, jump if you feel you want to
Jump, jump, jump if you feel you can.

Now for two actions . . .
Jump and clap if you feel you want to
Jump and clap if you feel you can.
Jump and clap if you feel you want to
Jump and clap if you feel you can.

Now for three actions . . .
Jump and clap and nod if you feel you want to
Jump and clap and nod if you feel you can.
Jump and clap and nod if you feel you want to
Jump and clap and nod if you feel you can.

Now for four actions . . .
Jump and clap, and nod and turn if you want to
Jump and clap and nod and turn if you can.
Jump and clap, and nod and turn if you want to
Jump and clap and nod and turn if you can.

Now for five actions . . .
Jump and clap, and nod and turn and shout hooray if you want to
Jump and clap and nod and turn and shout hooray if you can.
Jump and clap, and nod and turn and shout hooray if you want to
Jump and clap and nod and turn and shout hooray if you can.

Here is another favorite, also in the public domain, taught to me by Vicki from Broken Hill years ago:

When I was one, I used my thumb
Show your thumb.
The day I went to sea.
Make wave action across body to indicate ocean.
I climbed aboard a pirate ship and the captain said to me,
Make actions like climbing aboard and peeping eyes over the top of the deck; salute the captain.
"We're going this way, that way, this way, that way
Step forward, sideways, forward, sideways in wobbling motion while making ocean movements with arms across body.
Over the briny sea,
A bottle of rum to soothe my tum (a bowl of jelly to sooth my belly)
Pat tummy or make drinking actions.
And that's the life for me."
Give the thumbs up!

When I was two, I tapped my shoe the day I went to sea . . .
When I was three I hurt me knee, the day I went to sea . . .
When I was four, I slammed the door, the day I went to sea . . .
When I was five, I took a dive, the day I went to sea . . .

Feel free to ad-lib the rhymes for the numbers; ask the children to suggest variations.

Good friends Gary and Carol Crees have taught me many interesting and useful songs over years of friendship. I have adapted some of these to create new adventures. Here are a couple of suggestions:

- Use the song "Zum Gali Gali" (traditional dance from Israel found on *Jewish Favorites*) with a small parachute. Gather children around the edge to hold on and move in a circle, first to the right and then to the left during the chorus. Then lift the parachute up and down as you move inward and outward during the verse. The same can be achieved with some satin ribbons passed across a small circle to make a beautiful web in the middle. See if you can arrange it so each child holds two ribbons that are linked to two different children on the other side of the circle.
- Another version is an inner circle facing outward, holding hands with an outer and larger circle facing inward, holding hands. During the chorus the inner circle moves left, then right, and the outer goes in the opposite direction. Both circles step toward and then away from each other during the verse. It's very effective and beautiful. Obviously this version is for older children, and they can easily master the skills with a little practice and encouragement.

The use of the CD player, musical instruments and other devices

Let's face it, we can't do everything! Some of us can play an instrument, and others have not had the opportunity to learn; in the meantime we can use other equipment.

The important thing is to select suitable music or stories that will work for you. Don't leave it to chance unless you have a good memory for how something goes. Instead, listen before and see what possibilities present themselves. There is nothing worse than playing musical chairs with slow and boring music; it needs to be fast moving and noisy to generate the excitement needed. (My suggestion is to have percussion instruments available for children to play and gradually form an increasingly large band while the children who remain in the game fight it out for supremacy.)

Some stories on CD or tape lend themselves to great dramatizations and movement experiences. The most successful ones I have discovered are the *Hairy Maclary* series by Lynley Dodd. There are enough characters for children to have a turn without having to wait for too many repeats, and there are some excellent actions to use. When we use movement and music or drama time with young children, how can we raise their awareness of what they are doing?

Encourage children to think about and be aware of how they can improve their dramatization skills by thinking about how it feels to *be* something. Introduce some of the ideas that arise from the method-acting school of thought.

For instance, let's think about a drama for kangaroos. I mentioned this earlier, but I will repeat it because it is an excellent example and taught me a great deal about preparing children for drama.

> The visiting storyteller tells the children, "Before we begin the story, instead of jumping wildly here and there, let's slow down and think about how kangaroos move. They move many ways: on all fours, their back legs hopping forward to join their front legs and then stretching out onto their front ones again; they sit upright to listen, scratching their tummy, then flicking their ears in order to listen more carefully. They lick their forearms to cool themselves, and they hop quickly or very, very slowly, balancing on their tail in between forward movements.

You can use a piece of classical music that suggests kangaroos to you and invent a dramatic story using the music as background. Have you watched the giraffe eating at the zoo? Bring your observations to the group and share what you have seen, how the giraffe reaches up high for some food and then spreads its legs wide so it can reach the grass. Whenever you share what you know or have observed, you are encouraging the children to consider their actions in the drama or mime more carefully and deliberately.

Play mime games. Ask a child to mime being an animal or playing a game or doing something at home and request that the other children seated around the actor guess what he or she is doing. I have watched children making toast in a pop-up toaster or washing clothes in the washing machine, as well as being dogs and cats.

Here is a wonderful game:

The Train Game

(This game was taught to me by a presenter from Canberra in 1982 and has been one of the most useful games I have ever used.)

Place chairs, cushions or small plastic hoops on the floor in a train-seat pattern. Make sure there are enough chairs for every child but no reserved seating! Introduce the song:

> Train is a coming, oh yeah; train is a coming, oh yeah.
> Train is a coming, train is a coming, train is a coming, Oh yeah!

(This will become a chorus to call children back to the train between verses.)

Encourage the children to make train movements with their arms and hands. A wooden train whistle will assist you in calling the children back to the train, or a good toot-toot with your voice will work as well.

> We are going on a train ride to the zoo today. Are you ready? We will come back and sit down on the train each time we hear the whistle blow. Okay, off we go.

(Sing the chorus a few times to get it established.)

> Oh, I see some elephants. Can you get off the train and be the elephants?

> The elephants swing their trunks from side to side (play heavy sounds on the piano if you can or use a drum/tambour). They are very big and very wide.
> They put their feet like this and that. Their legs are long and very fat.
> They soak up water with their trunk and squirt it all over everyone!
> Toot-toot.

(Children return to their train seats for the chorus.)

> Now I see some tigers. Can you get off the train to be some tigers?

> Here comes the tiger creeping so very gently, very slow (play tinkly notes on the piano or use some bells)
> Quiet as can be, creeping about,
> Paws spread wide, creeping about.
> But, oh my, what a surprise when it ROARS and blinks its eyes.
> Toot-toot.

(Children return to train seats for the chorus.)

> Oh, I see some . . .

Ask children to suggest animals they might see and make up little movement rhymes spontaneously to suit the situation.

This game can go on and on as each animal suggests a different movement.

When the children are tired of the zoo visits, you can fly a rocket ship to the moon and experience being in low-gravity environments or being weightless in space, or go on a sailing ship and see a lot of whales and dolphins and sharks or sea birds.

This game also works well with the "Wheels on the Bus" song, and at each stop the children visit the park, go for a swim, see a movie or shop for apples.

Feel free to invent! You don't always have to use the Hebrew words in the "Zum Gali Gali" verses. You can ask children to suggest new words. *"What do you like to do in the sandpit?" "I like to dig."*

> Oh, we like to dig in the sand, in the sand we like to dig.
> In the sand we like to dig, oh, we like to dig in the sand.
> Zum gali, gali, gali, Zum gali gali
> Zum gali, gali, gali, Zum gali gali

If we do this, then we are able to keep the integrity of the verse's "shape" as it goes this way and then that way.

Cultural richness

Your mind should spin with possibilities. Gather music and stories from around the world to use.

Putumayo (www.putumayo.com) has a wonderful range of music from around the world, and these can be great places to begin. Buy some and listen.

There are so many possibilities.

Try to avoid focusing on one culture and instead be flexible and use a variety of music from different cultures every week. Return to favorites and do them again and again, but respond to what the children are talking or wondering about and invent new games to play about those topics.

Collect stories from varying cultural traditions and use them as foundations for dramatizations and movement experiences. Encourage the children to explore their creativity, inventing new movements and responses to ideas.

Being inclusive

It is so easy for us to have a lot of "hims," and not so many "hers" in the stories and games we invent. It's okay if we keep the balance and don't go overboard, but we need to be constantly aware. We need also to be aware of cultural clichés. All Italians don't wave their arms around when speaking; that is a generalization, a cliché. Japanese often bend forward to greet each other, but perhaps not always, and this can easily be a cliché. Let's try and be a bit more sensitive and aware as we explore different ideas and cultural traditions.

Remember to include children who have physical disabilities; make sure they get a turn in the game, have a turn in the drama, have a ride on the swing and sit in the sand to feel the texture. The other children will soon learn how to take care of their needs. I remember a little girl who finally learned to walk using two sticks, and she would scream with laughter as she was being chased around the circle in "Duck, Duck, Goose," but was hardly ever caught and never tipped over. Another little girl, in a small form-fitting fiberglass chair on wheels, would be whisked off the floor by a strong, masculine assistant and spun around the room in the games. He found ways to take her through the tunnels, over the bridge and even to ride on a flying fox! We wondered how she would learn these concepts if she had been deprived of the experience.

Inventing games and movements with young children

A colleague invented many games using small plastic hoops. It took us some time to find a supplier, but when we did, we bought enough for every child and a few spares. When first introducing games in a circle, or even sitting in a circle (it can be an interesting adventure for young children), hoops work beautifully. The adult spreads them around, and the children pop themselves into them. If you can't get colorful ones, you can make them with narrow irrigation pipes, wooden dowels, and glue. You can paint them or bind them with electrical tape to add color.

Begin with simple ideas. First ask the children to find their hoop and return to it. Select music that encourages vigorous movement, and the game begins with children getting up to dance around the room and returning to their hoop when the music stops (like musical chairs but without removing the hoops).

Encourage the children to jump forward out of the hoop and backward to return to it. Introduce sideways jumping out and into the hoop as well. Remember the physics theory about equal and opposite reactions? Well, the same applies with movements. Whatever you do with the left side of the body, repeat it with the right. For every forward action, make sure you include a backward motion to achieve a balance. This song works well with this idea.

Mr. Frog jumped out of his pond one day and found himself in the rain.
He said, "I'll get wet and I might catch a cold!"
So he jumped in the pond again.

Hoops make excellent placement helpers for playing counting games. For instance, five hoops in a circle and a large piece of blue cloth for a pond can be used for this game. (Once again, I have no idea where this song/game came from.)

Mrs. Duck was sitting on her nest, with five little eggs beneath her breast.
When one fine day she heard a "crack"
And out popped a little duck, "Quack, quack, quack."
"Come," said Mrs. Duck, "Let's go for a swim.
Put your feet together and jump right in."
"Oh, oh," squeaked the duckling, "Look at me."
And soon they were swimming 'round merrily.
(*repeat until there are no unhatched eggs left*)

I invented a game that we played for several years where children sat on eggs in their nests (hoops) and then went flying to particular music to find things to eat. An eagle would swoop by (one of the adults with long cloth wings), and the challenge was to get back to protect the eggs when the threatening music was played. I can still hear the shrieks of excitement and pretend terror!

Listen for music that has significant changes in tempo or volume, which suggests two characters and can be used for invented games and dramatizations. I discovered a wonderful CD called *Baby Mozart,* and one track suggested versions of "Giants and Fairies." (One side of the room occupies the giants' palace—they are afraid of fairies, you know—and when the fairies come out, they run home. The fairies' palace is on the other side of the room. They in turn are afraid of the giants and dance back home when the giants come out. The children quickly learn which music suits giants and which suits fairies.)

With the same music we played a number of variations: "giants and ants," "clouds and rain," as well as "Mr. McGregor and his rabbits."

A four-year-old, Anna, invents some words for Mr. McGregor to use in the game that fits the rhythm of the music exactly. "Shoo, shoo, shoo, you rabbits you. Shoo, shoo, and don't come back!" Look for the possibilities.

Take your cues from the children's reactions and play with their ideas.
Use old favorites like:

One elephant went balancing,
Step by step on a piece of string.
He/she thought it such tremendous fun,
He/she called for another elephant to come.

Two elephants went balancing,
Step by step on a piece of string.

They thought it such tremendous fun,
They called for another elephant to come. . . .

Ten elephants went balancing,
Step by step on a piece of string,
When all of a sudden, the piece of string broke,
And down fell all the elephant folk!

Search out and learn these songs and games and then use them as a basis to invent your own. The children will make a lot of suggestions, so don't be alarmed by the prospect.

Encouraging participation and invention

We touched on this topic earlier, but it's worth revisiting. It takes courage to participate, but when we have fun, we encourage most of the children to join in. Don't force the issue too early. Suggest they have a turn with a friend or an adult to get the first experiences out of the way, if that's needed, but play it easy and cool. There is nothing worse than being pressured in front of others. However, my experience tells me that the child who is not able to take a turn in a drama or movement game may not be ready for the rigors of big school, so keep this in the back of your mind.

Children do not need to be frightened, but they need to be challenged. So set up climbing equipment in new, interesting, and increasingly challenging ways over the year. Be available to assist when needed, and help children develop rules for safety. For example, one child should stand back while the child ahead climbs the ladder instead of pushing in too close; both could get injured, and it's good manners.

Ask one child to help another with a new skill. The instructing child will understand the process and can usually give helpful hints.

We all do this and we all do that

It depends on the environment you work in and the age of the children you work with, but yes, I do think there are good reasons to have some good old-fashioned group times. I don't mean boring, long-winded sessions; I mean lively, fun-filled sessions that children want to participate in. For a child who can't cope with being so close in a group, find a safe place on the outer edge or something quiet to be involved with nearby. Even small babies enjoy a little group time with adults singing with them, and older children will certainly love to gather together at times.

Involve the children in developing actions to songs or in dances and games. There are so many ways to do things. Let us not get so hung up on one way that it becomes the only way.

Be prepared to change direction, as this story suggests.

This morning I plan to read a story about an old tree; the conversation last week had been about old-growth forests where I had recently seen the Queen of the Forest! As we sing a couple of familiar songs and the children play along with an assortment of percussion instruments, one of the adults assisting me notices one child has turned his stick sideways in his clasped hand and is hammering it through his hand with the other stick, turning it over as he runs out of stick and starting again. What a fantastic idea, we agree, and soon we have shared his discovery with the other children. In fact, I even have a special song in my repertoire that will work with this really well, and soon we are playing along to "We've Been Working on the Railroad."

I have some pictures at home of a little steam engine and am able to enlarge them, laminate them, and share with the children the following day. Monique (my assistant) and I demonstrate how people used to hammer spikes into the train tracks using huge hammers, taking turns to hammer the spikes in just like Adrian had shown us was possible with the sticks. I hold one stick upright in my fist, and we take turns hitting the top of the other stick as we sing the song. It is a hit, and soon we all are joining in. Some children hold the stick in one hand to hammer with the other as Adrian had invented, and others are doing as Monique and I had demonstrated, with one person holding an upright stick and two children taking turns hammering. One small group even experiments with one child holding the stick upright in the center and two other children taking turns hammering the spike in. What fun!

Of course I don't read the story about the old tree; instead, we have a riotous time with "Whistle Up the Chimney," making the sounds Nan Hunt wrote for the rhythms of the various trains that thunder through the lounge room, down the hall and away into the night at Mrs. Milly Mack's house. Suddenly we have made a right-hand turn, and trains are back on the agenda.

Look for a child doing something original and encourage her thoughts and actions. Then share the child's inventions with the others. It adds to the fun for everyone.

Image of the child

CHILDREN ARE CAPABLE

We spread a large cloth on the ground. It has the hopscotch shape painted on it, and the children are learning the new game. They are practicing hopping from square to square, throwing the beanbag onto the next number and so on. There is a lot of laughter as they find it difficult to get back to the home space without putting both feet down on the 1, 2, 3 squares, but still they persevere. It's this ability to persevere that makes the difference.

In charge of the proceedings in another area, on another day, is Bailey, who has a wonderful understanding of the rules and the numbers on the hopscotch shape. He tells and then shows the child about to have a turn which square she should be aiming for, and when the beanbag lands on the correct spaces, he holds both arms above his head and shouts, "Howzat!" His encouragement and excitement mean that most of the children take a turn in the new game. Bailey is generous when the beanbag does not land where intended, and with a smile hands it back so the child can try again to get it in the right place.

Amanda is a bit cautious about the new inverted climbing frame we put out on the soft-fall area.

She approaches, determined to cross the obstacle, and yet is nervous. I admire the bravery that children exhibit as they encounter experiences for the first time—

Amanda cautiously explores the new climbing frame.

they draw on other knowledge they have, are trusting that what we assemble for them is within their ability level and that we are close by. She climbs up and over, and holding tightly she moves her feet forward near the middle and then transfers her weight forward and holds the other end of the frame.

A child, nervous to take a turn in one of the familiar circle games, is encouraged by another child, saying, "I can come with you if you like," and soon the nervous child finds new confidence, holding hands with a friend, to take a turn for the first time. I notice that the children know just when to do this; a few weeks earlier the offer would have been rejected, but today it's going to work.

We used to have a wonderful old-fashioned steel monkey bar, later removed by the safety squad. It was set into the soft-fall so that the taller children could actually touch the soft-fall when hanging from the rungs. We had had it for years without an accident. Each year I watched the children develop the upper-body strength needed to swing from rung to rung, bend their bodies up so they could sit on top of the monkey bar and other incredible acts of dexterity and bravery. I had such confidence in their ability. Something I loved was listening to a child explain to another child just how to do an action, or telling him that "it just takes time and practice. You'll be able to do it soon." Look for and expect the children to be capable!

Reflections, challenges and wonderings

Looking back over the stories in this chapter and others that pass across my memory as I write, I reflect on the importance of challenging but doable kinaesthetic experiences. I think about the children who have overcome their nervousness to participate, to try a new skill, to use new equipment, to cross the bridge, to climb the ladder, to try again and succeed. They are my heroes!

I wonder how we can continue to encourage children to try, to practice, to persevere, to take risks and to grow creatively. We make the difference, the way we approach issues or environments, our imagination and acceptance or the way we encourage children's new ideas—that's the key, I think. A child's body is the window through which he experiences the world and gathers impressions that he turns into concepts in his brain. Fingers help the brain grow, as do feet and toes, and back muscles and the muscles that focus an eye. They are all extensions of the brain at work and developing.

PUTTING IT TOGETHER

Let's see if we can pull the ideas together into a whole.

Connecting dimensions

From our earliest moments after birth to those last moments of our lives, our bodies are experiencing the sights, sounds, textures, tastes and smells that make up the world we live in. The small baby struggles to focus on a face, and then to smile, hold his head erect, reach forward to grasp intentionally, sit up, crawl, stand, walk, toddle, run, climb, jump, hop and skip. As we grow older we develop physical skills that will add richness to our enjoyment of life or bring us income that keeps us comfortable. We balance on our two feet. We sense our bodies in space and compensate for movement around us. We transfer our weight from one side to the other, from foot to foot (and in some cases from hand to hand). We change directions and avoid a collision. These basic physical abilities can save our lives in some situations. They are important. The body is what holds everything else together, and our kinaesthetic awareness and memory are essential for everything we will attempt in all areas of our life.

It's easy for us to draw a box around this dimension or that one, but the kinaesthetic dimension overlaps with all the other dimensions of our development and creativity. Children need space, opportunity, equipment and encouragement to develop the skills they will need for all their lives.

Creating new experiences and ideas

Listen to and observe children as they create new movements and responses to stimuli. Follow their lead and encourage further exploration. Be creative yourself and expect and value creativity in the children.

I watch James at the easels. He is familiar with the materials and equipment; he is often found in this area. He knows that we really like to keep some of his paintings to display at the center or put into his portfolio, and this day he is obviously thinking about how to take a painting home and leave one with us. Then I observe him placing a fresh piece of paper over his just completed painting of a chicken and some eggs. He rubs with the palms of his hands and the sides of his hands. He lifts the top paper off and reveals his invention: a print of the original. One painting is for us (he touches up a couple of places that didn't print as well as he would have liked), and one is for himself.

The sun is streaming in the window one winter morning, and I notice we can see right through one of the child's ears—he is sitting at just the right angle. After morning meeting time, I invite anyone who is interested to get a magnifying glass and look at my ears as I sit in the sunlight. Jack takes up the offer, noticing that there are tiny hairs inside the ear canal and then looking closely at my hair. "Can I pull just one out with some tweezers?" he asks me. I am happy to let that happen. I know this child is capable of doing just what he plans. He returns with a piece of white cardboard and a pair of tweezers. Using the magnifying glass, he isolates just one hair and gently pulls it from my scalp using the tweezers. He places the hair on the cardboard and exclaims, "Look! Even a hair has a shadow." I look; he is right. It does cast a shadow on the cardboard. I have never thought of that as being possible, but Jack has used his senses well. Soon he draws his observations.

TAKING CARE OF YOURSELF

How do you relax the best? Some people take their minds off their worries by engaging in physical exercise such as yoga or tai chi, playing tennis or golf, or just walking or swimming. Others find soothing music or painting and drawing to be the best way. I think what matters most is that we are so totally engrossed in the actions that we forget some of the worries we have. We had better take care of our bodies; they're what make us alive.

Pam Schiller (mentioned earlier in this chapter) reminds us of the importance of drinking enough water every day. She suggests having some every 90 minutes of our waking day. She reminds us to eat fresh, wholesome foods and not pre-prepared or fast foods, and she reminds us to have rest, especially good sleep. We know this, but how well do we manage this in our busy hustle-and-bustle everyday whirlwind? Take time out to smell the roses, listen to music, go for a walk in the park, visit the places you love, look way out to the horizon and pamper yourself whenever possible. When you do this, you can better do your job, and your job is the most important one in the world next to being a parent. You touch the future!

A couple of books and CDs that will assist your task are:

Schiller P, 1999, *Start Smart!*, Gryphon House, Maryland, USA.

The Baby Einstein Music Box Orchestra, 2000, *Baby Mozart*, The Baby Einstein Music Company. LLC.

4

EXPLORING MATHEMATICAL AND LOGICAL DIMENSIONS

Like a painter or a poet, a mathematician is a maker of patterns; but the special characteristics of mathematical patterns are that they are more likely to be permanent because they are made with ideas.

Howard Gardner

What do we mean?

This dimension is the ability to reason and calculate, to think things through in a systematic manner. We all have stories of children who have fascinated us with their interests in unusual things. I remember a little boy who knew just about everything there was to know about termites, another whose interest in insects and spiders continued way past his early years, and one who explored maps and mapping for most of the preschool year as he prepared for a summer trip with his family. These children stand out in my memory as does the child who spent the best part of 18 months digging and building water features in the sandpit (inspired by television's Jamie Durie) and another who gathered pieces from the preschool garden to make a special garden for small creatures to live in in his own backyard. I think about the child who explored the properties and interactions of water and air with containers in the water tray.

From where I am sitting at the moment, in part looking back over a lifetime of experiences with young children, I find myself reflecting on how we (the adults) can celebrate the wonders and wondering of children and thus bring about environments and experiences that will foster creativity in the mathematical and logical dimensions.

It's a painful truth that the majority of people working in the early childhood sector are women. This is not a sexist statement; it's an observation of fact. My experience with a large number of students studying early childhood education (almost all women) leads me to consider that we may have quite a deficit happening. Many of the young students have not had childhood experiences with wooden train tracks, blocks and other construction equipment. In recent years (I hope) this has not been the experience of young girls, but I was amazed when the girl child of a twin pair told me all these things were in her brother's bedroom and she never played with them!

There are a couple of considerations here. We know, for instance, that experiences in the early years, especially before eight years of age, are essential for the development of both logical thought and mathematical ability. A 2007 report about research at Macquarie University by Joanne Mulligan found on the Web tells us that:

> Pattern and structure lie at the very heart of school mathematics. A pattern may be seen as a numerical or spatial regularity, and the relationship between the various components of a pattern as its structure. The generalizations on which algebra is based are one type of pattern that children encounter in school mathematics. The underlying mathematical structures that children need to recognize include the base ten structure which underpins the number system. The early development of "pattern and structure" in children's mathematical thinking is critical to ongoing development of abstract mathematical ideas and relationships.

A series of research projects conducted over the past ten years have endeavored to find out why some children succeed and other children find math so difficult to master. They found that (Mulligan, Mitchelmore and Prescott, 2006):

. . . low achievers (in grades 2 and 3) were more likely to produce poorly organized representations (drawings, diagrams, symbols) compared with others. These children also lacked flexibility in their thinking and were unable to replicate structured models such as groups, arrays or patterns . . . these difficulties persisted right up to grade 5 . . . These students did not seem to look for, or did not recognize, the underlying mathematical similarities between superficially different situations—a crucial step in effective mathematics learning.

Their research also found that (Thomas, Mulligan and Goldin, 2002):

High achievers, on the other hand, used abstract representations with highly developed structures that were already well in place in grade 2.

What do the researchers suggest we do to improve this situation? The answer is quite simple—provide experiences that will encourage the children to:

- improve visual memory,
- identify and apply patterns, and
- seek structure in mathematical ideas.

Which brings us back to train tracks, puzzles, blocks and other manipulative equipment!

I believe that if most of the staff in early childhood centers are women, and if many of them have not had significant childhood experiences with these materials, then they will not necessarily understand the importance of these materials. I have a real story to illustrate my thinking.

A few years ago I had a student from the local university completing her third year of a four-year degree course. She observed some children putting together the wooden tracks from a well-known railway construction set. This student wondered aloud why the curved pieces of track would have track on both sides whereas on the straight piece the underside was left smooth. I asked her about her experience with the train tracks, and she replied she'd had none, not in her childhood, and not in her university course or practicum to date. I wondered how she could develop an awareness of the importance of such equipment without any experience and suggested she spend the next week with the tracks and some children who were experts on the subject! She came back to me with eyes wide, excitedly telling me what she had learned not only about the equipment but also about the effect of shape, direction and size on the completion of a workable track. My point here is that if we don't understand deep down inside ourselves the value of such equipment, how can we fully appreciate the skills and knowledge of the children? How can we encourage and support mathematical development and entice children who are reluctant to participate to join in?

After this event, and the discussion with the girl twin, we held a series of master classes for the children on building good train track designs and solving the inherent problems as well as classes on block building and exploration of other equipment. We invited skillful children to show what they could do and talk about the process. We encouraged them to take child partners who were less skilled and work with them over several weeks until almost all the children attending at that time became proficient, excited and capable problem solvers, pattern makers and engineers.

Most centers have a collection of geometric-type puzzles. The amazing thing about many of these puzzles is that they have a variety of solutions or rely on the pattern for completion.

A few years ago I had two very interesting children, one who came to the center Monday and Tuesday (a girl) and one who came Wednesday and Thursday (a boy). During the year they each noticed that the other child was creating some amazing patterns with one particular puzzle (I made sure they had access to the class journal so they could see what the other group had been doing). A friendly rivalry developed with a little encouragement from the staff, and each week the girl would leave her best solution (in photographic form) for the boy, who would create a variation and leave his solution (in photographic form) for her to see. Toward the end of the year the boy began attending additional days, and so these two were able to bring this exciting journey to fever pitch! Imagine how these children (and those around them who observed and were challenged) were able to develop awareness of pattern and structure.

We can make significant improvements quite simply by:

- providing time and space for extensive exploration;
- providing additional equipment to bring such exploration to life (small animals, people, cars, trucks, boats, pieces of fabric);
- providing a wide range of equipment in sufficient quantity for extensive exploration;
- paying attention and documenting children's involvement with these materials (validating their exploration and growth);
- sharing children's ideas with other children so all may benefit;
- providing a generous selection of interesting puzzles;
- encouraging exploration and experimentation with multisolution puzzles;
- providing a generous selection of interlocking, intersecting and other manipulative equipment;
- encouraging exploration and problem solving;
- documenting, documenting and documenting so you see progress happening, share your observations as well as reflect and plan more easily;
- validating children's work; and
- challenging children with a problem to solve or an activity to participate in.

Early awareness of math can also be stimulated with collage (making patterns), with painting (taking prints, experimenting with symmetry, creating patterns) and with clay (creating patterns with various implements). You will find some really useful suggestions in Williams, Cunningham and Lubawy (2005).

Remember also that the outdoor environment can be an extremely useful addition to the math classroom.

I observe Lachlan in the sandpit. He digs two holes and lowers long pieces of poly water pipe into the holes and pushes the sand firm to make the pipes stand straight. He collects a few pieces of smaller-diameter pipe and pushes them together with plumbing connectors, and lowers the newly made construction into the upright. It fits exactly! I ask him, "How did you know how big to make it?" He answers, "I measured it with my eyes." He continues to add other structures and then hangs some large pieces of cloth over the entire area to create some additional shade on the edge of the sandpit where the large shade cloth doesn't quite cover first thing in the morning.

A discussion about a visit to a local lighthouse results in our photocopying and enlarging a postcard, brought back by a staff member, so we can see the details. One of the girls has been experimenting with a block building design that began with a series of circles from the two smallest half circles through to the large. The lighthouse stimulates her to add a vertical dimension to her design, standing six arch-shaped blocks up but balancing on the large, flat circle foundation. Then she adds more blocks on the top section of the arches and finally a large, open triangle shape that encloses some yellow Plexiglas. The lighthouse is complete.

Other children soon use and extended her design to provide the ocean waves with blue cloth, some rocks (using small blocks), boats and a headland made with a pile of blocks covered with a green cloth and their lighthouse (using the former design) placed within this context. Hours of valuable play develops from the construction, discussion about lighthouses and design and the use or need for them. It extends to discussion about tides and beaches and how far light travels—and it began with a mathematical design, strong and balanced, valued, documented and shared.

I am astounded when Rhianna combines two quite different ideas we have challenged the children with. We begin with an idea using three different colored papers, one a whole piece, one a half piece and another one a quarter piece. The idea is to choose colors that complement or contrast with each other in the three sizes and place the half piece on the whole piece and then tear the quarter-sized piece of paper into small pieces to place on the half piece. (With adults I notice many of them discovering just how much space is taken between the torn-up pieces and how difficult it is to make the torn-up quarter fit into the space available on the half piece.) At the same time Lachlan is exploring the numbers on clocks. We have photocopied and taken away the hands before re-copying the blank clock face with just the numbers around the circle. Rhianna combines the two different ideas that have been discussed during the morning meeting time that day. She cuts the clock face into quarters, colors one quarter and then glues all four onto a large piece of paper. She comments to me when I ask her about her work, "I colored one quarter. Is that what mommy means when she says, 'We'll go at a quarter past two?'" Yes, she is almost five, and dividing the clock face into quarters has suddenly become a reality to her with a pair of scissors. My observations of this child over that year lead me to believe she has some special talent in the math dimension. Time will tell.

We are making biscuits one year when Cameron comments, "That tray will make 20 biscuits." I asked him how he can know this when we have only just started to put the mixture onto the tray. "Well, you can fit four across that way and you will be able to fit five rows down this way and that will make 20." Now grown up, he is working in the USA at the moment for a big information technology company, but we could see his talent when he was four.

Logical and mathematical thought can range from the most abstract notions of wondering about where the sun goes at night, to counting the number of trains and cars to be divided between five children who have built the track. The wondering and thinking are the most important elements, not having the answers, as answers can prevent us from wondering further. The pondering, imagining, searching for the pattern, talking aloud, and questioning "whys" are what make a scientist or mathematician.

Anna notices that the sky is clear and blue as she lies back in the swing. "Joy, where have the clouds gone?" I answer, "I don't know, but you are right, there are none this morning."

"Perhaps they slept in," she replies. Perhaps.

I ask another and older child Anna's question a few days later. John replies, "Well, you see, the wind comes along like a broom and sweeps them all into a huge pile, and then the sun vacuums them up." Anna and John are beginning scientists; they have some answers but are still wondering. Science is aided by the development of logical thought.

Stories and examples from the classroom

A race course for crickets!

The original idea is to see how quickly crickets can jump out of a circle. They are so fast we can hardly see it happening. "What will happen if we build a fence around them?" asks Harry. We give Harry the crickets to take care of for the weekend, and he brings them back for the start of preschool this morning.

Harry has been talking at home about the crickets and has come to the center with an idea that a race course for crickets is an excellent idea. We agree. How can we do it?

"We need something to put the race course on."

"It needs a high fence to keep the crickets inside."

"It needs to be high, higher than they can jump."

"It needs to be strong so they can't push it over."

A large Masonite board is dragged from the storeroom, and a container of Popsicle sticks is collected to build the fence. We suggested some white paper to define the race course a little better.

"How can we make the sticks stand up and not fall over?" I ask.

Jack remembers using clay recently to hold the fence and trees for a house he has been building out of small boxes. We like his suggestion.

The pictures document the story.

Jack and Harry begin the fence line. They roll clay and press onto the paper. They pay close attention to the corners.

Others join in, and the fence begins to take shape.

Amy sees a gap forming and adds more sticks so the crickets can't escape.

Zachary checks Jack's work. This should close the gaps.

The crickets run to the edge, to the corner, they climb; the children catch them and put them back inside the enclosure. The squeals increase! Crickets escape, and the children chase, catch and put them back many times. Not one cricket is injured.

The finishing touches are made.

"Perhaps the crickets are frightened," I suggest.

"We'll make them a house they can hide in."

The children use the egg carton the crickets were delivered in; several of the crickets scramble underneath to hide.

The children are happy to release the crickets in the garden later. We can get more another day.

Implications

In an article from the *Child Care Exchange*[1] that arrived in January 2007, I read:

---

[1] You can enroll for a daily bulletin from the Child Care Exchange by writing to them at exchangeeveryday@ccie .com and asking to be included.

In their *Exchange* article (July 2005); "Play and the Outdoors: What's New Under the Sun?" Susan Oliver and Edgar Klugman quoted Anita Olds, the late designer with a special gift for child-centered indoor and outdoor environments, as observing, "There's no way we can help children to learn to love and preserve this planet if we don't give them direct experiences with the miracles and blessings of nature." Oliver and Klugman go on to point out. . . .

"Imagine young children's daily lives if the range of their experience began and ended at the door into their school or child care center, only to re-emerge when it is time to go home. Certainly many would agree that something important was missing from their education. Yet, when they go home, today's young children are experiencing more and more of life indoors. As an early childhood educator who has impact on both kids and parents, you can be the first line of defense against a culture-wide loss of appreciation for the whole package of developmental benefits our children can only access if they have a healthy relationship with the great outdoors and its natural wonders.

"Spread the word to parents, administrators, and others who make decisions about how children spend their time every day. Outdoor play doesn't require a playground or a park or an hour or a warm, sunshiny day. It only requires a commitment to kids' healthy development. Nature is standing by—ever patient, available whenever we want—ready to nurture the young children in our care."

Increasing numbers of young children are spending a huge proportion of their childhood in child care settings, away from what many of us would think of as the traditional childhood of our own memories: the backyard, chicken pen perhaps, a family pet, wash drying on the line, snails happily munching new seedlings, plants popping through the surface, puddles and being splashed by overhanging bushes after rain, gurgling water down a drain pipe on the side of a building or even running down a gutter nearby.

It's a messy, perhaps even risky, environment, but it's real. It's where young scientists and mathematicians draw experiences that feed their investigative spirits. Our "*civilized* world is increasingly fastidious and cautious" writes Jim Greenman (1998, p. 71). We can so easily civilize the wondering out of children.

This article, also from the Child Care Exchange, will encourage your use of natural environments, I am sure:

In the *Ecologist* (October 2005) Edward Gill's article, "If You Go Down to the Woods," makes a case for the importance of restoring outdoor play for children. In part, he observed . . .

"Children are disappearing from the outdoors at a rate that would make them top of any conservationist's list of endangered species if they were any other member of the animal kingdom. So does it matter that kids aren't playing outside as much these days?"

"Let's start with health, and specifically with childhood obesity. Here, everyone agrees: playing outside keeps kids thinner . . . spontaneous play may be the only requirement that young children need to increase their physical activity."

"The physical benefits of outdoor play should come as no surprise. What's more remarkable is the growing evidence that children's mental health and emotional well-being is enhanced by contact with the outdoors, and that the restorative effect appears to be strongest in natural settings. Studies at the University of Illinois' Human-Environment Research Laboratory on children with Attention-Hyperactivity Deficit Disorder (ADHD) have shown that green outdoor spaces not only foster creative play and improve interactions with adults; they also relieve the symptoms of the disorder . . . contact with nature may be 'as important to children as good nutrition and adequate sleep.'"

"The great thing about many natural places is that they are ideal environments for children to explore, giving them the chance to expand their horizons and build their confidence while learning about and managing the risks for themselves. These places are unpredictable, ever changing, and prone to the randomness of nature and the vagaries of the weather."

CREATING CONNECTIONS

Let's look at some ways logical and mathematical dimensions overlap with other areas.

Introducing graphic literacy

It seems so obvious really. Young children are not yet able to write down their ideas, and so they draw, paint and construct them if we allow time, attention and materials that encourage it to happen. I would suggest at this point that you return to chapter 1 and see what Loris Malaguzzi says on this subject in an interview with Lella Gandini.

You will also see references to the challenges from Alise Shafer at an International Festival of Learning in Fremantle in chapter 1 that apply in this chapter as well. This shows the strong overlapping of dimensions in the whole child!

Children expressing ideas

A couple of years ago I had a child who caused my heart to leap with excitement as I watched the complexity of his play. He'd been an awkward little boy, finding movement difficult it seemed, lacking social skills, a bit of a loner when he first arrived with us, just after spring began. He stayed for the following year as well. By then he was five-and-a-half, as he told me.

My first glimpse of his playfulness and imagination comes when he asks for a paper bag to attach to his jumper, upside down, so he can be a mommy koala. He adds the little joey himself, after negotiating with one of the children to cut it out for him. (He can't cut well enough for his own satisfaction at this stage.) Soon I have a whole room of kangaroos and koalas, each with pouch suitably applied.

One day he comes rushing up to me. "Joy, Joy, can I have a glass jar, a rubber band and a paper bag?" "Of course. Let's go find them."

He attaches the bag tightly across the top of the jar, a little splash of water inside, and holds it fast with the rubber band. He leaves it on the bench and rushes back outside. Next I see he has dug a hole to catch a snake in the sand. It is covered with a lid of sticks, a kind of trap. One of the children has brought a rubber snake from home in response to a conversation about numbers of legs; it was securely caught in the trap. Next loud screams, and a rushing child to grab the jar and head back outside, muttering as he goes, "Thank God I made that antivenom."

Play is magic and real. If we provide time, space and equipment as well as interaction and support to play, the children will create ways to explore both math and logical thought in often astounding ways. We provide the environment for creativity to flourish.

Truth or exploration?

About nine months after having my head turned inside out by the words of Alise Shafer in Fremantle, I had what turned out to be an incredible and mind-altering encounter with children's development of logical thought in the sandpit one morning. Here is the story.

Dominic, Brady and Lachlan are digging in the sand one morning and find water. Instead of giving them an explanation about how Barbara (a work colleague) had watered the sand earlier that morning, I ask them:

"How did the water get into the sandpit?"

Brady says: "When the dinosaurs died, the water was still there, and when we put sand in, it means we have to dig for water. We want to tell everyone where to get the water."

Dominic says, "It's wet sand. The sun shines on the wet sand and turns the wet sand into water."

Lachlan says, "From the rain. It dries up and the wet goes down."

I question further, "Why does it stay in the bottom and not come back out?"

Brady adds: "Because the dinosaurs were nesting under the sand and they were everywhere. Then they died and we can dig for water. Sand turns into the water from the broken tank of the nesting grounds."

Dominic tells me: Because the tank is broken.

Lachlan suggests: 'Cause it's very wet underground. It can't come out 'cause there's a lot of sand on top.

I wonder, "What on earth do they mean?"

I ask the boys to draw me their ideas. The concept of graphic literacy is something new to me at this time, but I have an inkling I am on the edge of something very exciting.

Dominic draws the sandpit posts and the shade cloth on top. Then he draws the sand and the deep hole. He draws a tunnel in the sandpit and the deep hole. He adds a tunnel in the sand and a pipe connecting with it. There is a sun as well.

He tells me, "The water goes through a pipe under the ground, through a sand tunnel and into the bottom of the sandpit. It stays dry on top because the sun dries it up."

I can follow his logic. Drawing has helped him focus the theory so it made sense to others. ("The child is the physics professor, the exam is Friday. You'd better listen"; Alise Shafer's words were ringing in my head.)

Brady draws some children on top of the sand, a deep hole with water in the bottom, a lot of water in the rest of the sandpit, a pipe down the side, the tree, sun and clouds.

He tells me, "When we were digging for dinosaur bones (I suddenly remember a student burying bones for the children to find a month or so ago, so that's the context), we made a deep well and found water in the bottom. It fills the whole bottom of the sandpit, right across."

"There's a drainpipe down the side and water flows through it."

"The tree helps to melt the water. The tree roots help."

"The sun helps the tree to melt the water."

"You have to wind the water up from the bottom of the well."

Lachlan draws a big brown sandpit with a tiny patch of blue in the middle.

He tells me, "You have to dig a long time."

I ask him, "If you dig a hole over here, will you find water here too?"

He says, "Yes."

I ask, "And here?"

He says, "Yes."

I ask, "But where does the water come from?"

He draws the clouds and rain.

Later we throw the question open for other children to share their ideas.

"Some people are digging, and they pour water in. The water stays," Vincent tells us.

"A truck puts water in first and then sand on top," another Lachlan adds.

Eliza considers the question carefully: "A long time ago, there was a big pool and the water was still in it. They put the sand on top." Later she adds, "It might come from the frost."

"I think there was a big truck with a big river on it, perhaps 100 trucks," says Sophia.

There are many other similar explanations.

"Was it Barbara with the hose or was it the rain?" we ask the children.

"How do you know if it's been raining?"

The discussion goes on for days. Some children draw pictures about water dripping off the leaves and falling into the sandpit, trees turning into cement because the rain doesn't come, and reasons why wells in another sandpit are dry.

"The other one is shady. It means the sun can't dry up the water so much."

"How would we know if it has rained?"

"A water meter."

"How would you know if it has rained or if it was the sprinkler?"

"If it hasn't rained at home or we haven't heard the rain."

"It wouldn't be dry when we got to preschool. It would still be wet."

"Would the rain only wet the sandpit?"

"Everything would be wet."

"If we used the sprinkler, would everything be wet?"

"No, the sprinkler doesn't get everywhere."

The children begin to plan to make some rain detectors. Buckets taped to the top of poles, a plastic bottle with a traffic cone taped to the top, upside down and then strapped to a post, and another with a funnel stuck inside a long piece of plastic tubing running down into a plastic bottle, taped onto the swing frame. They record their own solutions on paper. The numbers they have added to their devices become important and are carefully noted.

The following week it looks like it might shower. I ask the three boys to predict how things will look outside if it rains. I only have time to listen to Lachlan before it actually begins to rain. He draws a picture of the swing frame with rain falling above it. I asked him if the brown swing frame will look any different when it is wet. He glues some blue cellophane over the drawing.

I wonder aloud what he means, and he takes me outside to show me.

"Bring some glue and blue cellophane, and a brush," he tells me. He collects a bucket and brush from the shed and some water out of the tap. We go to the swing frame.

He paints the wood with water and waits. He pastes the cellophane over where he has wet the frame and waits some more. Then he lifts the cellophane. It isn't how he expects it to look. I can see him puzzled. "It's not blue," he tells me.

He lifts the cellophane and looks again, "It's still not blue."

"What color is the rain?" I ask him.

"Clear," he replies, still puzzled.

A few days later, we talk again about the swing frame in the rain. I asked him what he was thinking about.

"They always make it blue," he says.

"What?"

"The water."

"Where?"

"In the pictures."

I can see what he means. I think he expected the swing frame would turn blue when the water hit it. He can see it didn't do this even with the cellophane, but he is puzzled by what he saw.

It's this puzzlement that is one of the essential ingredients.

Creating scientists and mathematicians

The environments we provide—messy, natural, rich with what Nicholson (1974, quoted in Greenman 2005 p. 248) calls "loose parts"—and the experiences we share with children can create wonder, questioning, exploration and problem solving or they can close the doors in a young child's mind.

The conversations we have with children during snack times, reading a story, pushing a child on a swing or lying on your back looking at the sky through the leaves create scientists and mathematicians. Planning for an exploration over several weeks or months at the children's pace (instead of our own adult rush toward the finish line) about the here-and-now topics that children choose creates a culture of learning within a community of learners. A theme, dedicated to a topic chosen by the adult and with predictable outcomes based on the adult's knowledge, is a different event altogether.

In "A Conversation with Howard Gardner" (1993), Howard Gardner talks about "teaching less and understanding it more." He shares the story of asking his graduate university students what happens when we toss a coin into the air. Their answers told him that they had lip-service explanations of the science involved, yet their real knowledge was limited. He wondered if they had stopped wondering at some stage and had just accepted the answers given to them and therefore never built on their knowledge.

Edwards (2001) explores this notion as well. He wonders how often we steal discovery and hypothesis from children because we are so ready to share what we think we have learned. I know I have often been guilty of this. I promise I will try harder.

Recording and documentation

The focus of recording and documentation needs to be the child, not the requirement to demonstrate to others. Record the conversations, work and play of children in ways that pay attention to what they are thinking about, learning about and wondering about.

Documentation can take the form of mounted panels that show the progression of an idea over some months in pictorial (usually using photographs but adults' sketches and children's interpretations also work well) form, or a book set aside for a project or perhaps even a daily journal that records many threads weaving in and out that day.

Where we often have multiple classes of children during the week, it is recognizably difficult to document the same way as we would if children attended every day and we only ever shared our days with 20 or so children. It is more difficult for those of us who touch 80 or more young lives a week. Documentation has to be manageable and pleasurable to the adults, validating what we do and showing others what young children are capable of. This works better than the "court report" style that we often see in journals that tell the story of the day in a predicable format of the story, the songs, the craft and so on. Perhaps it is time to consider a more reflective and connected approach to represent the connective curriculum.

Curtis and Carter share some marvelous ideas and practical examples in their book *The Art of Awareness* (2000). They started me on a new series of steps in my own journey.

Documentation can be as simple as an explanation of an event or a series of events over an hour, days, weeks or months as children's interests develop, or it can record conversations and children's graphic literacy (as in the case of the dinosaur bones found in the sandpit as discussed in another story in this chapter).

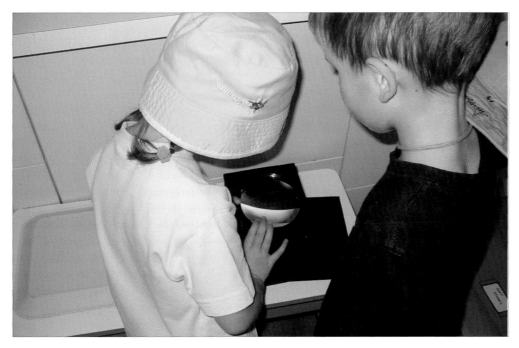

Lily and Sam look at a moth.

Lily finds a dead moth. Sam watches with her. "It looks little, it looks big," she tells him as she moves it under the magnifying glass and looks carefully. She puts her hand under and out from the magnifying glass several times as she and Sam compare and observe sizes of the moth.

Some fantastic questions

We so easily overlook the best questions. They often slip by unnoticed when we are eating morning snack or trying to settle children down for a story.

"Joy, look at those ants," Connor says. I am not ready to hear him; we are running late, the families will soon arrive to take the children home and it's the last afternoon for the year. I want to read a favorite story. We are trying to get children's shoes on and make sure all the bags are packed, ready to leave. There are final cuddles to enjoy as we say good-bye. I don't want to listen to his question.

He continues. "They stick to the ceiling and don't fall off. How do they do that?"

Right. Now I am listening. What a terrific question. Do we have time? Yes! Too bad about the story.

A quick introduction to Connor's question and his suggestion for everyone to take a clipboard, some black pens and paper and draw the ants and tell us how they stick to the ceiling meets with approval. The children are familiar with the clipboard routine by now, and so it only takes a moment. Most of the children are interested in Connor's question, but a few prefer to complete some puzzles they missed earlier or to read a story quietly and comfortably in the book corner. Questions often sneak up on us.

"Look, the trees are kissing," Amy observes as we sit under a canopy of leaves for morning snack. Indeed, the branches from one tree meet the branches of another and almost entangle, they are so close. It's late summer and the leaves are at their glossiest.

I pick up one single yellowed leaf that has fallen that day. "Look at this one. Do you think this is from one of the kissing trees?"

Some kids agree and some don't. Lachlan adds, "They'll all fall off soon."

"Why do the leaves fall?" Anna asks.

"Good question," I say. "Let's see what happens in the next few months and then we can work out why."

Or perhaps . . .

"You scared of thunder?" asks Naomi, munching on a carrot.

"No, I really love thunder," I comment. It's true actually.

"I am," says Isabella.

"Well, I used to be until we went camping before we came here," says Naomi.

Her family has recently arrived from Arizona. Not much thunder there, you would think.

"We were putting up the tents when we saw a storm was coming. My sister and I were scared of the thunder, but Dad said not to worry. It was just God clapping his hands."

"God must have been very pleased about something," I reply.

"Yeah." She munches. "He was allowed to play with his flashlight as much as he liked."

Perhaps we can bring this idea to life, we think. The next week we provide torches, large pieces of spray-painted blue cloth, a broom handle, musical instruments and willing participants. We place some children behind the cloth. It is hung over a broom handle between two adult chairs. We give the children torches so they can take the role of God. Others are near the piano to be the thunder with instruments, and a couple of adults with rainbow-colored streamers are ready to dance. I tell Naomi's story with the piano . . .

"One sunny day, a family went off, went off in the desert to go camping," I sing.

"They took some sausages, they took some bread and they took their camping gear too. Just as they started to put up the tent, they noticed the sky was darker.

'What if it rains,' Naomi asks. 'The tent will keep us dry,' her dad says.

"Late that night when it was very dark, Naomi saw a FLASH FLASH FLASH."

The children behind the cloth flash their torches.

"And they heard a CRASH, CRASH, CRASH."

The children with instruments make a lot of noise.

"And a FLASH, FLASH, FLASH, and a CRASH, CRASH, CRASH!

'Don't worry,' her dad says. 'It's just God clapping his hands, 'cause he gets to play with his flashlight all night.'

"Naomi and her sister, her mom and her dad sleep all night and in the morning the rainbows dance."

The adults with streamers make beautiful rainbows around the room.

A few weeks later, leaning against an outside wall, Isabella tells me, "You know Naomi's theory about the thunder?"

"Yes."

"Well I don't think it's true."

"Oh?"

"My sister says it's caused by electricity."

"Yes, I have heard that. What do you mean electricity?"

"You know, lights and stuff."

"How do you think it happens?"

"I think God has got a very long extension cord!"

More than just counting

How often we add a counting song or rhyme to our daily routine and think we have addressed math. Repetitive counting and even one-to-one counting on our fingers is a start, a good start, but not the whole story. Math is a way of thinking about patterns and predictability; it's about developing a logical attitude as we wonder about a whole range of things, find common patterns emerging, look for similarities and differences, think about solutions and answers to questions and then observe some more. They are intrinsically intertwined.

Watch as children explore the concept of symmetry for instance. This side matches that. It can be a drawing or painting, it can be a design of blocks lying flat on the floor or a tall construction, it can be with two buckets of sand or water being carried by a child, it can be in the steps of a hopscotch game. Watch as children explore the relationship between symmetry and balance as they test the boundaries and then see the tower fall or try to hold themselves steady in a game of Freeze.

It can be music. It can be about the beat, an exploration of time, so often missed in our conversations about math!

> *It begins with Amy. . . . She is playing the wooden African zylodrum and finds that the large box behind it also makes a delicious sound. Tap, tap, she beats a rhythm on each, comparing the sound. Next she adds a metal tray, turning it upside down, a plastic chair, the "washing machine" and an upturned wooden bowl and finally an upturned large plastic tub. She moves from one sound to the other, experimenting with the sound and the beat. She makes a series of complex rhythm patterns using two sticks.*

It begins with Amy.

Lachlan takes up the challenge.

When she is satisfied that she has exhausted most of the possibilities, she leaves the area and Lachlan takes up the beat. He begins with bowl, washing machine, large box and upturned tray. Two sticks, complex patterns, experimenting with the sounds. There is soon a whirl of movement. The idea grows, and soon other children join the fun.

I'll let the pictures tell the story!

Other children gather to take up the beat.

We can see the pleasure! Let's rock around the clock.

Materials, provisions and experiences

It sounds like a joke, but the reality is that we are often the stumbling block when it comes to using the wooden project blocks! We imagine many reasons why we can't use them—we don't have the space, they are dangerous, they make a mess, no one will pack them away, we can't see what children learn, they do the same thing every day, they are noisy, only the boys use them.

I refute all of the above statements—blocks (in all sizes) are a necessary ingredient in a quality program. They cost thousands and yet they are worth millions! Millions of experiences and experiments, millions of opportunities and challenges, millions of dramatic play delights and millions of mathematical calculations.

Dr. Tom Lowrie presented some interesting research in 1999 (*Lego loss reignites traditional vs electronic toy debate*) that tells us that young children need to work with three-dimensional equipment more often than they need to be in front of computer screens. They need the three-dimensional experiences so they can hardwire their brains to see three dimensions, he tells us. The flat two-dimensional screen (that we can imagine is three dimensional because of the hardwiring we did as children) will not achieve this for children. Tom says in the article:

> Just sitting kids alone in front of computer or TV screens, using them like electronic babysitters, doing automated tasks for hours on end is little better than letting them sit and stare at a blank wall. No matter how interactive the game is, it's always the computer that's in control.

You will find the complete article using the Web site address in the references.

To understand the three-dimensional elements of math, children need to hardwire their brains to accept the images. A friend's son attending school explained to his mother one afternoon that the flat drawing of a cube on the page was actually a cube and that the box she had used as an example was not!

We need to look carefully to see the way children use their math skills, to predict exactly which block or piece of track will go here or there and find ways to encourage and support their learning. If we notice it and record it in some way, or comment on it, the children know we value their ideas and growing awareness. I think that this development of the sense of *can-do and do-know* helps children begin a confident relationship with math.

Cultural richness

Cultural diversity can begin with the earth—enjoying the pleasures of the sights, sounds, smells and tastes of the earth; being one with the earth; being all of one people from diverse places. It's a philosophical viewpoint I suppose.

> *Barbara (a work colleague) collects small bags of sand as she travels Australia on long-service leave. She brings them back to share with the children; we all observe the array of wonderful colors of the earth. I have a container of red sand from Central Australia and spread it on a large white table for the children to explore the color and texture with dry finger painting. They create large swirling patterns in the sand and then bring the elements together in a smooth pile ready to swirl again.*

> *"In some places in Australia the people paint their skins and the walls of caves with paint made from sand like this and grated rock," I tell the children. We combine some white clay, water and some glue to make a paint that will stick well to paper. We only have one color of clay available at the time, and the children are eager to create another earthy color. We find half a brick left over from the playground redevelopment and use the grater to make a fine dust to mix with water and glue. It works beautifully. The children paint on the black paper we provide and also on themselves! I wonder if this will be a problem later when they go home, but the children take care of this themselves, washing their legs at lunchtime when they begin to feel scratchy. I am amazed that the paintings*

reflect what I knew (but had not yet shared with the children) of Aboriginal painting styles from a number of regions. Of course, this makes discussion and further exploration of Aboriginal art techniques a topic for weeks to come. We will return to this story in another chapter with another purpose. This time it's about the context. We took the opportunity. You can too.

A large hand-carved wooden bowl from Africa is added to the environment. It holds salt, filled almost to the brim. A perm comb from the local chemist shop is added to use as a rake as were some seeds (haricot, lima, red kidney beans) to make patterns, and the children have yet another way to explore the smells, textures and colors of the earth. At the same time they are able to develop their understanding of pattern and structure.

A large wooden bowl and some wild bird seed, a scoop made from a coconut shell, and another scoop that was a gift from a friend in Sarawak and was hand-woven by parents at this friend's school as a way of raising money is made available for the children. The children sit around the bowl to fill, pour, trickle and sift the seeds. We place a rug beneath the bowl to catch spills.

To see the world in a grain of sand
And a Heaven in a wild flower,
Hold Infinity in the palm of your hand
And Eternity in an hour.
                    —William Blake

Perhaps cultural diversity is also buildings and clothing. We can gather picture books that depict people and places and building styles. Not books designed for children necessarily, but big books with wonderful pictures that are often on sale. We see calendars used for a similar purpose. They add to the background, and children absorb the images every day. It's not about "doing" a theme; it's about living in the world all the time.

It's deceptively easy to approach cultural diversity in a thematically based manner, such as "We are learning about Africa this week!" Now, Africa is a wonderfully exotic place, but I hesitate to think we could ever "do" it in a week in whatever way we chose. It is diverse, the peoples are diverse, and we could only ever touch the edges of the cultures and its people, grasp a tiny sliver of the threads of cloth, a teaspoon of the flavor, a tiny glimpse of the land. A lifetime of curiosity and learning and we might have some idea about the complexity of Africa. That's what we hope to set up, a lifetime of curiosity. I wonder then if we can approach the topic both logically and in a variety of contexts, such as this short story illustrates:

Exploring the relationship between the mounds of sand and the mold used to create them, Diana exclaims, "It's just like Handa's Kraal." One of her favorite books was the delightful big book Handa's Surprise.

The children's play will reflect the value the adults place on cultural richness in their choice of stories, pictures, artifacts, materials, languages spoken, music played, dances danced and songs sung as well as foods eaten. However, when we place these naturally and easily in the context of the everyday lives of the children we meet every day, the richness doubles in strength.

Being inclusive

It has been important to me to include as many real children in the stories in this book as possible. One of the children in the race course for crickets has autism, yet he is right at the center of the action. You will no doubt also notice that the girls as well as the boys are investigating, problem solving and thinking logically. It's an attitude really. If we see the child first and not the label, then the way we interact will be inclusive. If we examine our attitudes and realize where the bias lies, we can more easily overcome it. It's not possible to be totally free of bias, but we can make significant inroads, I believe.

Image of the child

CHILDREN PLAY

Nicholas has enjoyed the Brio train track for seven months. He comes to the preschool two days a week, and most days he uses the train track. After all this time I am surprised when he turns to me with a huge smile and tells me, "Look, these pieces are the same." Sure enough, the two long straight pieces of the track are the same. I wonder why he has not noticed this before, and why today is the day he shares what he knows. I ask him what other pieces are the same, and he sorts through to show me several pieces, sorting them into groups of length and curve. Then he is puzzled. "These two are the same. Look, when I put them this way, they are exactly the same (he places the curve pieces on top of each other), but when I put them next to each other, they look different." Indeed that's how they look, the angle of the corner distorting the appearance of the length of the pieces.

Reflections, challenges and wonderings

We so often SAY, "Play is a child's work" or "Work is child's play" or other standard statements about play. We SAY we value it. However, what do we do?

TALKING WITH THE CHILDREN

Lilian Katz (1998, p. 36) challenges us when she agrees with Bruner's observation that up to 80 percent of interactions in early childhood settings are directive or managerial, rather than conversational or thought provoking. Let's listen to what we do, and see where our conversations fit in this equation.

I watch with interest a work colleague at the water tray. She sits quietly and watches as a girl puts her hands into the blue water, lifts them out, puts them in again and pulls them out. Wendy doesn't comment, ask questions or give advice; she waits as it feels the right thing to do, she tells me. Eventually the questions come from the child. "Wendy, do grown-up hands change color when they go under the water too?"

ROUTINES AND PACKING AWAY

Many of us have experiences of centers where the children are constantly packing away, being interrupted for another experience or activity or where the routine is rigidly followed. There is nothing wrong with routines. We need them so that young children feel safe, so they can tell the passing of time in a predictable manner. But we often go overboard, don't we? How flexible can we be? The children face many years of routine and constraint. This short time that they are young could be such a delight, full of magic and mystery if we let it.

If we do need to use the space that blocks are used in for rest time, then of course we will need to pack away. However, can we move the blocks to another place or can we be more flexible about where rest time happens? For instance, if the weather is nice and there is sufficient shade, can we move the beds outdoors some days, just for fun?

DOCUMENTING

Taking pictures or making sketches of the wonderful block and train track or other constructions will validate the work of the children who were involved and encourage them to greater achievements the following day. A research student of mine reported on a crawling baby interacting with her documentation. The student had noticed the little girl stack a few blocks and took a photograph. The student printed the picture, mounted it and laminated the documentation, placing it at child's eye level on the floor. The child crawled to the picture, sat and thought for some time, then gathered the blocks, created a new design and waited for the photograph to be taken. It was. The process repeated over many days, and each time the child created a more elaborate building. She knew the process and was part of it.

HOW DO WE ENCOURAGE CHILDREN TO PLAY?

How do we arrange the environment so that children can make choices of materials to use, will be given adequate and flexible amounts of time to play and will be encouraged to extend their play with the sensitive support of adults? How often do we cut short a child's practice, become impatient or interrupt?

PUTTING IT TOGETHER

Once again, let us cast our minds back over this chapter and bring the ideas together.

Connecting dimensions

You will no doubt have noticed in this chapter that the lines are blurred. It is not *only* intentional; it is the only way I can bring the ideas to you. These ideas have developed over a long time, taught to me by the children, pointed out to me by researchers, other presenters, my staff and my own children and grandchildren. In *Preschool Math* (2005), Williams, Cunningham and Lubawy have tempted the reader to explore math in a scientific manner with a wide range of materials across the curriculum. To play with Gunilla Dahlberg's (1999 p. 10) words, we "wanted to bordercross" the curriculum. We suggest music and games, songs and stories, art and craft, dance and drama, water play and sand play, building and cutting, and many other tempting morsels with our minds quite firmly focused on math. This chapter in particular and this book in general develop many of the ideas appearing in the *Preschool Math* book.

It's so easy for us to think inside the familiar and predictable box, preparing environments and experiences based on our own interests or experiences. Many of us are familiar with setting up and planning for a theme, and many of us only feel comfortable when we can predict the outcomes. It is rewarding though when we develop the awareness and courage to follow children's interests and explorations and allow our imaginations to create new possibilities that we can present to the children.

The development of logical thought is essential. Encouraging children to develop and explore the possibilities and record them with their graphic literacy devices helps the young child to think about what came before and what came after, as well as what might happen next. It suggests to the child that she can think about the causes and that her answers do not have to be "right." One fundamental observation about scientists is that they are never finished looking and wondering, they are never completely satisfied with the answers and they can devote their whole life to finding out more about a topic. That is fully developed logical thought. It begins in the sandpit and ends up in space; it begins with building a block tower and becomes a grand architectural delight; it begins with a ramp built for small cars and ends with a huge bridge; or it begins with folding a piece of paper in half and becomes the human genome project!

Creating new experiences and ideas

There are hundreds of books with fantastic ideas, more than we can read in a lifetime, but they help us imagine what is possible. Our own imaginations, however, are even more limitless, and we can access them in a second. We can draw on the power of the children's inventiveness as well or the ideas of the people we work with. The shower is a good place to clear space in our minds so we can invent. Our sleep sometimes presents us with ideas as our subconscious works with the images from the day. Let the ideas flow.

The best ideas come from really listening and watching the children at play. What are they doing? Do they comment that the water disappears into the sand? Do they notice that it's much cooler under the sand than on top of it? What can we provide or suggest that might help? How can we provide additional materials another day without giving them the answers but provoking thought and interaction?

The water flows into the plastic and creates a waterfall, but what if some large, flat river rocks could be added? The children create an imaginary water pump to make the fountain, but what about providing the power for the pump to work? What could be provided to create the representation of power lines, the lights and the light poles?

It doesn't matter if the children totally ignore the materials you provide today. They might notice them tomorrow, or if you present them in another way, then they might become intrigued. You might have to add it to the list of tried but untrue possibilities.

TAKING CARE OF YOURSELF

Creativity and imagination are fragile things really. To take care of the children's creativity, it is essential that we first take care of our own. When the airline steward reminds us, "Adults, please attend to yourself first," we are being given some of the most important advice possible. We can only feed our own creative imagination if almost everything else is being taken care of.

So, is imagination important? What is it and how do we nurture it?

Montessori (1973, p. 175) was convinced that imagination was essential. She said:

> If man's mind were limited to what he actually saw, his outlook would be dreary indeed.

And (1973, p. 174):

> Is the child's mental horizon limited to what he sees? No. He has a type of mind that goes beyond the concrete. He has the great power of imagination.

Ashton-Warner (1963, p. 26) comments:

> Children have two visions, the inner and the outer.
> Of the two the inner vision is brighter.

When we have staff who are or we ourselves are stressed, overworked, downtrodden (it makes me think of Maslow's hierarchy of needs actually), threatened, tired, tied to desks by paperwork, dictated to by owners, overregulated, overinspected and enclosed in environments of plastic and artificiality, overwhelmed by color, noise and movement, then we have staff who cannot provide what the children need to develop their imaginative talents. The children need open, receptive environments that encourage diversity and exploration. We need to develop imaginative cultures. We destroy imagination when we place a model of a finished article in the center of a table and then get the children to make (I hesitate to use the word *create* here) what they see. Don't laugh; this is still happening in some places.

We destroy imagination when we plan our programs in enormous detail, stick to them and repeat them every year or in alternate years, with no regard for what is happening in the immediate environment, the questions that children ask or experiences adults or children may have had.

Conversely, Broinowski (2002, p. 123) states in his conclusion to his research on the topic:

> (that) early childhood educators . . . require a disposition which is conducive to enchantment, imagination and creativity . . . that to provide an enriching program for young children it was important to ensure that staff had a strong sense of their own professional journey and would constantly explore their creative imagination as educators.

Take care. You matter!

Some resources that will help in your journey:

MacDonald S, 2001, *Block Play: The Complete Guide to Learning and Playing with Blocks*, Gryphon House, Maryland, USA.

Rockwell R, Williams R and Sherwood E, 1992, *Everybody Has a Body*, Gryphon House, Maryland, USA.

Rockwell R, Sherwood E and Williams R, 1983, *Hug a Tree*, Gryphon House, Maryland, USA.

Sherwood E, Williams R and Rockwell R, 1990, *More Mudpies to Magnets*, Gryphon House, Maryland, USA.

Williams R, Cunningham D and Lubawy J, 2005, *Preschool Math*, Gryphon House, Maryland, USA.

5

EXPLORING NATURALIST DIMENSIONS

Nature can heal, renew, revitalize, and energize us. Nature can evoke latent potentials and reveal deep learnings about the self.

David Lazear

What do we mean?

There used to be a magnificent stand of eucalypts beside the mountain road between Kiandra and Cooma. My heart would literally race with excitement as we neared this section of one of my favorite drives. We always clambered out of the car at this space to stretch our legs and talk to the trees. Peter would comment about tree hugging and so on in a lighthearted tease.

There was something special about this place. I felt a strong sense of peace, relaxation and inspiration—I could literally breathe it in. Then came the horrendous fires that swept through the Kosciusko National Park and on to Canberra. My wonderful trees then stood like blackened witnesses to the carnage. Many of them were marked with a pink ribbon to show they were considered dangerous and would be removed soon. The entire stand was destroyed. The first time I visited, not long after the fires, my heart just sank with despair—I could imagine their pain. Every few months when we find an excuse to go that way to the coast, we get out of the car and talk to the new trees. I take photographs and hope to collect the story of regeneration of the forest. I encourage the tiny saplings to grow and be strong while the blackened reminders of their glorious past stand close by guarding the new growth. The place is still sacred to me, blackened or growing. Can you call to mind special places like that? A waterfall, the expanse of a valley, the way a river meanders around a corner, a rocky outcrop, a headland or lake? When we suggest to people (during workshops) that they take a magic carpet ride to anywhere on earth right at that moment, it will most often be a natural place rather than a human-created space.

When we bring all our senses together in one place to appreciate the wonder of a natural environment, we are exercising the naturalist within. Think for a moment about the children in your class who are interested in and collect bugs, bark, leaves, flowers, and rocks, and who know a lot about animals. These are the naturalists. This chapter is about how we can encourage and nurture the naturalist creativity. They may not all grow up to be another version of David Attenborough or the late and wonderful Steve Irwin, but we can bring out those qualities in the children and ourselves very easily.

We experience this dimension when someone gives us a bunch of flowers, when we plant a new tree or walk in the park. It may be what we enjoy most when we have a barbecue outdoors at home or, as I sometimes do, just sit quietly and watch the sprinklers in the garden late in the afternoon (when I am permitted to use them) or, more wonderfully, the rain falling. Howard Gardner (1996, p. 3) defines a naturalist as being:

> an individual who demonstrates expertise in the recognition and classification of the numerous species—the flora and fauna—of his or her environment.

Stories and examples from the classroom

My husband, Peter Law, tells me he will deliver some rosemary and oregano leaves one morning. (I had phoned with a request; the children have discovered some of the perfumed leaves in the garden and want to chop the leaves and make a perfume stew. We don't have rosemary or oregano at the center, but we grow some at home.) Peter encounters Lachlan, magnifying glass in hand, flashlight tucked under his arm, peering in the bushes. Peter asks him, "What are you doing?" The reply: "I'm doing research!"

A child peers into the bushes looking for baby snails and leaf-curling spiders.

*In Lachlan's case he **is** doing research. His entire year has been spent examining, drawing, collecting, finding out information on the Internet at home and making books on various topics. It is Lachlan who calls me over, whispering for me to be quiet and leading me, both of us creeping, to see a tiny butterfly emerging from a cocoon. "We can't call the others," he tells me. "They will make too much noise and will frighten the butterfly." Instead, we take photographs and share the story later when the tiny creature has safely flown away. Lachlan saw what was happening and knew the importance of leaving that butterfly alone to safely dry its wings before flying off.*

Connor has a small box of soft-fall bark, twigs and leaves. I wonder why he has collected them. "I'm going to take these home. I am making a home for crickets in my garden." I talk with his mother, and sure enough, in a shady place, under some bushes, he has arranged his collection in the hope that crickets will soon take up residency.

The outdoor spaces surrounding early childhood centers can be a source of such naturalistic delights. A good old-fashioned digging patch or a small garden, or a collection of large pots to grow vegetables adds another dimension.

Monique (work colleague) finds an interesting leaf on the Camellia bush beside the front door. It has some bumps on it, and we think some of the children might be interested in looking more closely. . . .

A few years earlier I had discovered that a circle shape drawn on a piece of paper helps the children focus on what they see in the magnifying glass. We used this knowledge for a new adventure.

We place the leaf and a few other interesting articles on the cloth-covered table, and make clipboards, paper in the shape of a magnifying glass, the freestanding magnifying glass and suitable drawing utensils available.

I introduce the materials and tell the children, "An artist, just like a scientist, looks and draws, looks again and draws again, and then looks some more." I wait to see what will happen. I predict that Taylor and Jack will gravitate to the area, and I am not disappointed.

It is interesting to see how Taylor translates what she is observing onto paper, focusing at first on the bumps that attracted Monique to this leaf in the first place. She doesn't stop there though; she puts the entire thing into context, the context she knows so well: a house, a bee, a red-backed spider and a flower.

Taylor looks and draws and looks again in scientific fashion.

When Jack joins her, he discovers that another leaf (a geranium leaf) has a dark line around the edge and takes it to the light table with the magnifying glass so he can see the darkened line more clearly. Then when he has drawn this, he focuses on the camellia leaf, and looking carefully with the assistance of the additional light from the light table, he can see the tiny insects that are causing the bumps. They soon become part of his next drawing.

A colleague, Kirrily, introduces drawing from nature with a group of children at her center. She brings a beautiful large drawing-portfolio book to display the photograph of the interesting object and the children's artistic representations side by side. Over the year the children have become used to drawing what they can see, making representations with art materials and talking about the object. Soon other children, not so artistically inclined, begin to gather interesting natural objects and bring the stories of where they found them to the group. A new group of naturalists begins to emerge, one who sees, appreciates and wants to collect and classify objects.

The ability to recognize and classify sits at the heart of this dimension. Lachlan collected information about spiders as part of his research year—spiders that bite or sting, spiders that build nests in hollows and under rocks or spin webs, spiders that attack other spiders and so on. He classified the information as he collected it, and could talk about particular classifications of spiders easily. He also had a well-defined sense of humor, as the next story illustrates.

One morning Lachlan arrives with a large black rubber spider and invites me to be part of the conspiracy with him. I am happy to oblige as we place the frighteningly real-looking creature on a part of the branch overlooking the sandpit. Neither of us gives any warning, and so when we hear some loud shrieks and later equally loud laughter, we know the other children have spotted it. Sometimes naturalists can have a lot of fun.

Children can use their naturalist knowledge to intensify the play possibilities available for themselves and others.

Implications

As we head into adulthood, we are faced with decisions about the world that surrounds us. If we expect our citizens to value the animal and plant world as well as the manufactured one of our own invention, we have to have in place avenues for children to develop an awareness of the natural world. When we appreciate, we value; when we don't, we squander!

Our world is faced with some serious decisions about whaling, greenhouse gas emissions, protection of old-growth forests, biodiversity of food crops as well as planted forests and sustainable agriculture (Suzuki 2003). The naturalists among us lead the way, perhaps a little way ahead of public opinion, but without their lead we would have devastation happen more often. I think back to the days when farmers would pull a chain between two tractors and clear the forest to plant crops and then look at my own father who carefully cleared small sections of land and left others as forest. I wondered why he would do this, and his answer was that trees were there for many purposes and he would try to walk softly upon the land. In hindsight, I should not have been surprised; he knew every species of tree that grew on the farm, he knew where the biggest and oldest trees were and he knew the native animals and plants as well as the sheep, pigs, chickens, cattle and horses we domesticated. He sat up nights on end to feed orphaned baby lambs, tucking them into little beds made from cardboard boxes in the kitchen with hot water bottles to keep them warm on cold nights and stoking the wood fire to keep the kitchen warm. He was a bushy, perhaps deep down even a greenie. He touched my soul forever anyway.

We have a responsibility to the future to encourage the creativity of the naturalist among us whenever we can.

CREATING CONNECTIONS

This dimension of the naturalist touches all other dimensions at some point. Together these eight dimensions that Howard Gardner (1983) identified in his research make us whole. For some of us our natural abilities lead us one or two ways more than others, and this is what makes us unique individuals. Our society needs this mix of personalities and possibilities.

Classification

At the core of being a naturalist is the ability to recognize and classify. Pam Schiller (researcher, author and friend) commented in one of her presentations that there was an even more everyday application to being a naturalist: the people who set up supermarkets classify the stock into varying categories, and that is why we, mostly, can find what we are looking for! I had never thought of this before.

However, for the purist, it mostly concerns being able to recognize, value, and classify the natural environment. David Lazear, in his book *Eight Ways of Knowing: Teaching for Multiple Intelligences* (1999), reminds us that we don't even need to be able to see to become a naturalist. Some well-known and respected leaders in the field have used their sense of touch alone. We'll need to remember this when we look at including all children regardless of ability, gender or ethnicity.

We can encourage children to develop this ability to classify in everything we do within our center. Are we packing away the building blocks after a good long play session? If we provide classification systems so that these blocks go here and those blocks go there (it could be photographs or other pictorial representation of the blocks), we are encouraging children to use their classification awareness. If we ask

John to collect all the curved blocks this size and Julie to collect all the short straight blocks, we are further encouraging classification systems to develop as part of the ordinary everyday routine.

Perhaps it is time to gather the children for morning snack or lunch, and we want the children to move freely, not rushing or pushing, to go to the toilet and wash their hands. We need a way to slow them down so they wait a few moments for their turn. Let's look at the colors the children are wearing, what kind of closures they have on their footwear, the children who have decorations in their hair, are wearing shorts, have pockets or zippers, buttons or buckles. We can use these to help children understand the idea of classification.

The favorite guessing game of "20 questions" is good for understanding classification: "I am thinking about an animal. Now, I won't answer yes or no to a question that asks me if it's a lion or a monkey unless we are near the end of the game and you are getting close. Instead, ask me if it has fur or hair, or fins or feathers. Ask me if it is big or small, or ask me if it walks on land or swims in the ocean, and then we can play the game." It takes a few attempts, but soon the children who know how to use classification systems begin to ask questions that give them the category the secret animal might belong to. Mostly, a group of four-year-olds can solve the problem before we get to 20 questions.

A complex puzzle, pulled apart and mixed up before being completed, gives opportunities for classification. "First we'll try and find the ones that go around the outside edge," the adult says, or "Let's see if we can find the biggest pieces first and put them in; the little ones can go in later." These are all classification systems ready to be applied in new situations.

Help children remember new classification facts. I was drawn to this knowledge with my friend and coauthor Dr. Bob Williams as we looked at varieties of oak trees in North America. "There are red and white oak," he told the group of fellow travelers. "These leaves are from the red oak. See how they are pointy at the edges? They are sharp, not sharp enough to prick your finger, but you could imagine they might. That's one way to remember they are red." Classification made remembering much easier.

Natural environments and exploration

"Stand back, stand back," says Gregory. "Don't hurt that frog. If Mr. Noah saved that frog, we had better look after it." This is music to my ears.

A burrowing frog has suddenly emerged from deep within the sandpit. It is very large, in brown tones and soft with big eyes. As we watch, the frog slowly screws itself backward into the sand and disappears. Gregory wants to grab it at the last moment, but I am afraid he will damage this precious creature and ask him not to. He understands my request and complies easily. It has been quite a journey, this one about Mr. Noah!

Barbara (work colleague) at the time is on long-service leave for six weeks on a bus tour around Australia, and we have been plotting her course on a wall map. At the same time it has begun to rain after some years of drought. It rains every day for a week or more, and the children start to be concerned about floods. I read them a story in a big-book format about Mr. Noah and the ark. Their interest almost overwhelms me; they love this story. I remember we have a small hand-carved ark with animals; it has sat on the shelf in the storeroom for years and years untouched. I bring it out, and we make up new versions of the familiar story, acting out episodes we imagine might have happened, like Mrs. Noah trying to get the wash dry or telling Noah to get rid of the red-backed spiders.

The children start to bring stories or pictures about Noah and his ark. We experiment with making things waterproof after one question is posed to us. The story says that Noah applies pitch (tar) within and without; we wonder why he would do this. The wondering guides the experiences and experiments we share.

We measure cubits and then string string lines to show the length, width and our estimation of the height (as tall as this hickory tree, the sign read) for adults to visualize the immensity of the vessel. Then this group of children (who attend just two days a week) begins to make a book about Mr. Noah, and each child has the task of adding animals that need to be saved from extinction. The book keeps growing as children remember animals that should be included, and they use their classification systems to guide them.

Cats: Okay, let's have lions, tigers, leopards, jaguars, mountain lions. One morning Sarah dashes in and starts drawing immediately, importantly. "I just remembered the snow leopard; if we forget to put it into the book, it might become extinct."

The project continues for seven months. In fact, one of the siblings who comes the next year talks about it too; it had been a great topic at home. "You think the ark was big? Well, it goes from the railway station to St. Vincent De Paul's shop, but the Titanic was really big and went all the way to Woolworths," he tells me. Each time I think the topic is finished, another child brings something in and the children relate it to the ark in some way.

Gregory receives the conservationist message—to him, if an animal was saved from the flood, it should be taken care of now. Tears of joy fill my eyes.

Molly is also a naturalist—another year, another group of children, and another center! I seem to be able to remember the naturalists easily.

She finds a snail and brings it to one of the adults and asks for a magnifying glass. This is soon supplied, and the adult suggests she get a see-through easel for the snail to climb on so Molly can look at the underside to see how it moves. However, the adult forgets to moisten the Plexiglas and the snail soon dries and falls onto the cement.

Molly is upset; the shell has a hole in it. She thinks the snail will die in the sun without a full shell, and soon she finds an umbrella and is sitting beside the snail, protecting it from the sun. A small group gathers as Molly talks about the snail and how it became injured, about the moisture it needed and the protection of the shell. Along comes Joshua. He has not heard the conversation so far, and he uses a classification system from home—he stamps on the snail with his foot, killing the creature. "Why would you kill an innocent little creature? It has a right to live just like you," Molly asks him, tears filling her eyes. We explain that at Joshua's house the snails eat the seedlings in his mother's garden, and she kills them because for her snails are a pest. Molly sniffs but accepts the answer we give.

The next day Molly begins to search for more snails. We gather and hold a meeting to ask what the children already know about snails and where to find them. There are some unusual answers, but we accept them as being correct at the time.

The hunt is on! About 30 snails are gathered in a short time, and suitable play environments are created for them, with leaves, grass, mirrors and water sprays and little bowls of water. Heads hover over magnifying glasses to watch them eat, move, defecate, hide and slide back out. "I wonder," says Trish, one of the adults, "if snails always like to crawl upward." Molly is standing beside her with six or eight snails crawling up her arm, all in the same direction toward her elbow. Instantly Molly bends her elbow, and now her hand is facing up, and we watch as the snails slowly turn and head back up where they came from, upward toward the raised hand. "Yes," Molly says. "So, where do you find the smallest, smallest snails?" I wondered. Soon we have the answer, right in the very center of the agapanthus plants. "I didn't know there were baby snails," Callum tells me. "I thought they were all the same size." Classification encourages wondering and reflection as we sort and re-sort according to our knowledge. This is what naturalists do.

Recording and documentation

As the children shared their knowledge of snails, one of the adults wrote their words down. Some children drew their ideas, and we made a display about snails as we knew them to be. Gradually over time, the children's ideas changed and grew and we added the new ideas to the documentation on display. The children could read the ideas and follow the changes as they happened. "We used to think this, and now we think that . . ."

Our ideas change over time no matter what age we might be. The consensus changes also as we gather more information and as a society we document these ideas in many forms, from art on cave walls through to the latest paper given at a sustainability conference.

My own thought is that if we document the children's wonderings and thoughts, their play and conversations, we are recording something really important and the story of their development is contained within the learning story. Record the learning story and the development details ride for free on the learning bus. My observation is that when we record the child development story, it lacks context; it's often boring or is very predictable and uniform, dictated by the checklist we have been working from. The learning story is about wondering, about working out, solving problems, working together, saying our thoughts aloud and making predictions. It's about a child's play with others or his solitary exploration, but the child owns it. The *learning* story is full of mystery for us as adults. We wonder where it is leading and how we can help, and this is the story worth telling in our documentation. It can be about one child, a small group or even an entire group now and then as children embark on new discoveries. Naturalist learning stories are immense!

Listening to children's ideas

The ancient Greeks wrote about an earth mother goddess named Gaia. In 1979 James Lovelock documented 20 instances where it appears that the earth is a self-regulating organic system. Peter Russell (1983) suggests that the earth is an independent organism and has its own life wholly apart from the human species. Is this possible? If it is possible, what does this mean for humankind? Will the earth self-regulate and destroy whatever damages it, meaning us? Is this what happens in natural disasters, or do they happen for other reasons? Worth thinking about, isn't it? Knowledge and ideas about our natural environment and our impact upon it often change over short periods of time. We don't know everything either as individuals or collectively. Every piece of new knowledge brings more questions, it seems.

If we don't have all the answers, then the children's ideas must have value. Let's listen to them.

> *"I know what causes the wind," Ethan tells me. "It's like this. The trees are standing near each other, and one says, 'Gee, I'm hot,' and suggests to the other trees that if they were to shake their branches and leaves it might make a cool breeze so they could all cool down. That's what causes the wind." I like his reasoning.*

Personally, I am still working on the earth's moon phases. I am using the term earth's moon, because some friends at NASA tell me that there is a project in the pipeline to take another Earthship (new name for spacecraft) to Earth's moon in 2019 or 2020 to celebrate 50 years since the original moon landing. I realized then that the word *moon*, meaning our moon, was no longer appropriate; we have to consider the moons that orbit other planets as well, so now I am a bit more specific. Each time I almost have the mystery solved, where I can draw it, make a model and explain what happens, another question pops up. I thought I really understood it just recently, but no, I have noticed something else, and now I will try and work out why the sun lights that particular side of the waning moon in the way it does. It doesn't fit my previous model somehow and needs more research, as Lachlan says.

> *"The sun walks over the mountain and around to the other side of the earth while we have night," Naomi tells me. I wonder how the earth doesn't get burned from the sun's footsteps. "He's wearing shoes!"*

A friend tells me she is disappointed with her drawings. "They lack perspective," she tells me. I laugh with her, not at her, and reflect that it took centuries and centuries for artists to discover the rules about perspective and she expects just to know how instinctively? Likewise, for centuries humans thought the earth was at the center of everything. Some lost their lives because they questioned this, and others were placed under house arrest. Now we know that our sun (called Sol) is at the center of our own little solar system but that *everything* is much more complex. Surely we can listen to children's ideas and allow them a few short years of creating rules about nature and then re-creating them as new knowledge and questions occur to them. This is how we encourage naturalists. We stifle them when we give them all the answers and take away their wonderings.

Peter and I were walking beside the local lake recently, trying to predict which night around the full moon we would see the seemingly big (we *now* know it's the same size higher in the sky later in the evening if we measure it against our outstretched hand) bright orange earth's moon we so love. At the height of summer we found we had to walk after sunset on the night after the official full moon on the calendar, but we wondered if this would be the case in winter. More walking to do later this year. We met a friend walking the other day and shared our wondering. He looked puzzled. "I don't think I ever wonder about anything," he told us. How sad that made me feel. We love to wonder!

Cultural richness

So many of our cultural experiences are based on our senses of taste, smell, sight, touch and sound.

> *I ask a parent to please share with us the numbers from Nepal. (The children have been collecting all the forms of the numbers they can find to make clocks.) She brings a calendar that hangs in her kitchen near where she cooks. The children comment about the smells on the paper, and we ask her to bring the spices she uses in the cooking so we can smell them and see if we can identify them with our noses against the paper.[1] We can! What a treasure the calendar becomes for us: more than a search for numbers, soon also an awareness of cooking traditions. It leads the children to ask her more questions about living in Kathmandu, and each question she answers, each artifact she brings to share, each story she tells encourages more questions. We talk about Mount Everest and Sir Edmund Hillary and Sherpa Tenzing Norgay. "I am going to climb Mount Everest," vow several children, inspired by the film I shared with them about Hillary's historic climb. We bow and wish each other "namaste" (more like "Take care" or "Good luck" than just saying hello). We learned the word earlier in a song, and then in the film we heard people in villages calling out the same greeting to Hillary's son as he embarked on a journey in his father's footsteps. The children turn excitedly when they hear the greeting and comment. The children have much to classify as life in Nepal becomes more familiar to them.*

---

[1] Recently at a center I observed some children using discarded out-of-date spices from sprinkling jars as a marvelous addition to their collage. Wonderful idea.

There are so many cultural traditions to learn about. Sometimes we have to wait a few years before we meet a parent from this or that area of the world, but we can use what we do have as often as we can. When nothing appears to be available, use your own collection of information from previous visits and previous people. Share your interest in the natural world, the people, plants and animals of the world. Your interests will rub off on the children, and this is what we do well—spread enthusiasm and visions of peace!

Being inclusive

Until I read David Lazear's comment about it not being essential to see to become a recognized naturalist, I would have approached this section quite differently, and I am thankful for his timely reminder to the contrary.

All children, regardless of their ability or disability, gender, ethnicity or socioeconomic status, can become naturalists! It's the attitude, awareness, desire and some wondering that matter most. Very young children know what tastes they like and what they don't. They have begun to classify before they have the words to tell you what they are thinking.

Children a little older know that they should keep their fingers away from the spider curling in a leaf, because some spiders might bite them. They know that some animals are wild and must be treated carefully and others can safely live with us.

> *Simon tells me after a crocodile attack is in the news, "Don't people know it's the crocodile's habitat and to be more careful?" He adds, "Poor crocodile, it gets the blame when it was the person that was stupid!"*

Materials, provisions and experiences

Good quality, "real" equipment really helps children explore their naturalist tendencies. I found some large magnifying glasses that stand by themselves over the object, and others that have little feet that can be extended so they can balance. (These also had plastic tweezers held within the handle that were enormously useful to hold or pick up things.)

I discovered that small baskets or dishes are useful to hold collections of tiny objects found in the outdoor environment on naturalist hunts and make a difference to the learning environment.

An assortment of perfumed (but nonpoisonous) plants to pick, pull apart, cut up and pound with mortar and pestle will add variety. Natural environments with real grass and trees with bark that peels off, or leaves that drop all year or in autumn, hickory nuts and pinecones are wonderful. Bring shells you have collected or ones you can buy in the craft shop. You can buy bags of small polished stones and other river or beach stones that are interesting. Combine them with brushes and some water so children can experiment with the way things look when wet.

"Joy, look!" Jayden shows me a dampened pelargonium leaf under a magnifying glass outside in the sunshine. "It looks like a thousand diamonds." I look. He is right. Now, would I have thought to dip the leaf into some water and then look at it in the sunlight? Probably not, but the child did.

Collect snails, dig up worms, look at cicada shells, and explain what is dangerous and what is safe to the young explorers and naturalists so they can move with confidence. Mix sand and water, oil and water, mud and water, cornstarch and water—just mix. Follow the children's interests as much as you can, but don't be afraid to bring your own wonderings and fascinations with you.

Image of the child

CHILDREN LEARN IN CONTEXT!

I know from my own experience that my success in learning something new is influenced by the context. The context makes the new learning make sense, or it is where the wondering began. I learn best when I need to know something; then I can listen and watch or experiment until I have the answer. At other times I just switch off, get frustrated and angry or feel overloaded with too much new information.

Perhaps it's like this for the children. Our task is to invent, arrange, manipulate or create the context, and then the children will want to learn. Our task is also to listen and observe carefully so we know what the context is for a new direction of inquiry or small project.

I recently heard someone refer to the outdoor space as the "learning laboratory."

We all learn about our world in the context of what is happening. My reality is different from your reality. A body of knowledge in Alaska is very different from a body of knowledge in New York.

Billy has limited language. He has been attending speech therapy for some years, and still he is difficult to understand. He is understandably reluctant to talk. I find that he is interested in reptiles, and we embark on a voyage of discovery. He has something to talk about, and so his conversations just take off. Forget teaching individual sounds out of context; let's talk about something the child is interested in. We can often reach to the core of a child when we use the naturalist dimension.

Reflections, challenges and wonderings

A parent/geologist came to talk with families one evening about his work. I set our collection of rocks on the table for him to talk about. I was interested to know how a geologist sees the world and what tools he uses.

As he lifted each rock in turn, he didn't make a diagnosis immediately. He thoughtfully and slowly picked it up, turned it over, examined the surface texture and color, felt the weight, sniffed the rock and then licked it. He told me, when I asked, that a geologist uses as many senses as he can to help notice the fine details, and then from this he can usually place the specimen into one of the categories. He moved through the collection, moving the ones that belonged together into small groupings so that the classification happened before our eyes. Smell and taste as well—who would have thought about using them?

> *Some time later, some of the children become interested in volcanoes. I have a collection of rocks that came from the foot of a volcano in a canvas bag. They don't all look the same, but I wonder if the children will comment on the smell. I invite them to examine the rocks, and they, like the geologist, pick them up, measure the weight and size in their hands, turn them over, look closely at the details and then spontaneously sniff them, and when I give them permission, some even taste the rock. They tell me they can smell the volcano in the rocks, that even when they look different they still smell the same. When I add a collection of petrified wood, they do the same and tell me these have a different smell, and when I test their idea, I find they are right. So easily we present interesting items but then eliminate some of the senses from our range of inquiry. Perhaps we can make objects more available for complete analysis. From this observation of the details, the children construct their own classification systems. The system they use might not be the same as the 35-year-old professional, but it's a system, and we all have to begin somewhere.*

I was thinking about wood. A collection of bark, cuts of timber, twigs, small logs, objects made from wood and a collection of driftwood found beside the ocean or on the banks of a river—how are these items the same and how are they different? Will they look, taste, smell, feel and sound the same or different?

We can spread this wondering to groupings of many things: flowers, shells, acorns and hickory nuts, fibers and feathers. Such items should not just be beautifully displayed to look at but not touch—we should explore using all the senses that are available and safe.

PUTTING IT TOGETHER

In chapter 8 you will discover varying states of consciousness, and one of the highest states is described as feeling as if we are one with all there is. Naturalist experiences give us an opportunity to become one with all of creation.

Connecting dimensions

This chapter has been about encouraging naturalist creativity. We don't have to know or understand everything; we can sit beside children and wonder just the same. We can ask, encourage their observation, document their thinking and help them put it together in a new way.

This chapter has also been about exploring the world around us, mostly the natural world in real ways—wondering, observing, collecting, using all our senses to gather information and recording our thoughts in some way. This dimension touches all others through the senses. Rather than a theme or unit of work on "the senses," I suggest we actually use them to gather information about all sorts of things in the context of what children are interested in. The naturalist dimension is a constant source of adventure—be adventurous.

I wonder when I notice children acting out inappropriately in enclosed and limiting environments, where they are separated from the natural world and natural elements, surrounded by plastic and other artificial materials, if what is really happening is that the child's spirit is reacting to its reality. I wonder, then, if we made small but significant changes to the environment, we might reveal the child within. If life might become more peaceful and satisfying for the child and everyone else in the room. Try adding new and interesting natural environments and elements to your center. Enlist the help of others who might be interested if you feel you need support.

Margaret writes to tell me that the children have been watching a duck sitting on eggs just over the fence from the preschool. She gets duck and hen eggs and an incubator so the children can observe more closely what happens. It isn't because it is spring; it is the children's interest that leads the exploration.

Another colleague writes that the children notice the caterpillars eating the bushes. The center is able to get some butterfly eggs delivered, and the children watch as the tiny caterpillars emerge, need feeding, change, and fly away as new butterflies. Can anything be more rewarding?

Another colleague tells me about an excursion to the local nursery after the children comment on the new leaves on trees after winter. They returned from the nursery with several hundred dollars worth of pots and plants, and these were the focus of almost all their endeavors for the months to come. This is real stuff, authentic stuff, naturalist stuff, and the finest of endeavors.

Creating new experiences and ideas

LISTEN, OBSERVE AND REFLECT ON CONVERSATIONS!

The children have been gathering small interesting items from the garden to look at under a magnifying glass. It's called a Tweezer Treasure Hunt. They use tweezers to pick up the tiny objects. Each child or small group has a small cardboard circle to focus their attention onto a small area of the playground. Some children find a seedpod, and when they return inside to the science bench (aka table), the adult splits the pod open to look inside.

They exclaim as they find several seeds, and Monique (work colleague) comments that these seeds might grow if they plant them. She notices that one child does not understand the link between seed and plant; it has not been in his experience until this moment. He is curious. She finds Eric Carle's book *The Tiny Seed and the Giant Flower,* and they read it together. Later they get seeds, a sandwich bag, some cotton wool and a dash of water and create a small test tube to watch germination happen. Over weeks they grind seeds to make flour, grow broad beans, measure the growth each week and create charts together. The other children are interested and participate, but for one child it's an eye-opening adventure taking him places he has never been before. Look for these moments.

TAKING CARE OF YOURSELF

There is a fine balance between having a wonderful naturalist environment that requires you to be in attendance every day, including weekends and public holidays, and having an environment that doesn't ever need weeding or the grass being mowed! My colleague with the hen and duck eggs knew it would take a time commitment from her, so she enlisted the assistance of staff and interested families until the project reached completion. The efforts were well rewarded!

We can't, however, commit to such wonderful adventures every day and every week; be prepared to look for the small and simple things as well. It can be simply the eye or hair color of staff, children and families that attracts attention at first and then reaches into the realms of beards and why hair goes gray or falls out as we age. This can tick along quietly without a lot of additional out-of-hours commitment.

Sue is about to sweep the debris from the hickory tree from the pavement. It's that time of the year when this tree drops hundreds of hickory nuts. Instead, broom in hand, she stops what she is doing and brings out some black cardboard, brushes and PVA glue in containers. Would the children like to collect some of the specimens onto the cardboard, she wonders? She sweeps the debris into small piles so this task is easier. It's a very popular experience; the area is soon swarming with children eagerly gathering the hickory nuts. Later in the day when the glue has dried, we bring the specimens inside. The first thing we notice is how shiny the cardboard is from the glue, and the second thing we notice is the smell. How would we have known this had the hickory nuts been swept up and put in the rubbish bin?

The storm has passed at last after much noise and lightning. The bravest children sit with me so we can watch the progress of the storm together from the safety of well inside the room. When the rain stops, we can hardly wait to get outside to examine the puddles left behind and look to see how the bark has changed color on one side of the trees and less on the other. We look at the water gathered in the swing seats, feel how squishy and wet the grass is and look at our reflections in the puddles. We measure the depth with our bare feet or against our shoes or even with a stick and marvel at the rain.

The vision of creativity I most want to share with you is this ability to marvel at the small things!

Some favorite resources you might find helpful:

Edwards C, Gandini L and Forman G, 1998, *The Hundred Languages of Children*, Ablex Publishing, USA.

Elliott S (Ed), 2008, *The Outdoor Playspace Naturally for Children Birth to Five Years*, Pademelon Press, Castle Hill.

Suzuki D, 2003, *A David Suzuki Collection: A Lifetime of Ideas*, Greystone Books, Vancouver.

Rockwell R, Sherwood E and Williams R, 1983, *Hug a Tree*, Gryphon House, USA.

Beginnings are lacquer red
fired hard in the kiln
of hot hope;

Middles, copper yellow
in sunshine,
sometimes oxidize green
with tears; but

Endings are always indigo
before we step
on the other shore.

"Life's Rainbow" by Sheila Banani

EXPLORING LINGUISTIC DIMENSIONS

What do we mean?

The ability to use language to express meaning, share insights and ideas, be able to inspire others, understand others, tell a simple story, remember and tell a good joke, react appropriately to stories and poetry or plays with different moods and learn new vocabulary or a second language is using the linguistic dimension.

Pause and think for a moment about the way Bob Dylan, Cat Stevens or Neil Diamond use words in their poems put to music. How do they challenge you to listen attentively, think outside the box, or find pleasure in their music (or perhaps grimace at the mere mention of their name if your tastes are different)? Words are used to share a vision, to encourage, to show leadership. Winston Churchill promised the British people would fight on the beaches and never surrender. John F. Kennedy promised a person would land on the moon by the end of the decade and Martin Luther King Jr. (1963) shared his vision of racial equality and harmony in his famous "I have a dream" speech. It's eerie to think that the power of words and the way people deliver them can cost them their own lives, as in the case of two of the above people, or can move a nation to war, cause people to commit atrocities or to pull together in enormous feats. Think also of the power of words in a movie you have seen, or a book you have read, that has moved you to laughter or to tears. It can be a combination of music and the word, but for me it begins with the idea made word.

Stories and examples from the classroom

Ken is a young boy from a Vietnamese family, learning English as a second language. His sister was with us a couple of years earlier. She had been a very eager learner. Ken is a little harder to get started for some reason.

His idea of painting is a splash of color, something simple. I have watched him a number of times and think it is time to see what else he can do.

Often we step back, we don't want to interfere with creativity. Here it goes.

"Mmm, this looks interesting. Can you tell me what your painting is about today?" I ask.

Ken replies, "It's a goal post."

"What sort of sport?"

"Soccer."

"Is it grassy or just dirt under the goal?"

He adds grass across the bottom of the page and under the goal.
"It's grassy."

"Who is playing? What colors are the teams wearing?"

"It's the Storm and United," he tells me, adding a few players in the right colors.

"Who is winning?"

"The Storm." He smiles.

"Anyone watching the game?" I venture another question.

"Yes." He adds spectators on the sideline.

"Is it raining or is it a sunny day?"

"It is sunny." He adds a sun, some blue sky, and one cloud.

"Ah, now I know what you are telling me about," I say. We hang the painting up to dry.

"Do you like soccer?" I ask.

"Yes."

"Do you play too?"

"Yes."

"What do you like about playing soccer?" (I have finally worked out a question that does not have a yes/no answer; it is a talk-more question.)

"I like running fast. I like kicking the ball, I like scoring a goal and I like playing with my friends."

"Yes!"

I could have said, "That looks interesting. Good work," and hung the painting to dry. I didn't. I talk with Ken instead. Over the next weeks he talks to me about soccer, where he has played, which games he has watched on television, who has won and what he was thinking.

Katz observes (1998, p. 37) "Because the teachers' and the children's minds meet on matters of real interest to both, teachers' minds are also engaged."

Implications

In *The Hundred Languages of Children* (Edwards et al 1998), Lilian Katz (p. 36) reports on some 1980 research by Jerome Bruner that indicated that of 10,000 teacher-child interactions, he observed only 20 percent of the interactions as being conversational; the rest were directional—about milk time, or giving instructions, about packing up, washing hands and the like. Katz (1998, p. 37) adds that her own observations and research agree with Bruner's findings. Indeed, she says:

> When children are painting or drawing, teachers seem very reluctant to engage the children in any kind of conversation at all. When children are filling in worksheets and workbooks, teachers are understandably eager to give positive feedback, and therefore frequently say things like "You did well," "That's the right idea," "Very good" and similar positive comments.

She contrasts this with her observations from the schools in Reggio Emilia, and this is perhaps the key to encouraging creativity in a linguistic dimension.

She reports (1998, p. 36) that in the U.S. the content of the relationships between the teachers and the children when not about the ordinary mundane and routine moments is about the children themselves.

In Reggio Emilia the teacher-child relationship is focused on the work the child is doing rather than routines or the child's performance.

> Adults' and children's minds met on matters of interest to both of them. Both the children and the teachers seem to be equally involved in the progress of the work, the ideas being explored, the techniques and materials to be used, and the progress of the projects themselves. The children's roles in the relationships were more as apprentices than as the targets of instruction.

Let us pause to think and talk about our own experiences. What does she mean and what does it mean to us and our practice? What are the implications?

> *A group of children is gathered around a table working on the project for the day. They have been asked to color in and then cut out a pre-drawn butterfly as one part of the exercise; the other part is to complete a stencil that puts the life cycle of the butterfly in order on a page. The task requires the children to cut out, color in, and rearrange the adult illustrations in correct order on a new piece of paper.*

I began to wonder if the children were attending to the information on the paper or concentrating on the skills involved with coloring inside the lines (this seems to be such an important skill to learn it is practiced endlessly at the request of adults) and holding the scissors correctly so they will cut easily, or worrying about how to place the newly cut images so they will fit onto the additional page. I doubt they were thinking about the life cycle of the butterfly actually. If we watch TV programs about science, the first really obvious thing I notice is that they have the real-life example of the object in front of them. They draw literally from real life, document carefully what they observe and then think about what it might mean.

They dissect or pull apart and draw again what they observe and think some more. Do we ever do this with young children, or do we skip ahead of them and provide other people's observations of the reality? I also wondered where the interest in butterflies had come from. Had the children noticed some on bushes? Had the children found a cocoon or caterpillar? Had there been a program on television about butterflies that stimulated interest? Or was it (and I suspect this is the case) that the teacher had reached that part of her program that said it was time to do a theme on butterflies?

I began to think that we should stop "doing crafts" completely. Is this where we go so wrong? Let's think about it. When we invent a nice craft activity, we arrange the materials; we know how they will look. What else is there to say but "put this on that and cut along here"? Imagine the opportunities for linguistic discovery that are missed when we do this. Instead of talking and wondering about the life cycle of the butterfly, the language becomes one of instruction. Are Bruner and Katz right, do you think? I know when we first encounter these ideas they can seem a bit challenging, especially if our experiences up until this point encourage us to plan particular craft activities for the children to enjoy. If we turn it around though and provide a range of materials (including craft) for children to express their knowledge, imaginings and wonderings—and take away the expectation of "craft"—we might find it a whole lot more satisfying and foster creativity in all dimensions.

We speak of the children using *One Hundred Languages* to express their learning. One of these graphic languages is collage and craft materials; let's encourage the children to use these languages to express their thinking. If we learn to do this, I suspect we will find our conversations with the children taking on more meaning for adult and child. Lilian Katz (1998, p. 37) continues her observations:

> Because there are no formal prespecified lessons that all children must learn, teachers can create activities that can contribute to developing children's more appropriate understandings of the topic. Thus the content of the teacher–child relationship is rich with problem setting and problem solving. . . .

> A program has intellectual vitality if the teacher's individual and group interactions are mainly about what the children are learning, planning, and thinking about.

Professor John Edwards, at the Early Years in Education Society conference in Perth in 2000, spoke about the things we steal from children. He wondered if we steal conversations, words, thoughts, ideas, perseverance, and interests in our desire to "teach." I wonder about this too. Do we present answers and not ask questions? Do we steal wondering from children? This paper is available on the Internet (Russell and Edwards, 2006).

It's not just about talking with children. It's also about the environments we create to encourage thought, wondering and conversations. Is it our fear of losing control that's the problem? I can identify with that. I used to think that I must be a dreadful teacher because the children would suddenly take off with an idea in the middle of the story, and eventually we'd get back, but perhaps I wasn't keeping the lid on it! There was never absolute chaos, but there was quite a bit of to and fro happening, spontaneous stuff. Now I see that as being successful. I feel more relaxed about it.

We have some students from a local university drama department visiting us; they want to know what the children are interested in so they can write a play for them. We are reading Big Rain Coming *this morning. We have read it a few times before. We have looked at the illustrations, how many times there were three of this or that on the page, how many words in the title and how many times the titles appeared. Today the conversation is about the sun and planets, about Jupiter being the protector, about the sun rising and setting and the way shadows fall even at night. The children are on fire. The book takes about 30 minutes to read. We pause and talk about every page. It is so exciting. The children experiment with new words; they extend their vocabulary, learning from me and from each other different words they can use to describe their thoughts and wonderings.*

Can we encourage language instead of keeping the lid on it?

CREATING CONNECTIONS

We know that the learner makes connections as she gradually adds more detail or knowledge to her understandings about a particular subject; that is one of the definitions of learning, to make a connection. However, we can be a little too subtle sometimes waiting for the learner to see a connection, and sometimes, but not always, we can point out the connection to the child and give him a shortcut to knowledge. We do have to be mindful so that we are not always doing this, as it takes away the power of awareness and sudden enlightenment, but we can sometimes assist in making the connection more obvious.

The art of good teaching is the ability to provide materials and experiences, to encourage discussions and to provoke wondering so that the learners can more easily make connections for themselves.

Recently talking with a group of adults, I commented, "It's very cool this morning. I wonder why?" An answer came immediately from one of the group. "Because it rained last night." "Is it always cooler after rain?" I asked. Another person in the group added to the discussion. "I lived in Darwin in the wet season, and it rained every day, but it never became cool like this. It would slightly cool for a little time and then get hot and humid again." The group continued the discussion about rain, humidity, wind directions, low pressure troughs and cool changes for some time. Weather is a complicated series of connected concepts, and for many of us it remains a complete mystery. For others it is a source of wondering and learning.

The importance of words

Talking with children is about learning the language, using language to express ideas, to form concepts, to test hypotheses, building a piggy bank of words. Dr. Brian Cambourne (a former lecturer at Charles Sturt University—Wagga Wagga) told of the boy who was reading about keeping guinea pigs and rabbits. He stumbled on the word *hutch*. It wasn't that his reading was poor, Brian told us. More likely it was that he did not have the word in his piggy bank. He had a guinea pig deficit rather than a literacy deficit.

A colleague (thanks Janine) talks about "the invisible backpack." Her thoughts are that as we experience throughout our lives, we put items into our invisible backpack for later use. You never know when something will be interesting, useful or just the item needed for new learning. Let's keep putting ideas in the children's linguistic backpack.

A Talaris Research Institute (2005) report entitled *Look at the Big Bubbles*, on recent research about how families teach their children to talk, has lessons for us all. First, I would note that the more self-conscious we become about it, the more "teacherish" we become, and the worse we are at the job. Try to relax and be natural.

The research indicates that just talking with a young baby teaches vocabulary. Talking a lot. Talking—when bathing, changing diapers, feeding, sitting together, and building with blocks or rolling over—matters. In the first three years especially, just talking is the most important feature. The more the parents talk to their children, the better the child's conversations in terms of variety and richness. In fact, by the age of three, children from families that talk the most have an average vocabulary more than twice the size of children from families that talk the least. Even at six years the children still have the advantage. This is a challenge for most of us, because for many of the early years the child does not talk back to us much.

Talk about the past and the present. Plan for tomorrow. Talk about what is happening. And:

- just talk;
- listen;
- be nice;
- give choices; and
- talk some more!

The research found that the less talkative parents were more inclined to give negative feedback than the parents who talked a lot. Is this what happens in centers also?

What happens when families (or adults in a center) are watching television or talking to each other instead of talking to the children? If young children are with us a good percentage of the waking day, then what are our responsibilities to help them develop vocabulary?

A huge gap exists between the kind of talking we often do with children as a teacher and the natural stuff we do as a parent. Remember that talking is a two-way street! Are your conversations going one way? Creativity is best served when we remember the children need to practice their words, pronunciations, meanings, inferences and semantics. We model and encourage, but the children are the learners.

My friend and mentor Dr. Yvonne Winer tells me that we should listen to ourselves reading a story and reflect on the type of words we use, how we phrase them, the questions we ask and what we point to as "the teacher" and then how we'd do it as a parent. Are we reading "to" or reading "with"? This idea suggests something about the way we talk with or to children as well. What metaphorical hat are we wearing, and do we always have to wear this hat? Is it the right one?

I remember a conversation from years ago with some friends when we started to reflect about the conversations we have with our friends or other adults. One of the dinner party guests told about a long drive with another dinner party guest where an amazing story of intrigue and romance was divulged. "You know, when she finished telling me all this over a few hours, she never once asked me to recall the details; she just waited for my natural response." (Both of the guests are educators in various realms of academia, and of course I won't give their names!) "Why," she wondered, "do we do this to the children? Is this being real?" It was the first time I had thought about being real, being authentic with young children. Until then I was "the teacher" who "knew stuff," and I had a role to play as the controller of all learning! How much of our talking with children is cute?

In the University of Maine Cooperative Extension Bulletin #4077 (2007), the writers draw our attention to *acceptance* as being especially important. When adults threaten, command, preach or lecture to children, it gives children the message that they don't count, they can't do anything right. The researchers urge us to remember that accepting does not necessarily mean approval; it just means we understand where the children are right now in their development.

They suggest we use what they call "door openers" instead of using phrases that stop further conversation. For example:

- I see.
- Oh.
- Mmmm.
- How about that!
- Really?
- Tell me more.
- Say that again. I want to be sure I understand you.
- No kidding!
- That's interesting!

Marie Clay (1985) from New Zealand, the founder of Reading Recovery programs, writes about encouraging children to talk more with our conversations, and she recognizes it's a particular struggle for children who speak English as their second language. It is so easy to ask questions that have a single word answer. How can we phrase what we say to encourage the child to talk more?

Jokes and other experiences

How easily do you remember a joke? When asked to tell a joke, many women reply with "Oh, I can't remember them." I wonder if this is really what the problem is, or is it that in our culture women who tell jokes are often frowned upon? Humor is important though. It reduces stress, can get a message across more subtly, and can break down barriers. Let's find ways to remember jokes better (telling them to someone almost immediately works well, as if in the act of speaking the words our brain puts them into memory) and let us also encourage the children to share their humor with us.

Anna tells me: "See those trees (pointing to some pine and hickory trees)? They are evergreen. See those trees (pointing to the deciduous trees we are sitting under at the time)? They are NEVER green!"

She tells me another worth repeating. "What did Mr. Armstrong say when he found bones on the moon?"

"I guess the cow didn't make it."

Songs, poems, games, stories, drama and dance

Bradley and Bryant (1983) report research about children learning to rhyme and the important connection rhyming has with learning to read. Children who don't understand, can't hear, have no experience with or can't make rhyme happen stand the real risk of having trouble learning to read. So, if the home or center relies on the television to teach the child to talk, then how much importance is placed on rhyme?

How often do you use stories that rhyme and nursery rhymes in your daily work? How often do you make up little songs that rhyme about ordinary everyday things? If you are doing this often, well done. If not, it's time to take the risk. It really will be worth it.

Here is a little game with a couple variations to add to your repertoire.

I'm thinking about, I'm thinking about, I'm thinking about a special word.

I'm thinking about, I'm thinking about a word that rhymes with . . . cat.

Or

Oh, gallop away and gallop away and gallop away today, today.

Oh gallop away and gallop away and stop with your hands on something that rhymes with . . . bed!

We are finding that children go off to school with quite a good knowledge of the letters and letter names. However, do they understand the function of these letters? The work that letters do in making sounds is really important to learning to read. How are you doing with this?

Another variation!

Oh, gallop away and gallop away and gallop away today, today.

Oh gallop away and gallop away and stop with your hands on something that starts with . . . "th."

Many may be familiar with the song "Ants in the apple." Well, how about using a variation that targets the names of the children in your group? Use the sounds the letter makes in this version of the game.

B is for Bradley, B, B, B
C is for Connor, C, C, C
M is for Mia, M, M, M!

The children love using their own names as the reference point for all literacy, so it is a good place to begin with recognizing sounds.

Using CD player, musical instruments and other devices

It is so easy to think of linguistic richness in terms of only the spoken word and forget the other events that make up a day with young children that can also encourage creative use of language.

Stories are available on CD or cassette tape. Listening to these while resting provides a chance for children to turn off their other senses, close their eyes, stop moving as much, relax and listen. At the same time, the children are adding words and phrases to their vocabulary piggy banks or invisible backpacks. We need to remember not to rely so heavily on the prerecorded story, however, that we never provide other experiences.

Instead, we can invent stories as well that introduce some new ideas. Here is one worth playing with as a starter. You can change the events to the drops falling on a swing and ending up on Alexandra's pocket, or falling on the luggage as it is being put in a plane bound for Albuquerque to see Jamie's grandparents! The *shape* of the visualization story works, however. Experiment.

High in a little, white, fluffy cloud, in an otherwise clear blue sky, were two little raindrops. They were named Drippo and Droppo.[1] They have many adventures as you will see, but this is one that happened to them the other day.

Drippo and Droppo were relaxed and sitting quietly when they noticed some more raindrops arriving. They knew some of them; some were cousins they hadn't seen for a long time; others were new friends to make. They played a game of ring-a-rosy together, and then they found it was getting crowded and they didn't have enough room to move without bumping into someone else. "Oh, I'm sorry," said Drippo when he bumped into Droppo. "That's okay," said Droppo. "We are all getting excited."

---

[1] Thank you to my friend Peter "Team" Henderson, otherwise known as *Bong Bong Hat Band* and also *Pete the Plumber,* for inventing the names of these wonderful characters and sharing the idea with us.

Well, they were getting excited. There were so many raindrops now that the cloud was getting to be huge, a tall tower reaching far into the sky. Some parts of the cloud were quite dark, and there were some soft white bits right on top of the tall tower. The little raindrops started to really bounce about, jumping up and down with excitement; they knew that soon they would be on another adventure in the water cycle.

The cloud grew very cold. The raindrops started to shiver, and then suddenly Drippo and Droppo felt themselves starting to change shape. They had six corners. They were white and they were fluffy little things, not like a raindrop at all. They started to fall from the sky, softly, slowly, swaying and floating in the wind. They tried really hard to stay close to each other as they always had, and soon they were getting very near to the earth. They could see the top of the mountain: glistening white, ragged peaks reaching like fingers up to meet them. Drippo and Droppo found themselves landing gently on a bed of soft snow that had fallen earlier, on a steep slope of a ski run.

"Wow, I love this," gasped Droppo. "I just love it when we turn into snowflakes. It's always such fun." Well, that was true. Sometimes they landed on a tree, settling on a branch and staying there for weeks and weeks, watching all the people underneath having fun going down the hill on their toboggans, sleds and skis or throwing balls of snow at each other. Sometimes they turned to ice on a leaf, making the leaf shine with a thousand diamonds when the sun shone. Sometimes they melted and ran down into a little creek that became a fast-flowing river passing through machines to make electricity for people in the city and on farms, but today they were in for a special treat.

Just as they settled onto the snowy slope, a skier came whizzing by. It was Stuart.[2] He was a very brave man and a fast skier. They would be safe with him, so they jumped onto his boots and whizzed down the slope with him—over the mogul bumps, sliding from side to side, holding on tightly so they wouldn't fall off. When Stuart stopped to rest near the bottom of the mountain, they crept up and into his boots and settled down, warm and cozy on his bright red socks, and stayed there, sleepily, quietly, resting.

After some time Stuart trudged home through the deep snow. More little snowflakes tried to take a ride, but when Stuart reached his front door, he took his boots off and only a few little drops went inside with him. Two of the little drops were our friends Drippo and Droppo. Stuart made himself a cup of tea and sat down, taking his socks off carefully, hanging them on the back of a chair. Now he could warm his toes by the heater. "Mmm, that feels good," he thought to himself.

Drippo and Droppo stayed on the socks for quite some time. Then the heater started to make them feel sleepy and floaty. Soon they were floating, holding hands, up to the top of the curtain near the door, and when Stuart opened the door the next day they drifted right out the door and floated up, up, up, back to the cloud. "That's the way, little raindrops," smiled the sun, warming them and helping them find their way home. "You'll go on another adventure another day."

---

[2] I have dedicated this story to the incredible courage of Stuart Diver, the only survivor from the Thredbo landslide.

Every time we play games, sing songs, read a poem, or tell a story we are adding new words to the children's piggy banks or backpacks. For me, it's important to find a few really enjoyable songs and repeat them often. This way the children become familiar with the words and actions, as well as the musical qualities. Experiment with using songs that are perhaps a little more difficult than you think the children can cope with. For instance, we began an exploration of rock-n-roll music after a conversation about learning to play the guitar one day. I found the children loved the words, even the words they didn't understand.

One really foggy morning, about the time of the "sun's birthday party" we had planned for the winter solstice, I introduced "Turn On the Sun," recorded many years ago by Nana Mouskouri. At first the children loved the chorus, playing along with the percussion instruments, and then they learned the chorus. They listened to the verses, and we began to explain what stevedore, lawyer, engineer, steeplejack and so on meant. We even talked about "warm emotions" as being those feelings we get when we do something special for others.

Cultural richness

It's important to talk with young children about diversity. They encounter it every day, and when we ignore the topic, they think we don't understand or don't know.

At first discussions may be about physical differences, and then gender, skin color, hair color and texture, eye shape and color. Later children become aware of other people with disabilities. When we create an environment rich in possibilities for exploring diversity, we help children develop concepts about who they are and about the separateness of others, and allow and encourage conditions in which children feel comfortable initiating conversations about differences.

After September 11, we waited for the children to talk about what they had seen that morning on the televisions at home before coming to preschool. There was not a word about it until morning snack when I mentioned it. It was like a floodgate opening. They had seen it all right, but until we mentioned it, the children were protecting us from what they had seen. Once it was out in the open, we could then talk with the children about their fears and feelings. We encouraged play and painting to express their ideas. We learned a lot and were able to help the children work out what was happening.

Don't assume that the children don't know about something because they have not mentioned it. You can easily communicate that subjects are taboo and off-limits by your silence. Instead, be available and approachable. Share your own feelings and encourage children to express theirs in suitable ways, such as with music, drama, art, collage, block construction and dramatic play. Reassure children with your words; show you care and that their feelings matter.

The Web sites that offer helpful advice for talking with children change frequently, so instead of offering details, I suggest you access new articles via your search engine. I found several that offered advice about talking with children who have experienced trauma, for instance, and these could be useful to you also. One that was current in 2008 entitled *Talking with Children When the Talking Gets Tough* (Myers-Wall, 2008) was particularly useful. You will find the address in the references.

On a more positive note, we can easily include words from a variety of languages in our everyday classroom experiences. We can include the words for "hat" that we are familiar with or have collected from families and friends. It might be simply the various ways to say good morning, or hello, thank you, excuse me, or the names of colors or shapes in a variety of languages. It adds richness to our language environment. We don't have to know them all at once. We can add to them gradually.

For me, cultural richness and celebration of diversity work best when in context. Talking about people who love us is an opportunity to read *Mama, Do You Love Me?* a story set in an Inuit culture about unconditional love, or the Masai version, *Papa, Do You Love Me?* or *On Mother's Lap* (the details for all of these books can be found in the references list at the end of the book), also in an Inuit context but this time dealing with sibling rivalry in a delightful way. Perhaps the conversation is about grandparents who live far away and are coming to visit. A story with a Korean influence in the form of a faraway grandparent is explored in *Dear Juno*. We are fortunate that stories from a variety of cultures about ordinary moments in the lives of people have been made available to early childhood professionals. They are a great place to begin.

We have to beware of tokenism and in some cases the reality of experiences other than the ones we are familiar with in our own family groupings. For instance, Alma Fleet (2001) warns us about using a unit (I hate to even use the word *theme*) about pirates. She speaks of the reality for some families of being attacked by modern-day pirates while trying to escape from the atrocities of local warfare and seek refuge in a new land. These pirates are far from the storybook one-legged, hearty character with a patch over one eye and a colorful parrot on one shoulder that we often associate with the concept of "pirate."

Perhaps, however, the conversation can be steered toward "treasure," Fleet suggests, and exploration of what treasure means to us. Is it a special person, a wonderful pet, marvelous experiences caught in photographs or gold, silver, diamonds and rubies? It might be a fragment of a garment or blanket that survived with parents or grandparents on a long march to freedom across Europe. A far cry from pirates perhaps, but a better opportunity to explore diversity in a more sensitive and honorable way. We may really enjoy the excitement of the recent pirate movies, but is that a good reason to have pirates as an educational and romantic theme?

Edward wraps a piece of blue cloth around himself. I comment that he looks like some people in a coffee-table book I had recently found at the local library. He turns the pages, commenting on the buildings, the people, jewelry and dress. He finds some other cloth and begins to dress his friends. Soon I find the small group of children building with the project blocks, using the book as a reference beside them. I notice Jethro engrossed in study as he compares the architecture of his own building with that which he sees on the page. "It's the Egyptian king's castle," he tells me. I have not mentioned Egypt; that connection comes from his own knowledge. "It reminds me of that book The King, the Mice and the Cheese," *he adds. I think about it. Yes, I see the connection. That book has a crescent and star above the castle. The ideas spread, awareness builds, tolerance and understanding increase. You will find another reference to this event in chapter 1, illustrating that each story has several implications for our awareness. In this instance language is the key.*

Being inclusive

The words we use are the scaffolding for our thoughts, and they define our culture. That is why in recent years we have attempted to bring about the use of inclusive nonsexist, nonracist or nonageist language. Language can breed distrust, contempt, hatred and prejudice, but it can also encourage and support love and humanity. It's our choice how we use it.

There are a few hints from the *Do's and Don'ts of Inclusive Language* (Davis, 1998) that will help us keep an eye on our own use of language.

For instance, unless we are talking about someone specific, we can, as the article suggests, avoid singling out a person's "gender, race, ethnicity or other personal traits or characteristics (such as sexual orientation, age, or a disability) when it has no direct bearing on the topic at hand," thus avoiding the promotion of stereotypes.

The children have been enjoying using white ceramic clay for some time. We have demonstrated how to make "slip" so the children can successfully attach arms to bodies by scoring the surfaces and applying wet slippery clay in between. Soon some of the children are experimenting with black cardboard and a mixture of white clay, water and some white glue. They wonder if we have another color they can use. We don't have terra-cotta clay, but we find an old brick and find that by grating it we can manufacture another color with water and PVA. I have a small collection of precious soft rocks that can be ground to produce ochre and demonstrate the connection.

I am amazed to see the children experiment with the natural paints on the dark paper and their own skin in ways that remind me of some tribal art forms I am familiar with or have been given by friends over the years. The children's interest suggests we do some further exploration of cave paintings in various countries; the ways people paint their skin for performances in several cultures; how artists used to grind rocks and minerals to obtain colors before contemporary paints and tinting methods had been invented; as well as looking at a selection of Australian Aboriginal traditional art. We don't just "do" tribal cultures. We embrace them in the context of all people having ways to express ideas and use materials.

We should avoid, as the Davis (1998) article reminded us, singling out women because of their physical beauty, or a person with a disability using an aid. We can avoid words that encourage others to think of people as being victims, and instead of saying someone is *courageous* (because of a disability), we can say they have been *successful* or *productive*. This article is worth downloading. It has excellent suggestions that we can use to audit our own language use.

Writing words with children

Some spiders have been seen in the garden, curled up inside a leaf, and others have created some interesting webs that glisten in the frost. Jack chooses clay, pipe cleaners and some smooth river pebbles to create a spider. I notice the texture in the clay created by his knuckles.

Jack uses one of his graphic languages to express ideas about spiders.

The next week when the children meet again, I show them the picture of Jack's clay spider in the journal and suggest they observe and then draw what they see in the garden. We read Aranea. A Story about a Spider by Jenny Wagner, looking at the way Ron Brookes (the illustrator) has used fine black pens to draw the lines in the pictures. A box of clipboards, some fine black pens and clean white paper (the basic ingredients) are provided, and many of the children go about their work.

We notice that many of the children are writing their names (this is usually where print awareness begins, either recognizing the letter or being able to write the letter) on their work and others are exploring ways to write information. Emily uses a red pen to tell everyone that some spiders are dangerous. We observe, however, that she begins at the top of the page and writes invented words from left to right consistent with our culture!

Callum explores fine black pens and the world of spiders.

The temptation as adults is to rush children with everything. Alise Shafer at the Fremantle Reggio Emilia conference, "An International Festival of Learning," November 2001, reminded us to start at the beginning and not jump ahead to an adult experience. She told the participants that children need to learn about paper, how it tastes, feels, sounds when torn or crumpled, absorbs water or not, is fragile or sturdy, before they can appreciate what it's like to draw, paint, fold, paste or cut. This idea is well applied to children learning to write words. We so often want to rush them instead of allowing them time to play with ideas, explore skills, and experiment with writing forms. Let's slow down, allow play to happen and from the context of the play, conversations, wonderings and investigations encourage writing to emerge. In early childhood centers it is inappropriate for adults to conduct formal lessons on the letters of the alphabet as they do in school. The children in school are in a different environment and are at a different age and stage of development, and there is plenty of time for this to happen. Younger children learn holistically and through their direct experiences and in the context of themselves and their own play. Yes, we need to have a literacy-rich environment, a lot of stories, letters and numerals (as well as words) available for children to see, touch and rearrange, and then encourage and enable each child to work with his or her own construction of literacy awareness and skill. The context, as always, is important. Let's put writing into context by creating shopping lists, taking messages, writing signs, making invitations and cards, writing names on paintings and drawings, finding names among a pile of name cards, listening to names and sounds of letters.

Emerging literacy

Literacy is the use of symbols to represent the ideas we express in language. Literacy has evolved from pictorial symbols on walls telling the stories of heroic feats, through to early writing and nonspecified spelling (just read Chaucer and Shakespeare to see how Old English experimented with spelling traditions), to the myriad of standardized words we find in the languages of people around the earth in a variety of symbolic forms.

Many children around the world are learning English as their second language, and this has implications both for becoming literate and numerate. For other children their family backgrounds may be anywhere from very limited to ones that offer an extremely rich language environment. Some children have three books read each day and parents who talk with them; but other children have not seen a book, never see anyone read or have families that rarely talk with them. As educators in early childhood environments, the challenge is to provide a range of activities and environments that will enhance, encourage, stimulate and enable children from all backgrounds to thrive linguistically.

Mem Fox says we need to read three books a day MINIMUM to a young child!

I say we also need to repeat favorite stories again and again. Let's read aloud a whole lot more. This can happen in small groups, or with individual children, in larger groups or even the whole group; just read aloud. With interesting but not overdone voices, play with the lilt and alliteration of the language, play with the words, play with the title, but read aloud!

Apart from this, however, what can we do to encourage linguistic and literacy creativity?

I like to use an image from my own childhood of "the family maiden aunt." In my own case it was not actually a maiden aunt, but instead she was married to an uncle. She had no children of her own and had come from a culturally enriched family background. My own family, while loving and generous, was a farming family—we were a big distance from other people, towns, children and experiences. Aunty Muriel was my treasure trove of enriching experiences. She was available to several nieces and nephews who all benefited from her loving extensions of our knowledge and experiences. She took me to the theater, she read stories, she told me about art and artists, showed me pictures and took me to galleries. She sang songs, played opera and classical music on her gramophone, talked about the world and its people and used fine china and silver cutlery! She taught me to knit, crochet and embroider.

She taught me how to sew and wear a hat! She read Rachel Carson's (1962) *Silent Spring* in its first edition and talked about environmental issues long before they became buzzwords. Imagine if we could use this image to enrich the language and literacy experiences of young children we see each day.

Context is essential

Literacy emerges in the context of language and literacy-rich environments. Literacy emerges in the context of conversations: involved conversations and authentic conversations, not ones that direct children to get a drink of milk or put their shoes on but from the wonder of ideas we as adults encourage children to create in their own minds. Then children have reasons to want to record their ideas using words. They want to learn to read because that's where all the information comes from.

Children need to be emotionally attached to language and literacy. Yvonne Winer convinces me of this when she demonstrates what she means by starting to tell me a story in Afrikaans. I can work out the first introduction line, "An old man went walking, walking, walking," from the lilt of her words, but then I am lost. It's difficult to listen; I soon turn off. Imagine how difficult it must be for children who cannot hear well or are distracted by many other ambient sounds in the room (thundering air conditioners, noisy fans, other children, adults cleaning tables and stacking chairs). Imagine how difficult it is to become literate when we don't understand the language being used. See what you can do in your environment to encourage children to become emotionally attached to literacy and language.

Listening, guessing and predicting

Literacy emerges from children learning to listen first, and then to guess and predict what words might come next. They soon learn about "book language" and begin to use words they have heard in books in their own spoken language. Books and stories that rhyme encourage the children to guess and predict.

Remembering what we know about literacy and language development, we add another few books to the spider investigations. One book is particularly popular as it combines an interest in the creeping little creatures and a love of rhyme that is also developing within this group of children. I watch Adam clasp his hands in delight as each line rhymes. He can anticipate the word that comes next and is delighted when he finds he is correct. Even for children who have had difficulty learning to articulate words easily (and this is the case with Adam), it is important to generate a sense of rhyme. For Adam a combination of a natural musical intelligence, combined with excellent kinaesthetic ability, makes rhyme even more poignant. It is the key to the literacy door for him.

Participation is important

We have read Mem Fox's The Magic Hat *many times, enjoying the playful rhymes, the lilt of the language. I turn the page, and several children spontaneously call out, "Stop," right on cue. They are participating in the delight of emerging literacy.*

The big book version of Mr. Brown's Magnificent Apple Tree *is a favorite. The children count aloud the number of apples left on the tree and wait for "Plop" to appear in delightfully large red letters. I later observe Jack reading this story to his mother when she arrives to collect him one afternoon. He has the big book on the floor and turns each page to tell her the story and then, with a sense of mystery and adventure, suddenly turns the page to reveal his favorite word and shout, "Plop." The literacy and language connection is magical for him. He will learn to read easily and well. He is participating not only in the group but also with the book lying there on the floor.*

We all do this and we all do that

Every time we read, tell, create or dramatize a story, we are providing the essential building blocks for literacy and language development. It doesn't matter if the group is three children or 20. What is essential is that the children can share the experience with the story and with each other. There is a certain thrill, however, in sharing a special story with a larger group, an excitement and murmur of comments, questions asked and ideas shared. A small group crushed together on the lounge and reading slowly, intimately with many asides, meandering and commenting, is equally as wonderful. They are both so good. Let us continue to do both!

Children have been selected to play the parts of all the dogs in Hairy Maclary *from Donaldson's Dairy. One child partly hides behind the adult chair. He is ready to pounce and hiss in his role as Scarface Claw (the toughest Tom in town). The other dogs are waiting their turn as the cassette player tells the story. The children taking on the roles of the much-loved dogs bark and wag tails and wander on down to the far edge of town.*

The story is well-known and has been chosen because it has a number of characters and has to be repeated only a few times for everyone who wants a turn to have one. ("No, we can't all be Hairy Maclary in one day. That's too many repeats," I tell the children.) Lynley Dodd makes rhyme an art form in her wonderful stories. When children have the chance to participate in making the story come alive, we add another dimension of interest, attachment and excitement to the development of language and literacy.

Image of the child

CHILDREN PRACTICE

According to Eisner (1985), learners need time and practice for the development of new skills. Therefore we need to remember to provide materials, experiences and activities that will be available for extended periods of time (with minor changes) to allow the children to return again and again to practice, refine and develop. Reading the same story, using the same name cards and dramatizing favorite stories all contribute to enriched linguistic environments. Instead of searching for the novel, let us create ways in which the familiar can be used in new and interesting ways.

Rather than using short-term, adult-invented "themes" (often repeated from year to year), the enriched language and literacy environment will provide for long-term exploration of "childhood themes" (that is, those wonderings that children create for themselves as they mature, the why, why-nots, the how and who, what's fair and just).

Reflections, challenges and wonderings

I listen to Sue, a work colleague, as she talks with children as they paint or draw. Her conversations flow so easily, and the children listen and respond on paper.

"Is your mommy wearing a dress or pants?" she asks, and the child adds clothing detail to her painting.

"Oh, I see ballerinas are dancing without arms these days," she comments to another child. The child laughs, hands over face for a second of delight, and replies, "I forgot them!" She adds some arms to her dancer.

I think we often get a bit precious, stand back and don't talk with children when we could because we are afraid of getting in the way or stifling their creativity. Perhaps we don't need to do this. Perhaps we can suggest, make comments, ask questions and wonder with the children about things worth wondering about, like where does the wind come from, why do we have clouds, why does the moon change shape and where does lightning come from? It's the quality and authenticity of the conversations, combined with the warm and generous relationship we hope that children share with us, that provide the opportunity for creativity to flourish.

PUTTING IT TOGETHER

Here we are at the end of this chapter. We have traveled together on a journey into the context and complexity of language and literacy. We have shared experiences of children using graphic languages to express ideas, and we have examined the ways children become aware of letters and numerals, listen for rhyme and the sounds that letters make and bring this and other knowledge together to become literate. The word, the creativity of language, however, is the most important factor. Without the words our development of ideas and forming of concepts is sadly lacking.

There are many helpful Web sites, articles, and publications available that will give you further ideas for successfully improving the quality of language in your center. An article from the University of Maine (2007), for example, talks about "winning ways to talk with young children." Ann Pelo (2007) in her amazing book *The Language of Art* gives excellent examples to encourage adults when talking with children about their art. Seek out such publications. Share the ideas with your staff or colleagues.

Listen attentively

Get rid of distractions and pay attention to what the child is saying.

Do not pretend you are listening when you really are not. Either ask the child to wait a moment so you can listen or make another time available.

Use more dos than don'ts

Now, this is especially interesting: we often forget the "don't" in what someone says, so "Don't run" becomes "Run" and so forth. Ask someone to get a loaf of bread but not to get a certain brand of it and he or she will come back with that exact brand! For younger children it can be difficult to understand the negative anyway. Say, "All those children who do not have their shoes on . . . ," and you will get the reply, "I have my shoes on, I have my shoes on," as a chorus from a group of four-year-olds. Phrase instructions positively instead, which gives better instructions that children can understand. Use the negative once children are familiar with it, and lead up to it carefully and slowly, introducing them to this new idea in time.

Use "I" messages, not anger, to communicate thoughts and feelings

Instead of saying, "You made a mess," try saying, "I need help picking up now," and instead of saying, "I'm really mad at you the way you ran onto the street," instead say, "I am really afraid you will get hurt when you run into the street."

Make requests simple

Don't give too many instructions at the same time. Think about a time when someone was giving you directions on how to get somewhere in a strange city. Did they give you too many turns? I know I can't follow. I have to draw it, or at least have time to visualize the turns. The harder I try, the more I can't do it. Sometimes we can use our fingers to help us remember three steps, but please keep it simple.

Make sure children are listening before speaking

Children concentrate on one thing at a time, so use the child's name and then ask the question or give the instruction.

Connecting dimensions

The drawings, paintings, collage, and block buildings we see children create are expressions of ideas that may one day become spoken or written language. We create connections with the children by enriching their environment, family-maiden-aunt-style, with our own experiences, artifacts and materials. Bring your own stories to share. Tell about the holidays, your family, the garden at home, your hobbies and your own wonderings.

Language is essential; it supports thought and defines our culture. It overlaps with all other areas of our development as human beings. Listen for the ways that children make connections, encourage them, comment and record their connections and share with other children. That way we can encourage creative language cooperative communication communities.

TAKING CARE OF YOURSELF

It is not possible to record all the conversations from a day, but we can record *some*, and that has to be an improvement on throwing our hands into the air and giving up! Do what you can and do it well. Document the learning that is happening, in pictures or drawings, if possible, and with words to tell about the experience and the children's conversations.

If we remember to work within our limits, or perhaps stretch just a little, we should not be so easily defeated by what we dream of but cannot possibly achieve. Give yourself brownie points for what you are doing, and set your sights just a little way ahead but not so far you cannot possibly achieve your goals.

If you can simply improve the quality of interactions where you work, so that conversations are more authentic, interesting and respectful, then you will have achieved a wonderful amount. If you can help children hear and make rhymes, then you will have set them up for easy literacy development. If you have made stories interesting, then you will have attached the children to literacy emotionally, and that matters! If you have fun and play word games, make jokes and laugh a lot, then you are extremely successful and creative linguistically.

A few favorites that might support you:

Schiller P, 1999, *Start Smart!*, Gryphon House, Maryland, USA.

Schiller P, 2001, *Creating Readers*, Gryphon House, Maryland, USA.

Silberg J and Schiller P, 2002, *The Complete Book of Rhymes, Songs, Poems, Fingerplays and Chants*, Gryphon House, Maryland, USA.

Silberg J, 2005, *Reading Games for Young Children*, Gryphon House, Maryland, USA.

Winer Y, 2005, *Stories for Telling*, Pademelon Press, Castle Hill, Australia.

Life's most urgent question is:
What are you doing for others?

Martin Luther King Jr.

EXPLORING INTERPERSONAL DIMENSIONS

What do we mean?

Living in a social world with others is not always so easy. It seems easier for some people and more difficult for others. It will be rare that we live an isolated life or work independently without having to interact with others; mostly we live, work and/or play with other people. There is much to learn as a young child that will enable us to happily be part of a group, but it takes time, good experiences and at times a lot of patience and forgiveness on both sides for this to develop. Harsh words and actions wound us, and it takes time for these wounds to heal. Learning to forgive others and ourselves is crucial in the development of interpersonal dimensions.

The two relationship dimensions, this one and intrapersonal dimensions, discussed in the following chapter, are similar and yet different. It's difficult sometimes to separate the stories and reflections, so please read these two chapters as if they were one with two parts. There are a lot of overlapping ideas, just as with musical and kinaesthetic dimensions. *This* dimension, though, is the ability to understand and discern the feelings or intentions of others. How do we learn this?

Imagine a world where we cannot make mistakes as we grow. Imagine a world where an adult remains angry long after a young child's small misdemeanor is over, angry out of all proportion. What makes us distinctly human is our ability to love regardless of actions and understand that another person is learning from the experience. So often our expectations are so high, impossibly high; we forget that we are all humans undergoing transformation as we learn and develop.

We expect a dog to do doggy things. We might be upset when it digs the roses up or pulls the sheets from the line, but we expect it to be a dog. A cat does catty things. Sometimes it comes when called, but often it ignores us except at mealtimes. A goldfish can't talk to us. We understand all this, but how often with children do we expect them to act like adults long before that can be possible? We all have to make a lot of mistakes first, and then we can learn from them, we hope.

Much is written about forgiveness in holy texts from varying religious traditions, from philosophers and wise people through the ages. Stephanie Dowrick brings these thoughts to her book *Forgiveness and Other Acts of Love* (1997, p. 291–92):

> Forgiveness deeply offends the rational mind. When someone has hurt us, wounded us, abused us; when someone has stolen peace of mind or safety from us; when someone has harmed or taken the life of someone we love; or when someone has simply misunderstood or offended us, there is no reason why we should let the offence go . . . (but when we do) in emotional terms, it is Everest without oxygen; Wimbledon without a racquet; La Scala without a score.

Our role in a child's development as a socially adept person is one of our greatest tasks each day with our own children and the children we encounter in our work. We can be the role model that makes a difference; the way we respect the dignity of a child teaches respect for the dignity of others. Our gentle approach and sensitive use of words, as well as space and time, teach a child that some things don't happen in a moment. We have to use our words carefully. What we do and how we do it matters.

My understanding of encouraging creative interpersonal dimensions is that first we need to make sure children are emotionally secure. From that security (later known as attachment) comes the ability to know, cooperate with and value others. It comes from inside us first.

Dr. Robyn Dolby's (2005) work on attachment theory grows out of Bowlby's writings (1958, 1969, 1973) that emotional security is essential for a person to grow to be an independent and competent citizen whose exploratory and attaching behaviors are in harmony. Watch a young crawling child sit on a parent's knee, slide off, crawl away and return a few minutes later. We see the beginning of this cycle of move-away-then-come-back happening repeatedly. As children grow older, the cycle gets larger, longer and wider. They move out of the family home, they move back and so on. When children return to a safe place, that safe place will usually be a person, the person the child is attached to. Having a safe, secure and warm attachment figure is important to a developing child. This is where a strong sense of self begins to emerge, and when we have this we are more likely to have a confident but sensitive human in a social world.

Robyn Dolby writes as she revisits the research of Mary Ainsworth et al. (1978) and others:

> Secure children cry when their parents leave . . . they are able to express their emotion in a straightforward and uncomplicated way, and this helps them get over it better . . . secure infants cry and when their mother returns they recover quickly and show no lingering distress.

Secure attachment grows out of close contact with a significant adult, and it's not just the hug that matters—it's the *way* the adult hugs. Hugging when a child wants and needs to be hugged and responding sensitively to a child's behavior makes the difference. When a child's emotional needs are met as a child, he or she is free to move on to independence, but when a child's significant adult always holds back a little, tries to toughen the child up before the child is ready, the child is always left wanting, always feeling needy, and this interferes with the development of independence and ultimately with growth of social interactions and fully developed interpersonal dimensions.

Stories and examples from the classroom

CHILDREN OFTEN SURPRISE US!

I got a phone call from an out-of-town parent asking to enroll her son. I have a vacancy and am pleased to welcome the family to a new life, new home and new preschool.

I then got a phone call from the former preschool teacher (with parental permission), during which I was warned that Tom was unpredictable and sometimes aggressive.

After a month or so, I am still waiting for his aggression to surface and figure that a new setting and a new home without the disruptions he previously faced means that he no longer feels stressed. Quite some time later the photographer is coming to take the annual group pictures, and a former child student at the center who recently moved away returns just for the day to be part of the photograph. The new boy has taken this child's place and so has not met her before. Tom notices Amy bending over a table making patterns with some small glass flat beads, fairy stones. He walks over with a chair and says, "You shouldn't bend over like that. You'll get a sore back. Here's a chair," placing it under her, touching her on the shoulder gently as she sits down. Tom returns to what he was doing.

I was totally enthralled and very touched by Tom's spontaneous and thoughtful action; when I told his mother, she was touched as was his grandmother. It would have been so easy to ignore his action, to miss it entirely; what a privilege it was to see, notice and be able to comment to him and his parent/grandparent. He touched my heart.

My mind wanders to another child, but the story is quite different. Matthew was born with a clubfoot that is now much improved after surgery to turn it around, and he is a large child for his age. He has been in childcare almost all of his short life so far. He is aggressive, in fact massively and unpredictably so. We have our work cut out managing him, making sure one of us is within arm's reach at all times and able to distract, interfere, redirect in a second. His flash point is very low. I start wondering why he is like he is. It seems outside the normal realms of aggressive behaviors that young children often display as they sort out emotions and the power structure, and learn that others have feelings and rights also.

I didn't know the exact cause of his behavior, but I wondered about his being clumsy. When he started to get up and walk, he often fell over or bumped against others. His newly reconstructed foot was not as strong or capable, coming out of months of plaster, as it should be, and he was a large child. I theorized that he often bumped and hurt others, unintentionally, accidentally, and that perhaps the other children retaliated, not understanding it was not deliberate. Was that how he learned to bump and bop and whack any child who came too close? I would never know what eventually happened to him; Matthew moved from the region the following year. But I often wonder with concern where his behavior has led him.

Another child, not yet able to easily speak his thoughts, also acts aggressively when other children move too close. It is easy to see what is happening: he doesn't have enough words to interact with the other children. He can't ask them to move back or tell them that he wants to play alone. Instead, he uses his fists.

Of course we arrange for him to receive some speech pathology and are able to access a specialist teacher to spend some time with him each week, but in the meantime we share strategies with the other children. We speak with them about personal space, about not crowding someone and about reading body language. We do many role-plays about observing body language. We use mime to help us with this task, and soon children are commenting on the body language of a child who is upset, has been hurt, is shy or is really excited about something. The strategies mostly work, and when they don't, the child who has ventured too close soon learns from the mistake.

Implications

A few come to mind. First, if anyone is unsettled, insecure or feels unsafe at home or in a childcare setting, it's going to be quite a task to get along with others easily no matter what age or stage of life he or she is currently in. Our early experiences usually define the adult we will become, and other experiences throughout our lives create sensitivities in certain areas: mistrust or trust, solitude or intimacy, dependence or independence. When our needs as young children or adults are met, when our parent or primary caregiver or, in the case of an adult, partner, is available, sensitive to our needs, does not react angrily or with disappointment or break the hug before we are satisfied, we will learn to be or continue to be independent and socially adaptable.

However, if parents (or the caregivers of young children at a center) for many reasons are not comfortable with giving such reassurance, are not organized themselves, have not had the experience of having emotional needs met as children themselves, draw away, put a child down too quickly or are not consistently available, the child will compensate in some way throughout life. A young child may avoid a parent's or caregiver's gaze, hide feelings, try to look busy to deflect interaction or, conversely, may be incredibly clingy and the attachment element of the equation is thrown out of balance. Adults in settings such as childcare centers and preschools may find it difficult to approach such a child constructively and may easily reinforce what has already been learned instead of acting as agents of change. Awareness, as always, is a great place to begin. Reflect on what you are seeing and how it's being managed. Can it be done better with more sensitivity and care?

Think once again about Maslow's hierarchy of needs (1943). It's a good reminder of what is most important. Is our timetable suitable more for us or for the child? Do we make a child more independent by withdrawing our support and empathy and setting them adrift too early? I think not. Instead, we could perhaps be a whole lot more consistently available, set aside the "chores" that we know need doing but can wait, and focus our attention on the children until they show us they are ready to move off to explore.

Second, if we have difficulties controlling our movements, others often misinterpret our actions and can react if we make body contact with them. A colleague, Elizabeth, tells me about a mother and child at her center. The child was incredibly active—he was constantly on the move, flitting from one area to another without interacting with the materials, the environment or the other children. He was like a whirlwind. Then one day she noticed what happened when the child and mother arrived each morning. The mother scooped the child into her arms and spun round and round and round with the misplaced idea that this would settle the child for the day. The mother, herself disorganized and facing many challenges each day with housing, relationships, employment and substance abuse, converted the whirlwind of her own existence to action and successfully set the child on a path of destruction. Intervention by some talented and sensitive adults, one sitting quietly in the same place each morning to take the child when he first arrived, before the spinning took place, a calm and reliable person able to devote all her attention to his needs, to help him organize himself and refocus his day, made a difference. We are probably all familiar with this scenario; it's not that unusual really. How we handle the situation matters.

Third, we need to be able to communicate well, and it helps if we learn to recognize others' body language as well as respect their right to their own space. Most of us are familiar with adults who get so close to speak with us that we want to step back to avoid our personal space being invaded. Our tolerance of invaded personal space depends on our experiences so far (I am told that submariners sit very close to each other, even when on dry land) and the experiences we have had with relationships thus far.

Successful interpersonal encounters depend on our giving and receiving nonverbal cues as well as spoken words of warning or encouragement. It's sensing rather than being told how another feels and adapting our behaviors according to what works best. It sounds easy, but it's not.

"What's the matter?" our partners ask us. We think we have hidden our emotions very well as we push the vacuum cleaner across the floor, very involved in being busy, or hiding behind the newspaper or book we are reading, the dark cloud of anger, depression or despair sitting above us, we hope unseen. "Nothing!" we say, pushing them away. The situation can be made worse if we continue to interrogate our partners, searching for what they have done to cause the dark emotions. I was reminded of this by my much-loved late husband, Stephen, one day when he told me that I should not think I was so important that I was the cause of *everything*—sometimes he just woke up feeling off emotionally and I was not *always* the cause; he'd get over it. However, we can also make the situation worse by ignoring what our emotional antennae have picked up. It's a delicate balance, isn't it, creating an atmosphere that will assist, a diversion perhaps, a subtle piece of emotional engineering without drawing overly much attention or appearing as if we are doing something. Oh dear, I wish it was simpler and that we never made mistakes, but we are human, and we all get it wrong sometimes.

As children have experiences and interact with caring adults who foster their awareness of others, they learn to read people's feelings and guess better what they are thinking. None of us ends up being a mind reader though, so we should also include words to express accurately what we are thinking and feeling, what we are planning to do, what we think is reasonable and so on. Observing others helps us sort out if they are telling the truth or hiding something from us, if what they are saying and what they are thinking agree with each other.

Recently, comments made by a visiting colleague made me think about the ways we learn to live with others. She suggested that when we prop children on a pillow so they can watch what is happening, we are removing any chance they have of learning to draw back from any aggressive, in-your-face encounters, and instead the children will lunge forward, hands flailing to protect themselves, and thus they learn this way of interacting. It made sense really; we are a product of many learning experiences along the way. Humans are not born with all the knowledge needed to get along well with others. We have to learn it, step by often painful step. We are not born sharing, and for many of us, myself included, we are sometimes able to do this and many times not. We learn to share by having a sense of ownership first: this is me and this is mine. Then we need to learn that others are much like us: they have feelings too, and it hurts when we pinch them just like it would if they pinched us. We don't like to have things taken from us, and perhaps others might feel the same way. It's a gradual awakening of awareness and respect for the rights of "the other."

If we have had good experiences with people sharing with us, and there have been enough pieces of equipment so we didn't have to fight over them, then we might learn to share, just a little at first.

> *There are many children gathered at the playdough table. I am sitting, playing, listening and talking with the children gathered there. A new child joins the group. Children move to the side to allow him access, and he brings a chair and sits down, but there is no playdough available. All except Jarrod keep doing what they are doing, but Jarrod pulls his playdough in half and passes the other half across the table to the new child. Jarrod looks at me, smiles and comments, "Now I have those warm emotions flooding back."*

You might ask what this is about: there was a connection. The children have been enjoying the song "Turn on the Sun," and we have been singing it and playing along with the chorus for months. Slowly we have added the verses and explanation of some of the words, learning what an engineer, lawyer or steeplejack does. One of the verses, Jarrod's favorite, is the one about "warm emotions coming back," and he has talked to me often about what this means. Today he knows inside himself the warm emotion of sharing spontaneously. All I can say is, "Wow!"

These are complex issues. Watch yourself and others in various situations. We don't crowd up the front of the classroom or meeting room. We try to sit down in the back, blend into the surroundings, and leave the front row at a presentation empty until the last people arrive and this is the only space left. We take care when visiting another's home that we don't sit in the "special" chair that is usually occupied by at least one of the adults, there are chairs made available for visitors and we take the visitor's role. If we do this, we are successful in relationships. But we may all be familiar with the person who visits us not understanding his or her role as a visitor; she heads for the refrigerator, turns off lights, opens doors and windows, turns on the television or takes up space usually reserved for us. We can tolerate it for a little while but will soon become irritable if it continues too long.

CREATING CONNECTIONS

No part of human development can be entirely separated from another; we are total, complex and vibrant beings! Thus, what we do physically, how we feel emotionally, the friendships we have, our ability to express our ideas in words or with graphic materials are all essential elements of the whole. This chapter, as with all other chapters in this book, considers aspects of human creativity but with the edges blurred.

Getting along together

Alanna is the only child in her family. Her parents are gentle, caring, and thoughtful parents, totally engrossed in her well-being. However, Alanna has not had many experiences playing with other children. One morning I observe her as she walks toward another girl building with blocks. Alanna knocks a few blocks as she walks past and then sits down right in the middle of the space the other child is building in. This is not a good move, and Josephine, engrossed in her own building, reacts, first with words, noise and then with some physical actions. Alanna is unprepared for this and doesn't know what to do. She just keeps on trying to muscle into the game without success. I move into the area to offer a little adult insight and support, perhaps to model suitable behaviors for both girls. I ask Alanna to bring me some long blocks so she can build her own building. Perhaps the two girls could build next to each other, I suggest. Alanna flounces off to sit under a large leaf on one of the potted plants, sitting there for some time before returning. In the meantime, with Alanna watching from her own safe little space, several children build alongside each other and finally begin to join the building together to create a city. Alanna returns. "Can I play too?" she asks. This works great. The others are ready for her, Alanna is more careful with her feet and elbows and soon the play is under way.

Our role is to create environments in which children may learn to get along with each other. It will take time (it doesn't happen quickly), space (crowding impacts on children's behaviors), suitable and sufficient materials (one big yellow dump truck is not going to work with five young children who would like to use it right now), modeling and patience. Let's help children on the outward exploration journey learn to interact with others, enter the game effectively, or find a place to play alone if that's all that is currently available, concentrate on the task and become involved in play of one kind or another and then return to the adult when necessary before embarking one more time.

I think that what I am observing is some excellent cooperative play between three three-year-olds one Friday morning. It sounds from a distance like it is cooperative, it looks from a distance like it is cooperative, but when I am able to sit closer and listen more attentively, I find this is certainly not the case. One child is pushing an ambulance with accompanying loud siren sounds, under and over the railroad tracks, another is building the railroad tracks and a third is making a structure for a fire engine. "Eee-aaaw, eee-aaaw," the sound continues. The track slowly becomes more elaborate, and the fire engine is added to the firehouse. The building child, a girl, moves away and begins to play with some figures and a dollhouse on her own. I notice how she sorts the people figures and arranges them carefully beside the empty house, lifting and looking at the furniture carefully before placing each piece in keeping with her image of a house. The ambulance boy moves so that he is next to her, kneeling at the house. He starts to add more furniture quickly and then adds some figures to the play. The girl moves away again, this time to a zoo area. She sorts the animals and sets up the pens ready to play. Ambulance boy starts to make his move. I distract him and encourage him to make better use of his ambulance, taking the injured child from the house to the newly erected hospital he was about to make.

I wondered how often this little girl had just begun to create a space to play alone, as she liked to do at that time, and how often she had been overcrowded with noise and movement. I wondered how often I had not really listened and understood what was happening, and reflected on how we could manage such situations in the future. We all need a little space at times. There is nothing wrong with quiet time in our own imagination. We don't always have to be at the party, we don't always have to be best friends, we don't always have to be social. Sometimes we need space alone.

> *Amy is very shy. We observe her playing alone for almost six months, beside the other children but not looking at them, often mirroring their play, but by herself. We wonder what to do and decide to give her time. After the preschool holidays, Amy's mother doesn't bring her little blanket back from washing. We use blankets, small sheets or beach towels on the floor for relaxation and imagination times. Current health practices dictate that each child must have and use her own blanket/sheet/towel. I think about Reggio Emilia and the little "nests" on the floor, where sometimes there is one child and sometimes two or three children nestle up together. The Italians are more interested in nurturing relationships, I've been told, and that cross-infection is not such an issue. I am tempted and finally give in to the temptation, suggesting that perhaps Kate might be able to share her large blanket with Amy if that is okay, as long as the two girls are able to relax and imagine. Out of the corner of my eye I notice a couple of other blankets disappear and there are requests for "Can we do that too?" I am in favor, so off we go with this new approach. Kate and Amy are observed the following day building together as they play their version of* The Lion, the Witch and the Wardrobe, *building the set with blocks so the characters can play out the scenes. A relationship is forged there and then on the shared blanket, and no one suffers any cross-infections!*

Sometimes our environments, the schedule or our attitudes get in the way of successful social interactions. How often do we take children from their spontaneous play so they can finish a task we have decided they need to do? How often do we break up play because it's time to pack away for morning snack, when we could perhaps move the morning snack to another place and allow children to wander in when ready or leave the play and return after morning snack.

I wonder if it's possible at your center to have small groups of children sitting in a variety of places for morning snack and lunch—in the shade, in the garden, picnic-style with friends. The adults can sit nearby to all the groups, and they might even be able to talk with each other, modeling suitable social behaviors. Of course, this may not be suitable for very young children and babies, but older children nearing school age should be able to manage their own food between them, friend helping friend. Children who cannot handle the freedom and feel the need to interfere with other children may need to be brought in closer to the adults from time to time, but you'd do that anyway.

I am thinking about providing opportunities in the everyday environment that can nurture social interactions. How often do we limit equipment and materials instead of having *more loose parts* available? Many of us have taken this to mean having everything out on shelves all the time, and I don't think this is what Nicholson (1974) meant. Rather, we can think about having more choices available on shelves, more (but not all) open and empty tables available and rotating materials and equipment

The girls' play continues into morning snack under a shady tree.

more slowly. We do not learn from novelty. Instead, we learn from constant or pro-longed exposure that allows us to create from the familiar. We don't need to alter environments every day, week or even every two weeks; instead, let us be flexible and make changes when we see the necessity for change.

Encouraging sensitivity, respect and thoughtfulness

Not all interpersonal behaviors come naturally. Many need to be taught, be shown to us, modeled or developed from experiences over time.

Each time we alter the flow of children to the bathroom to wash their hands before eating morning snack or lunch, we are teaching interpersonal dimensions. Every time we slow a rush by selecting children's names, the first letter of their names, names on flash cards (with photographs underneath at first), colors children are wearing, types of fasteners on clothing and shoes, those with and those without socks or shoes and so on, we are encouraging awareness of interpersonal dimensions. Each time we remind children that we need to allow children to go more slowly so they don't get crushed or rushed and we need to take it a little slower, we are teaching interpersonal dimensions.

Every time we stop a game because someone has a shoelace coming undone and it might cause an accident, or we stop the game while we attend to someone with a bleeding nose or play the game a little slower because one child has a physical disability, we are teaching interpersonal dimensions.

Whenever we notice that a child appears upset and we comment or take action, we are teaching the children to be sensitive to the moods, motivations and feelings of others. We can interpret. We can ask the child to explain what the problem is to the other children. We can search for new ways of interacting in the future so someone does not get injured or left out of the game, gets a turn or whatever is the problem. When we do this we are teaching interpersonal dimensions. Whenever we notice, comment and encourage thoughtful behaviors and give them a name and use the language of interpersonal dimensions, we are encouraging development of socially competent children.

I am not good at working in a group, I will admit. If someone asks for participants at a meeting or seminar to split up into small groups or to work on a project together, my heart sinks. I try to be the person left over at the end who will have to complete the task alone. I was virtually an only child; my only brother was 12 years older than me and went to boarding school about the time I was born. I lived on a farm that was 12 miles from town on a dirt road; the nearest neighbor was four miles away. I didn't go to school until I was more than six years old. The early years were spent doing my own thing in my own time and place. I still like it that way best. I like having friends and I am comfortable living in a city, but I still love my own personal space. I am not very good in crowds, and I don't enjoy small talk. Instead, I like to get to the nitty-gritty. When I read advice about teaching children how to work cooperatively in a group, I am personally challenged. I don't think I have ever learned to do it, or at least not willingly or well, so I am flying a bit blind here! My mind does, however, meander back to the North People's Olympic Games in Fairbanks, Alaska.

In the center of the indoor stadium, thick plastic covering the entire ice rink, stand three young Inuit men, each only about 5 feet tall. There is a leather ball hanging from the bar, and the height of the ball above the floor can be altered as the three finalists compete for the title. The plan is to stand on the dominant leg, hop on that same leg, then kick with the same leg to make contact with the ball, and then return, without falling to the ground, standing upright on the same leg. Try it; it is not a simple task. It's called the one-legged high kick. Soon there are two left in the competition, but the one eliminated remains to encourage the other two, and finally we have the last one standing. He is going for the new record, achieving a successful kick at a height greater than his own height. An eruption of applause signals that he is the winner and has broken the record.

What struck me was the way the competitors assisted, encouraged and talked with the record breaker. They wiped the floor so he wouldn't slip over and helped him visualize his goal, applauding like crazy when he was successful. If this was working cooperatively in a group, I liked it!

In an increasingly individualistic and competitive world, it is a challenge to allow others to come on a journey or to work with us. My suggestion is to look for children who like to work cooperatively, encourage them to participate in a project, add one or two other children who do not find this as easy to do and let the children who have mastered the skills help the others to learn from them. Look for opportunities and encourage participation. However, I acknowledge that for some children this is way outside their comfort zone, and my own thoughts are that these children have something special to offer society in their own individual way. We are not all the same!

It's interesting reading the details of brain research, learning that the frontal lobes are firing when we explore interpersonal dimensions and that this part of the brain has evolved over generations and is what makes us fundamentally human—it is essential for the future of our species. The higher states of consciousness, empathy for others, to dream of possibilities and make them happen, come from this area. Recent research I have either read, heard about, listened to or have seen as part of a documentary tells me that in young children the frontal lobes are still developing, and as we age they diminish. This is the reason why young children and older people often say the first thing that comes into their heads regardless of whether it will hurt someone's feelings; we are less inhibited at these stages of our lives. My own experience with people at both ends of the spectrum tells me this is accurate. The time for developing interpersonal dimensions is fairly limited. They are learned, used and then diminish over time. Let's make the most of this dimension while we can.

An interesting approach to the development of interpersonal dimensions comes from a physicist, John Platt (1980, p. 215), who writes:

> Whenever even two people start giving to each other and working for each other, these qualities and rewards immediately appear—greater mutual benefit, greater ease, and greater individual development at the same time.

Warm emotions are certainly coming back!

Reading body language

We are easily distracted—so often our own thoughts, problems, opinions, feelings and beliefs get in the way of good communication with others. It is almost as if while others are speaking to us our own words are being hurled back at them, forming a barrier to their words reaching us. How often do we need to remind ourselves to slow down and listen more? Observing body language, either with intention or subconsciously, can help the barriers come down if we allow.

I know that I often see body language and choose not to pay attention for all sorts of ridiculous reasons. This is why writing this chapter has been such a personal challenge. I think I have a lot of improvement to achieve in this dimension. I *choose* not to pay attention, I *choose* not to care, and I *choose* not to get involved. Is it self-preservation or simple selfishness? I will have to ponder privately on this a little more. It does not come naturally to some of us; we are all different and gifted with some of the dimensions and not the others.

In a circle game, we often notice the body language that tells us a child is eager for a turn, frustrated at having to wait or has no intention of taking a turn today. We can, as we ask children if they would like to participate and have the next turn, make mention of what we are seeing so the other children learn the language of the body. Be careful though, as you can make it much worse. Gently and sensitively done, it might just work.

"I see you are just bursting to have a turn, Tim, and find it difficult to wait. Do you think you could wait for just one more child and then have your turn?"

"Sarah, you look like you don't want to have a turn today. I can see the way you turn your head away when I look at you. It's okay not to have a turn, but you might like to ask a friend to have a turn with you, and that would make you feel braver, I am sure. Charlotte is looking at you and smiling. I am sure she would go with you if you liked, but it's okay if you don't this time. Perhaps another day."

I listen to a game. It's been happening for some time. It began with a small group of girls who set up house in one part of the room, moving furniture, dolls, dress-up clothes and cooking equipment to the new arrangement. They were playing "having a video party" and sent out invitations, made an afternoon snack, settled the babies in, had cups of tea and so on. Then some boys wanted to join the game, and the video was altered to take their interests into consideration and the game progressed. I am not sure of the link—I didn't see it—but soon one of the girls and one of the usually gentle boys were toe-to-toe in another area of the room. At first I thought it might be a video game, but then my other senses told me something was going wrong. I stepped in and stopped the play, calling "pause" and pushing the pause button on the imaginary video player. The two children stopped. I asked what was happening, and the stories almost matched. "We were playing a game, and we had to fight, but I didn't like the fighting and wanted to stop. I asked for him to stop, but he didn't listen and kept fighting me," Elizabeth tells me. Jack is almost in tears as he says, "Yes, that's true. We were playing a fighting game just like on the video, and I heard her say to stop, but I thought she was still playing. I didn't listen. I am really sorry, Elizabeth." I asked if he had noticed that she looked upset and hurt. He said yes he had, but he thought she was acting. They hugged; good friends forgive easily.

We often see this: a game starts and then goes horribly wrong. One child pushes another in a large ball, and the child going over and over inside suddenly feels scared and calls to stop, but the calls are unheeded. Our role is to step in and stop the game, to call attention to the cries to stop or to see the body language that tells us another is upset. "Does he look like he is having a good time?" I ask. "His face is red with anger, his eyes are full of tears, his fists are clenched and his back is hunched. He doesn't look like he is having fun to me."

It doesn't always work, of course; sometimes we have to wait for nature to take its course.

Two boys, good friends out of school and at the center, who travel together in a car pool, are fiercely competitive and often come to blows with each other over almost anything. I have tried and tried to get them to see reason, to use their words, to step back instead of into a fight, but after several months, I tell them I am not going to try anymore; they can just hurt each other. It happens a couple days later in the sandpit: one accidentally bumps the other, he retaliates, the other swings a punch, and then the fight is on. It continues out of the sandpit and across the garden, around a tree, on the path, becoming more and more aggressive. I watch and stay reasonably close, but they are of equal size and strength, and I think they need the experience of each losing their tempers. They do. Finally, with fingers up each other's noses and toe to toe, they start to cry and call for me to come help them. I pull them both into me, holding them close to me as they sob and sob. I think I may have cried with them; it has been very emotional. We wash faces and have a drink and move inside to a more comfortable place. I ask them how they feel when they lose their tempers, and their comments are about how bad it feels to hurt a friend and see him cry with pain. They agree that next time they will call for me to help them much earlier, and they do. Soon the sparring stops. They forgive rather than hit each other, and peace reigns. They are still good friends many years later.

Learning and inventing rules

Here are a few other ideas that might work for you. No promises, no formula—just some ideas that have worked for me over the years.

Nathan is a strong, lively and adventurous physical child. He loves to wrestle and box! "Oh dear," I think. "This is wearing me out." I unroll a large blue mat under the shade of a tree. I call the group to a meeting on the mat and explain that some children love to wrestle and box and others don't, and so this mat is the ONLY place that wrestling or boxing can occur, and any occurrences of it anywhere else will be dealt with fairly harshly. The threat is implied rather than actual. It is an "I will be very angry and have to think about what we can do if this happens" kind of approach.

Nathan positions himself on the mat ready for any participants, and for a few days some children do enter the space and take part in some solid child-child wrestling, knowing that when they call, "Stop," it will stop. It is a game ultimately. Soon, no children go onto the mat, and Nathan sits there for hours waiting fruitlessly. It is time to talk again, and he realizes something important: not everyone likes to be involved in the rough and tumble; it might be great fun with older brothers, but other children don't always go for it! Nathan stops.

It made me think, however, that perhaps those children who really like physically matching strengths might enjoy some other ideas we had up our sleeves.

Inside, sitting in a circle around a clear space in the middle of the room, we invite two equally matched children to participate in some sock wrestling. The rules are one sock on and one sock off each child. The game is played on the floor. Neither child is allowed to stand, and the idea is to remove the sock from the opponent's foot before losing your own. I ring a bell at the start of the round and give them 60 seconds before I ring the bell to stop. If they both still have a sock on, it is declared a draw. Any child can take a turn and can invite another child to challenge, but the invited child can decline a turn.

We had a noisy, exciting time, and all the while the children suggested rules to make it safer and fairer. Sometimes children have to have the experiences to make the judgments we have already added to our adult repertoire about suitable behavior.

An "economics" approach

It's basic economics at work really: one shovel is worth much and needs to be fought over; two shovels are worth a little less but still attractive enough to tussle over; but eight shovels mean there are enough for everybody without competition. It's the law of supply and demand.

One stroller and doll is a recipe for unrest; four of them are enough for everyone to have a turn in a reasonable time. Taking turns sometimes means having to wait—it does not always mean being first! This is a hard lesson to learn. Perhaps we never really do learn this one fully but only get it under control to some degree. We can encourage and model suitable behavior in almost any situation.

> "I am sure that when Nathan has finished with the fire engine he will give it to you next so you can have a turn, won't you, Nathan?"

> "I have a timer here, and I will turn it over. You can use that mincer with the playdough for five minutes, and then it's someone else's turn, okay? Here it goes!"

> "Wow, hold on there. That toy will break if you keep pulling like that. Let's see if we can work out a better way to make this work. What are your suggestions?"

A colleague (thanks, Wendy) told me that in her rural and remote area, many of the children have had little opportunity to socialize, and it can be quite an issue. She has insisted that instead of throwing a punch, the children have to come up with as many solutions to the situation as the number of years in their age. She laughed as she told me about one child, aged four, who told her when challenged, "I can just walk away and let him have the truck, I can keep pulling until I overpower him, I can suggest we take it in turns or I can just hit him!" My colleague's face said it all, and the child turned and said, "Nah, just joking. I can just let him have first turn and ask him to tell me when he is finished with it!" This might work for you too. Children often surprise us with the capacity to invent new rules, new solutions to try. Bring the children together for a meeting; explain the problem and ask for some solutions. Empowering children works wonders; you do not have to have all the wisdom.

Songs, games, stories, drama and dance that support learning

I love to share the story of *The Old Man's Mitten* in one of its many versions with the children. This traditional story, I think from Latvia, is about sharing a limited resource. An old man drops his mitten in the snow one morning when out with his dog, and a mouse, a frog, a rabbit, a fox and a bear discover the mitten in turn and try to climb inside for some warmth, finding it already occupied by the mouse who was first to arrive. The mitten of course stretches, but the animals have to accommodate each other, moving over and making space. A large cloth thrown over a table makes an excellent mitten, and putting the story onto tape allows it to be played over and over, pausing when necessary. The children soon take the roles easily as they become familiar with the story, and after a little while you hear them asking each other to please make some more space available and to be careful until the old man returns and the animals scatter, chased by the dog.

There are many such stories, one about a mushroom growing in the rain and animals finding shelter beneath it, and another about visitors coming to a house and sharing a muffin between eight and so on. These stories teach children about sharing space, making room, being careful and following rules. Include them both in your storytelling and your dramatizations.

One morning it occurred to me that the teddy bears and other stuffed toys available could take the place of characters from a story as a way to teach the idea of drama. Koala Lou took the role of the big ugly troll hiding under the bridge, and Crocodile took the role of Big Billy Goat Gruff, the Penguin as Middle-Sized Billy Goat Gruff and Possum as the Little Billy Goat Gruff. I manipulated all the toys the first time we told the story, and soon after the children moved the puppets and spoke along with the tape of the story, finally telling the story without any assistance from any adults.

Almost all the favorite circle games, such as "Duck, Duck, Goose," "Drop the Hanky," "What Shall We Play Today, I Wonder?" (a softer and more inclusive version of Punchinello) or even "Musical Chairs" involve turn taking, following rules, being safe with others, saving face when being caught or embarrassed at having to think of a new action. They are all worth playing; they help children learn how to interact appropriately, creatively, sensitively and bravely. Playing them regularly gives the interactive muscles a good workout. Use the interpersonal lens to examine the possibilities in games, as well as children's reactions and development over time. Collect games and stories or songs and drama or dance ideas, invent your own versions and create others from children's ideas.

Cultural richness

This might be a bit tricky actually as cultural differences indicate different rules of suitable behavior based on long-held traditions and practice. The culture might not even necessarily be what we commonly know as culture. It can be familial differences, or it can be place differences (you will notice this if you move from a rural and remote location to the city or vice versa; it's culturally different, the children have different experiences and expectations). It can be socio-economic differences as well. I encourage you to be aware of and sensitive to differences whenever possible.

I know a girl who spent her first six months in an orphanage and learned to be very reliant on herself and not as reliant or dependent as her wonderful, loving and willing adoptive parents would perhaps have enjoyed. It took time, but the bonds grew strong with time, love, patience and forgiveness.

I know other children who had a drug-affected sole parent and were often found dressed in diapers and onesies eating pieces of bread under bushes in the nearby park while they waited for their mother to wake up. We can't expect these children to react the same way as children who have been nurtured and protected from the world. These differences in family and place are cultural differences.

If in doubt, discuss your ideas with others in your area, run them by your colleagues and staff, and ask for assistance from families. What is it that they value, and what experiences have the children had? Children and families direct from a refugee camp or a war zone will have different needs than the average middle-class child from a secure home.

It's good practice for those of us who work with young children and their families to learn to walk in another's shoes, see through different eyes and feel different anxieties. It's a distinctly human characteristic as far as we know, this capacity to have empathy and sympathy for another person. Once again, some of us have well-developed skills in this area, and for others it requires some work, reflection, learning and courage to try something new.

Being inclusive

"Don't stare!" The adult grabs the child's hand and whisks her away. Well, how else do children learn about tolerance if they are never permitted to learn about difference?

I remember my embarrassment as my then four-year-old daughter gazed and gazed at a man standing in the bank. He'd had a leg removed for some reason and was using crutches, pant leg folded up and pinned, and he wore a turban! What a combination, I thought; she has never seen this before. The man took the initiative, telling me it was okay for her to look, touch and ask questions. He came to sit near us on the side as we waited for a teller. My daughter touched his face; she was interested in his dark skin and beard. She touched his turban. He told her what it did and how he put it on each day to hide his long hair. Then she touched his leg, and he explained he had had an accident on a motorbike and the doctors couldn't make it better. He was getting a new metal one soon and would be able to walk without crutches. He stood and suggested she play a game running under the space where the leg should have been. They both laughed; it was great fun. He met her needs, and she was satisfied. She didn't need to stare anymore; she knew about this stuff. I was so grateful for his understanding of a young, curious child.

Why doesn't Tanya talk? I have a marvelous young friend, a volunteer with me for almost 15 years, several days a week. Tanya was a former student when she was three and four, and as a young adult she approached me for work experience when she left school. This was so successful she has remained with us. Tanya has never learned to talk, but she can really communicate. Each year as new children enroll at the preschool, Tanya takes up her duties, taking care of everyone, another set of hands, eyes and ears, the solver of problems with simple suggestions and a lot of fun and laughter. She is capable and wonderful, and her presence enriches the lives of staff, parents and most of all the children she encounters in that time. "Why doesn't Tanya talk?" the children ask, and I reply, "She never learned to." I don't have to go into a lot of details, just state the facts.

Our acceptance of difference models acceptance. Our inclusion models inclusion. We make a difference. The more the child who is different can take center stage at appropriate times, be close to the adult, the more they are accepted. The cue comes from us. What we do matters. Answer questions honestly and openly but with sensitivity.

Andrew has leukemia. He goes to the hospital from time to time for treatment. His hair falls out, he has transfusions and he comes back to preschool. We ask parents of other children to take care that their children who may have infections remain at home as his immunity is low. We have the most amazingly positive response. "Why are you sick, Andrew?" the children ask. "What is wrong with you?" I encourage Andrew to share with drawings and in conversation his own ideas about what leukemia is like. He tells us about meditating and imagining the good cells are like tiny Pac-men eating up the bad cells in his blood and how he thinks this might make him get better. "Will you die?" one child asks. I hold my breath, but Andrew handles it. "I will try really hard not to, and the doctors will help me, but if I do, then heaven seems okay to me. I will help paint some rainbows." You will be pleased that when I last heard, his treatment had been successful, though I never saw rainbows quite the same way again.

We can be so careful not to stare that people vanish from our sight. It's like being ignored, becoming invisible. How would we feel if wherever we walked it seemed like a vacuum, that no one noticed us? A wheelchair-bound friend tells me she would rather people stared; at least she'd know she was real that way. We can be so careful avoiding asking or commenting that we never give the person a chance to share his or her life with us. It's like a barrier. Walk carefully, sure, but take time to see, to take chances to help children explore difference.

Some African teachers visit one day. Simon, so excited and wanting to be hospitable, asks if "one of those white men could read a story with me." I have no explanation for the white men part, but it was interesting that he chose a book by Ezra Jack Keats about a black boy named Louie for the visitor to read. The visitor was touched by Simon's open acceptance and attempt to cater to difference. Simon was only three years old.

Role playing

Role playing can be easily taught using mime, guessing what animal a child is pretending to be or what action the child is pretending to do, or even what machine the child is pretending to be. An adult can model some ideas and get the game started, but soon, with a little time, some encouragement and suggestions, the idea of mime will be a part of the everyday repertoire in the playroom.

Mime is then transformed into role playing. By pretending to be an emotion (in a context works best), the children explore ways to make this emotion become obvious using facial expressions and body language.

Explore, for instance, how it feels to be waiting for ages for a bus to come, looking down the road, shifting weight from foot to foot as you get tired of standing, looking at your watch, sighing and looking down the road again. If we introduce an idea and talk about the images we can see in our mind first, suggesting some actions that communicate the feelings and then help children concentrate as they practice their ideas, then we have some solid foundation for role plays. Adults can also do role plays, acting out a situation, encouraging the children to think about what was happening.

Experiment with ideas, take your cues from the children's reactions and try again. This is not easy at first, and it is not always possible with young children. You may be afraid it will get out of control, so there are other ways it might work for you.

Instead of acting parts, can we place ourselves inside a picture and imagine what one person is feeling and doing? Look for pictures of situations or emotions and ask the children to try to place themselves in the picture and tell what it looks or feels like from there. Use stories that help children reflect on what is fair or how to treat friends. There are many available—you will have some at your center or in your own collection, I imagine. Look for others. We all learn from stories—read to us, acted out, in movies or even as a painting.

Learning to listen and observe

So often we stand back, look over the heads of the children and, like the town cryer, observe, "Ten o'clock and all's well." From that distance that's a simple observation to make. How often are we completely off target though—all's not well, and soon we will hear sounds of distress and have to investigate further. We missed it altogether because our observation was too remote.

I investigated drawing the children at play as an attempt to better observe and listen. I found that a quick, simple drawing of the children helped me see so much better. I noticed how they were sitting or standing, who they were with, what they were doing and if I was close enough, what they were saying. I suggest you try this. It really improves observation skills, and after time the drawings will improve too. One artist parent commented after months of my drawings, "Your drawing really had movement today. Well done."

Children can resent us being too close, so we have to be a bit tricky, but they soon learn we are interested in them and with a clipboard and pen in hand we are recording their wonderful play and ideas. They like that and will often check that you have the details correct. Some children have used my drawings as a way of reconstructing a recently collapsed building; others can be seen, clipboards in hand, drawing the other children playing.

Take off your "developmental" cap. I would suggest we actually throw it out, but if you are more conservative, keep it near to slip on when you need it. Try to listen and observe the learning that is happening; record the conversation if you can; get little snippets of the play down on paper somehow: it will tell you a lot. Keep quiet yourself and listen more instead of always being the one in charge and doing the talking.

My daughter, Helen, told me about her youngest child. He goes to preschool and child care on different days of the week. One of his "developmental" record stories documented his ability to ride a tricycle, stop and turn. There was an accompanying picture to prove the story was accurate. Accurate it may have been, but it was not the whole picture. You see, Theo can ride a motorbike, and on the weekend he had started to ride over some small jumps, standing up as he maneuvered the bike! A teacher seeing him just one day a week could not possibly have the whole picture, and using the collection of preformatted, developmentally biased observation record sheets only made this worse, as it gave a sense of authority or knowledge that was in fact not present! What really mattered to Helen were Theo's social interactions. You see, he is the youngest child. He has amazing language, he asks loads of questions and he thinks and plays well. The best part is that he has encouraged a little boy who rarely speaks to talk. They chatter away together. Theo has found a way to draw out the language from this other child, giving him words, encouragement, exciting conversations and friendship. This is a story worth telling, my daughter tells me; I am inclined to agree.

Image of the child

THE CHILD IS A SOCIAL BEING!

Winter is often quite cold. However, recently we have had milder weather with sunny days, so it is no surprise when Thomas and a small group of friends head toward the shed to get some large wooden blocks. The carts are brought out first to carry the blocks to where they are wanted, and Thomas (very much the foreman) directs where the blocks should be placed.

There are about six children, mostly boys, involved, and the play continues. We stop for morning break on some mats outside. We bring out the easels, and other children explore ideas in paint. I sit on a big park bench and read stories to whoever wants to listen; Thomas and friends return to their play. We stop for a little story before lunch, have lunch and then Thomas and friends return to their game outside. A shadow puppet play about Five Penguins (inspired by the poem of the same name on the CD Wombats in the Belfry recorded by me with Bebe Jarratt) is happening inside, the children operating the tape recorder with the story and song, taking turns to operate the characters or to be the audience. Thomas and friends continue their game. Soon it is time to go home, and we leave the building for Thomas and friends to show parents as they arrive. It takes about 30 minutes for the adults to gather all the blocks and return them to the shed for the night, but it is worth it.

How easily do we interrupt play for our own purposes? Sometimes play concerns us because it can become noisy or boisterous. Sometimes we jump to conclusions too quickly.

A friend of mine from Northern NSW (thanks, Sonya) tells of watching a little boy squatting in the playground and then suddenly jumping on children as they went past. The children didn't seem upset at all, but she was about to stop him when she listened a little more carefully. This wasn't the way this child normally interacted. It turns out he was acting out The Magic Hat by Mem Fox and was "turning" the children into something else as they went past. The other children were happy to become giraffes and toads, it seemed.

We have to be careful not to jump to conclusions but to try to listen a little longer, observe a bit closer and be prepared for some surprises along the way.

Reflections, challenges and wonderings

How can we provide materials, activities and experiences that will allow and encourage the children to work/play with another child in a small group, or with more children in a larger group, developing skills for problem solving and conflict resolution as we provide peer models for children to learn from?

How can we provide experiences that will allow children to learn socially appropriate behaviors in a variety of situations, and to develop understanding and empathy for others?

How can we encourage children to form friendships that will support the development of self-esteem and confidence in social situations?

Let's hope the answers to these wonderings are found in this and other chapters!

PUTTING IT TOGETHER

In this chapter, as in previous ones, I have encouraged the reader to consider the whole child. While this chapter concentrates more on our ability to get along with others successfully, I encourage the reader to remember the other dimensions we have looked at along the way. Our ability to work across the dimensions is what gives our centers vibrancy. A creative learning environment is one in which the whole child is encouraged and provoked so that she or he learn and develop across a range of aspects.

Connecting dimensions

Just as in the other dimensions, there is tremendous overlapping. The experiences we have as young children allow us to explore ourselves as individuals as well as part of a group, to learn about "the other" as well as about ourselves. As our frontal lobes develop, we become more aware of how others feel; we observe them better; we imagine what it's like to walk in their shoes; we try and guess their motivations, intentions and perspectives; we can imagine ourselves in their position more often; we care about what others think and feel and we develop skills that show respect for another. We develop our socials skills; we become more interpersonally intelligent!

Our early experiences are important. Security in the home, a loving parent or parents, supporting friends and/or extended family make a difference, and social success brings about increasing social success. It's not automatic. We have to encourage, invite, allow, prepare for and nurture positive interactive dimensions.

We are reminded about this by Roger and David Johnson, and Edythe Johnson-Holubec (1988 p. 5:2) when they write:

> Children are not born instinctively knowing how to cooperate with others. And interpersonal and group skills do not magically appear the first time children and adolescents are placed in contact with others . . . these skills have to be taught just as purposefully and precisely as reading and math skills.

Think about choosing teams for an informal or formal game at school or in your center. The popular and skillful children are chosen first. Imagine what it is like to always be the last child chosen. If you are this child, how easily do you interact with the other children later in another situation? Have you ever been in this situation? What kind of pressure is on the less-able child when he does finally get his turn? Let's make sure we support and encourage this child's attempts and model acceptance of people doing their own best effort. The model comes from us! We can provide experiences that change the way people act in the future.

Think about asking children to choose with whom and in what order they go to wash their hands. This is a very successful and often-used practice, but are you making sure that the child most likely to be chosen last also gets to show his or her power? The child may need your help if speech or movement is limited, but you could use some flash cards with children's names and pictures to help with the task.

I find that if we are playing a circle game where the "it" child chooses the next participant, the boys will choose mostly boys, and the girls will choose mostly girls. This is permissible if we balance the situation well, and if we model that it's a good idea to choose a boy if you are a girl, and a girl if you are a boy so we get a better mix. What happens to the child who is often given the last turn? How must this feel if she or he is always the last one chosen? Let's make sure we notice and make necessary adjustments and make sure the often-left-to-last-child is the child empowered with the start of the game more often.

Is one child painting for hours because he or she doesn't know how to move away from the safety of the easel to play with others? How can we encourage the more socially skilled children to paint alongside and then invite the isolated child to accompany them? We can teach children to play socially; it takes time, effort, insight, patience and empathy as well as a creative and willing spirit.

Creating new experiences and ideas

Here are some ideas:

- A huge cardboard box, covered in white paper ready to paint, ready for some purpose or other, brings together children who might not always be found working together.

- A tall see-through Plexiglas easel with one child on one side and another opposite also encourages social interaction. Try having one child with paint on one side and on the other side a child as the artist's model. Who can resist pulling faces and making the other child laugh?
- Ask one child to "sit" for a portrait as several children explore ways to draw or paint the central child from many different angles.
- A fallen small branch from a hickory tree, standing upright in the middle of a pile of sand, or a discarded wooden telephone cable wheel makes an ideal decoration for the coming season. Small brushes take ages to cover the small twigs and hickory nuts with color. The "tree" can be hung indoors and suitable decorations made over the season to celebrate the colors we most often associate or see at this time of the year.
- Large floor puzzles that need three children to complete, the wooden project blocks and other manipulative materials, or a long cloth draped over a low-lying branch to create a secret space all encourage the children to learn to play with one another.
- Using the children's names often allows time for children to learn each other's names more easily. Use them at every opportunity: when handing out craft work at the end of the day, dismissing for lunch, in a game or handing out lunch boxes. Just do it often!

TAKING CARE OF YOURSELF

We all need time, patience, encouragement and sometimes forgiveness too. The most difficult person we often encounter is ourselves, and we are often the last to forgive ourselves our mistakes. Let's be kinder to ourselves!

Praise others—adults and children—using constructive praise, thoughtful and genuine praise and descriptive praise, not hollow "that's good" words.

Praise yourself when you have had a creative moment, a good day, and a wonderful idea, for overcoming something that had previously been a challenge, for bravery and patience, understanding and empathy and for your insights. Say, "I did a great job today." It's quite okay to praise yourself, reward yourself with something pleasant—a long soaking bath, some precious music, a walk in the garden or park, a long gossipy phone call, a clean and polished car (the act of doing it yourself or for and with a friend will leave you glowing for ages) or a good movie or book, an exercise or relaxation class, some creative cooking, time for a craft project, a good long run! Allow yourself to get it right as well as get it wrong. When it's wrong, it's not the end of the world as you know it. Relationships don't always work—sometimes they break. Turn the corner and get on with the rest of your life. Remain hopeful and have small things well spaced ahead of you to work toward and look forward to. Doesn't work today? There is always tomorrow. It will work better then. Pay attention to those people who really matter to you; they are worth your attention. Keep away from misery bags and negative people; they drag you down. You are special, and what you do is special. You are someone who touches the future!

Since life is our most precious gift,
let us be certain that it is dedicated
to the liberation of the human mind and spirit . . .
beginning with our own.

Maya Angelou

8

EXPLORING INTRAPERSONAL DIMENSIONS

What do we mean?

This is an inward-directed dimension.

David Lazear (1999) writes that the stages of consciousness begin with the body and its sense: becoming aware of ourselves in space and what we are experiencing through our touch, sight, smell, tastes and hearing. Comfort is important, as is a secure environment—it's a very basic stage, but it's essential. Without this in place the rest does not happen. It's similar to Maslow's (1943) hierarchy of needs, the base of the pyramid, but this time it is the consciousness pyramid.

From this consciousness we can move on to emotional awareness, considering "who am I?" This is an identification of the emotions and our unconscious needs (the desire to be loved, for instance), emergence of ego and our awareness that ego is different from the physical body. As we grow from this awareness of "I," we often become self-conscious. In young children this is when feelings begin to emerge and lead them toward thinking and intuition.

The next stage, according to Lazear (1999, p. 158), is more analytical: *"I think; therefore I am."* In this stage we develop a

> full range of psychological, intellectual and conceptual ability . . . human relationships, habit patterns, memory, personal history, self-image, and problem-solving capabilities. A sense of self-identity comes into full bloom as a separate entity . . . the struggle with authenticity, freedom, aloneness, and death emerges. We study our past, our problems, and our potentials.

Next we develop the awareness that we are citizens of the universe! Lazear (1999, p. 159) calls this transpersonal awareness. The incidents and issues we see on the news each night draw us into this awareness. We see how we are connected to other people's struggles, their pain and their joys; we may become more active in Greenpeace or Amnesty International or might adopt a child with a foreign-aid agency. Of course young children may be far from this consciousness, but we can often see elements of it emerging in their conversations. The ideas might come from home, and the words might not be their own, but the beginning consciousness is there. Let's not rush children into this, but ease them gently.

Let's begin looking at how others might feel and how we can help them, looking at what is right and just and how we can make a difference. In *Insights* (Fleet, Patterson, Robertson, 2006), several of the writers examine the ways that young children can explore social justice issues in new and interesting ways. These examples lead children toward what is known as transpersonal awareness. We can also explore the ways that beautiful music can transport us to another place and plane; it's working toward awareness that we are citizens of the world.

The last and highest awareness identified by Lazear is *I am one with all that is*, spiritual awareness, unity/spiritual consciousness. You might reflect on your own growing awareness of this in your own life. It can be God-consciousness. It can also be expressed in humanistic terms but at a greater depth than empathy. Lazear suggests (1999, p. 159):

the lure of becoming . . . the rising depth of spirit which energizes, motivates, heals, and empowers all other levels of our lives.

I have seen young children battling cancer using visual images invented by themselves or suggested by others so that they can assist their bodies' immune systems' ability to fight the invading cells. It's a young child's encounter with the highest form of consciousness, and I am often astounded by the ability to focus attention in these ways beyond what we would normally consider for a child that age. Perhaps we underestimate children, and that they can begin this part of their own journey at quite an early age when given the opportunity and encouragement. I will leave those thoughts with you.

I observe some small children at the edge of the local pool learning to swim: a line of tiny bodies sitting on the edge where their instructor has placed them, this time a little farther down the pool so they are in slightly deeper water. To them the difference may be huge; for an adult it's not so much. Some children may realize the water is deeper; others may not have considered this idea. The instructor moves along the seated line, inviting children to swim out to her and then back with her help. A number of children are eager to try their new skills, but I can see the little fellow at the end of the line is not going to do it. He has drawn his feet back from the edge and turned his face so he can avoid the instructor's gaze. She recognizes this and moves to him in a random sampling of children so that it's not one after the other across the line and he'll be the last. No, this doesn't work; he is not ready to trust her or himself with this new skill. She may have persisted, and he may have conquered his fears, but his mother steps up, makes a couple of cryptic remarks, takes him by the hand and they head off. The body language of the mother is that of anger or disappointment, perhaps embarrassment that her child cannot do what she expects. She is also pushing a stroller with a smaller child, so she is probably very busy. The child in his swimsuit tolerates his hand being held by his mother, but his body language indicates that he wishes he had just persevered that little bit longer and been successful. Now he feels his own sense of failure as well as his parent's disappointment. He avoids her gaze and looks back over his shoulder at the instructor wistfully.

How often has this happened to us? We are nervous about trying something new, we resist, we walk away and then we look back over our shoulder at the lost opportunity for growth. We meet someone who loves to dance. We feel silly dancing, but we are challenged to make the effort or walk away.

Stories and examples from the classroom

A friend tells me with some delight about a child she has been encouraging to paint. She tells me:

I have noticed that Jai never goes near the classroom art area, and one day when he is between one play experience and another, I invite him to join me. He resists, just a little, not so much that I can see it is the wrong time, but just a little—a hesitancy about something new. I encourage and invite him again and assure him that it will be fun, telling him he can use any of the colors. He puts on a paint smock and comes closer, picks up the brush and, choosing green, makes a huge swirl toward the top of the page. "Wow, look at that," I remark. "It reminds me of that big tree out the window. Look how the green swirls when the wind blows." I don't think his intention was to paint a tree, and perhaps I should have stood back and not made the remark, but I wonder if we stand back too often. Jai smiles and looks at me. He likes what I see in his painting. I suggest that he might like to see if the tree has a tall trunk. Jai selects brown and makes a long mark under the green swirl, a trunk. He is pleased with himself; he is making meaning. Our conversation is also making meaning. My comments matter to him because we are friends and he trusts me. "I wonder what else might be near the tree?" I ask him. He adds some splashes of color, turns and tells me "birds." It is a wonderful game we are playing, back and forth, conversation and challenge, support and endeavor. He adds some other splashes of color to the page. I hold back on suggesting more ideas; perhaps he needs a little space right now. The next week when we meet, I am excited because he comes to me and asks if I will come with him while he paints. The journey continues for Jai. He has overcome his fears and is now an empowered and successful young artist on one of life's great journeys, making meaning on paper.

Implications

Lilian Katz (1998, p. 36) writes about adults talking with children in a number of contexts:

> When children are painting or drawing, teachers seem very reluctant to engage the children in any kind of conversation at all.

I believe the "don't interfere with children's creativity" instructions are misunderstood. Interfering with children's creativity is making a model for them to copy, creating a stencil to color in and cut out or giving step-by-step instructions on how to make a giraffe. We can share art techniques; show how to use the side of a pastel or tip of a brush, how to glue things together, use a stapler, choose the best-sized brush for the job at hand, wash a brush between colors and employ other techniques. We tell the children it's about a technique, not about "make it like mine." The conversations we have with children in any part of the early childhood play/classroom are important; the art area is no different. Katz (1998, p. 36) continues:

> When children are filling in worksheets and workbooks, teachers are understandably eager to give positive feedback, and therefore frequently say things like "You did well," "That's the right idea," "Very good," and similar positive comments.

This is where the problem arises—when the adult has a preconceived idea of what the finished product will look like. We all have flashes of "I know, we'll make . . ." in the shower before we head off for another day of working with young children, but I urge you to cast these thoughts aside and replace them with "corks, which would be interesting to add to the collage I was watching Lachlan making . . ." or "Stephanie

Time and space to reflect

As we get older, our experiences accumulate so we can look back, see patterns in our own and others' behavior, and reflect a little about what works for us, who we are, what we are like. I encourage you to ask yourself a few questions:

* Am I more than my occupation?
* Am I more than what I do?
* Am I more than my relationships?
* Am I more than my skills and talents?
* Am I more than my faith?
* Am I more than my culture?
* Just who am I? Am I a combination of all this and more?

Let your mind drift back to your childhood. If your own childhood was difficult, try to focus on some good memories. Acknowledge that the bad memories have played a part in your development, but let's not let them overtake you.

So, what are your earliest memories of self? My own very early memory is sitting in a high chair and watching my older brother put his head behind a tea towel hanging on a line in front of the woodstove. I was alarmed at the sudden loss of his head and screamed. He of course continued the game for some time until my mother rescued me. When I consider child development theories, I realize I was very young at the time. Did I know then I was a person in my own right? Was I self?

When did you realize you were a "self" and that others were their own "selves"?

I think this awareness might actually take some time to realize; it slowly happens over the first five or six years of life. What is your story? When you observe the children in your center, how aware are they that they are separate from others, and how does this influence their play? How can we assist their development of sense of self?

How has your image of yourself changed over your lifetime? I am not talking just about a positive self-esteem. Rather, I am talking about an honest self-esteem, not over inflated and unrealistic or overly diminished in an effort to be humble. Remember the stages of your own development, how you got to be the person you are today, and the person you might still become one day. How much have you changed? Not just physically but mentally, emotionally and spiritually as well? How does this awareness of your own human development assist you in understanding young children? Humans have much to learn over a lifetime, and young children are beginning that journey. How can we help them develop realistic and positive images of themselves?

It occurs to me that using empty, easily obtained praise has inherent problems. Pam Schiller (1999, pp. 106–7) suggests that we use authentic feedback instead. She suggests:

- Reduce the amount of praise you provide; replace it with feedback.
- Use encouragement instead of praise.
- Help children learn to evaluate their own efforts. Let them critique themselves.
- Focus on the process as opposed to product.
- Be careful not to set children up for failure.
- Use a natural voice . . . be specific and sincere.
- Invite children to select their own rewards.
- Allow children to have more choices. Choices increase intrinsic motivation.

Dr. John Edwards (2000), giving a keynote address at a conference in Perth, used these words when he asked us to consider *the things we steal from children*:

If I am always the one to think of where to go next.

If where we go is always the decision of the curriculum or my curiosity and not theirs.

If motivation is mine.

If I always decide on the topic to be studied, the title of the story, the problem to be worked on.

If I am always the one who has reviewed their work and decided what they need.

How will they ever know how to begin?

If I am the one who is always monitoring progress.

If I set the pace of all working discussions.

If I always look ahead, foresee problems and endeavor to eliminate them.

If I swoop in and save them from cognitive conflict.

If I never allow them to feel and use the energy from confusion and frustration.

If things are always broken into short working periods.

If I and others are allowed to break into their concentration.

If bells and I are always in control of the pace and flow of work . . .

How will they learn to continue their own work?

Both Schiller and Edwards open a can of worms, don't they? We will return to some of the elements later in this chapter. Meanwhile, consider what makes you happy. What makes you sad? During your reflections on this question, consider how it is for the children you encounter each day. What brings them happiness and what makes them feel sad? How can we help them develop their emotional awareness, strength, stability and tenacity while still being aware of the rights and feelings of others?

Emotions have names; let us share the names with the children so they can use language to describe their feelings. Emotions are real. They often motivate us to action. How can we share ideas about controlling some of our negative actions but at the same time acknowledge the emotions?

Can we influence our own emotions? Consider a morning when you wake feeling blue. For many of us, the *occasional*[1] bout of depression is a reality, a result of tiredness, alcohol intake, relationship difficulties, employment problems, financial realities, a painful anniversary, health issues and so on. We can allow ourselves to wallow into deeper and deeper depths, or we can choose to alter our mood. Music is marvelous therapy, but if we play music that is extremely upbeat right now, it will merely annoy. Instead, if we use music that is blue, like us, melancholy, as a place to begin, we can attach ourselves to it more easily. We'll shed tears, and this is good therapy; the hormones we release while crying are beneficial. Then, over time, if we increase the tempo, change the style of music to a more upbeat example, our mood will follow. This is not my invention. It is suggested by David Lazear (1999) in *Eight Ways of Knowing*. It works. You can find out more about taking the brain from Beta (the most familiar; we operate at this level most of every day) through Alpha (we experience this in deep relaxation) to Theta (just prior to sleep or before we wake) and into Delta (we experience this in deep sleep) brain frequencies in response to music on page 111 of his book.

If we know this for ourselves (give it a try), how can we use music to assist children with their own mood swings? When the children are happy from running in the wind and we bring them to the mat for a story, can we expect them to settle down immediately? Will it work if we use relaxation techniques right at this moment, or does it work effectively if we bring the children's mood down slowly, acknowledging where they are and then shifting the mood with music and movement until they are settled, quieted, relaxed, receptive? Try some of these ideas and see what happens for you and the children you are with each day.

Relaxation and massage

Learning to relax, to be focused within, to quietly observe our own thoughts and feelings does not always come naturally to most of us. Many of us have to learn the techniques that enable this to happen. Young children can explore these ideas when led quietly, patiently, slowly over time to find a quiet space within themselves.

You might begin with the exploration of sound as a means of focusing attention. At first you may need to introduce some simple listening games, such as "The giant and his treasure." This is played with a child blindfolded safely and gently, so the giant is blind, and he/she guards a box of treasure in front of themselves sitting cross-legged on the floor. The adult asks one of the children gathered in the semicircle in front

---

[1] Please note, if you believe you are suffering from recurring depression, seek medical help. The suggestions offered here are for momentary mood swings.

of the giant to creep forward slowly to steal the treasure. To make it a little more exciting, the child may have to carry some bells and keep them quiet, and the giant may have an old stocking filled with crunched paper to form a sword! Another game is "Lion the Jungle King." Children are seated in a circle. A child is selected to crouch face down on the floor, not looking but listening. Another child creeps alongside, and everyone sings:

> Lion the jungle king, sleeping in the midday sun.
> Comes a hunter run, run, run.
> *The creeping child speaks the last line.*
> Guess who has caught you just for fun.
> *The crouching child tries to identify the voice.*

Another simple game called "Who Am I?" might also work well. A semicircle of children gathered in front of the adult, one child is chosen to stand and snuggle in close to the adult, with her or his back turned to the other children. The adult points to one of the seated children and asks the child to say, "Who am I," as loudly as possible. The standing child tries to listen to and identify a friend's voice, or find where he or she was sitting from the direction of the sound.

Using imagination time (relaxation, rest, after lunch) can be an excellent addition. Suggest that the children lie quietly, so quietly they can hear the sounds outside the center. Suggest they take their ears on an imaginary walk to find the sounds and bring them back. Encourage the children to try to identify the sounds they hear but not comment until they are sitting up once again. You will be surprised what they can hear when they concentrate.

Smells might assist children to focus their attention within. Use the lovely smells available in the playground, or bring leaves and petals from home or a neighborhood garden. Some people use essential oils as well; a word of caution, however: not everyone can tolerate all essential oils. For example, lavender, much loved by most people and considered safe, can cause severe headaches in some people. Use all oils and incense cautiously.

Smells can be experienced and identified while cooking or cutting fruit. Talk with the children about the words they can use to describe the smells. Language is an important tool for identifying feelings and thoughts. Expose children to the words.

Of course taste can also be used in a similar way. Encourage children to taste slowly, carefully, think about where they can taste (different parts of the tongue taste different qualities) and what they like or don't like and why. Use language to describe tastes. Our language does not have many words to describe tastes, so children might want to use "It tastes like . . ." in their description, much like adults do when tasting wine!

The texture of fabrics might help children settle into relaxation and become meditative. Collect pieces of interesting fabrics; ask families to bring in pieces they are happy to contribute. Encourage the children to feel the fabrics against their cheeks or on their hands, scrunching and releasing, passing from hand to hand slowly, letting the fabric dangle slowly.

You may choose to accompany this experience with music that suggests gentle and quiet movements. Once again, share language that describes the textures the children may encounter. Encourage the children to settle down, become quiet and focused on the task at hand. It's this ability to focus attention on a particular aspect that brings a meditative, reflective state, and this encourages children to explore awareness of themselves in new and creative ways.

Sight can also be an interesting meditative device leading children to concentration and quietness. If you have access to a data projector, an overhead projector or a slide projector, you can use these to project an enlarged image onto a screen or plain light-colored wall. Choose photographs of landscapes you may have taken or pictures that you find interesting and inviting. Share your thoughts with the children.

There are many wonderful books available that focus children's attention on particular items in well-known artworks; these could be useful. You might also find it useful to search for common elements in the illustrations we find in the incredible array of children's picture books. Very quickly children will find common elements in the works of Eric Carle, for instance, or Pamela Allen. The idea is to help children focus attention on something small and be quiet and still.

Use posters of paintings and suggest the children travel inside the painting and become one of the characters and tell the story of what is happening. A painting by Pieter Breugal called *Children's Games* is available on the Internet and could be useful—the children can be challenged to imagine they are one of the children in the painting and role play that game, either alone or with a friend. (This idea came from Yvonne Winer.) You will no doubt identify others that will become your favorites because they work. Once again, it's about helping children to bring their attention to something small and focus for a little while just on that. It's about identifying a technique that assists us to become still and quiet and look inside ourselves.

River stones, polished, available from a hardware store, too large to swallow and too small to be a danger, are excellent for children to learn the techniques of massage. At first they can use them on themselves, on their arms, legs, chests and tummies, and faces; then they can learn to use them on their friends, gently, acknowledging personal space. There are excellent opportunities to talk about "safe" places to touch and "unsafe places." The children will have insights they can share to establish the group rules. Accompany the massage with music. Allow time for the children to learn the technique as well as enjoy what they are doing.

Experiment—perhaps silk cloths will feel just right, or ribbons, feathers or commercial massagers. Children can sit in small circles of six to eight children, so that each child has another child's back in front of them to draw on and massage with the river stones. It works on several levels: the children develop attachments to each other, learn to respect personal space, acknowledge safe touching and settle down to a receptive quietness.

David Lazear (1999, p. 150) reminds us:

> Creativity is not a given at birth, rather, it is a dynamic process that can be learned, taught, and improved throughout our lives.

Aesthetics

The development of an aesthetic awareness takes time. It may change over time as our vision changes and we mature, or as we encounter new experiences. Our role is to encourage young children to develop their own unique aesthetic sense in an environment that has beauty, order and light. The environment needs to be uncluttered to allow children to see more clearly. An environment where everything the children have made for the last two years is on display, hanging from the ceiling, or crowded onto walls does not encourage aesthetic awareness. The community the children live in may have some excellent as well as hideous examples. The community may be cluttered with signs and colors, or their own homes may be chaotic, so let's provide something special in our centers. If you are not confident with this aspect, ask someone else at your center who does have a strongly developed aesthetic sense to create displays. Experiment and see how things look. Ask others for comments. Be courageous.

There is a lot written about aesthetics. It is a complete topic in itself and can be a philosophical way of thinking. If you are interested, go exploring and see what you can find on the topic for yourself and your own development.

Cultural richness

Photographs gathered from around the world introduce cultural aspects to children. For instance, we admire the whitewashed walls and blue shutters of the Greek Isles, but would that work in our neighborhood? We wonder at the unique houses designed by Gaudi, but would they fit into our city? We love the adobe walls painted in exquisite colors with amazing patterns in a number of different countries but hesitate to build something like that ourselves in our community. We can, though, bring these images into our centers for the children to look at and explore notions of who they are and where they live in new ways, using the introduced pictures as a contrast. In the same way we can use pictures of people—football or basketball players or runners, rap or ballet dancers, puppeteers, hunters, soldiers, musicians, artists—dressed in varying ways or with bodies painted in unique patterns, and look at ourselves against this background of diversity. Who are we? Who am I? Am I a bit like this person and a bit like that one? Am I not at all like that person?

One year I had a boy in my class whose grandfather collected hats, and over a few months we looked at the hats and the people who wore them. It took us into some interesting territory, occupations and beliefs, countries and cultures. It also presented us with an excellent opportunity to look at De Bono's (1992) ideas about six hats in a very practical and hands-on way, considering how we might act or feel when wearing a particular hat. You might find something else that encourages the children to put themselves literally into the life of another to see how it feels. Let the idea sit with you for a while and see what happens. Your imagination is the key!

Egan (1992, p. 1) says:

> Imagination is the capacity to think of things as possibly being so; it is an intentional act of mind; it is the source of invention, novelty, and generality; it is not implicated in all perception and the construction of all meaning; it is not distinct from rationality but is rather a capacity that greatly enriches rational thinking.

Dr. Ian Broinowski from Hobart, writing his PhD thesis "Toward Creativity in Early Childhood Education" (2002, p. 123), concludes:

> Educators with a strong sense of enchantment, imagination and creativity inspire children to become creative and imaginative through their learning and development. They also offer rich and educationally rewarding programs that develop children through natural curiosity, interest and wonder in their world, and they offer relationships that benignly influence these young lives.

Being inclusive

Once again we are challenged to make sure that children are encouraged in ways that suit their development, to treat them as individuals and allow them to be themselves. It's a delicate balancing act between encouraging a child to move beyond his or her comfort zone and try something new and challenging and our efforts to "make the child fit in." There is no one-size-fits-all answer to this conundrum. It's more about our recognizing and acknowledging respectfully the individual differences that make us human.

There are reasons to encourage a child to take a turn in a game, to make friends or play with another child, to join a team, to dive into the water and overcome fear, to hold a paintbrush and cover the page with color and express ideas on paper. At the same time, we need to be aware of just how far we can push today and be patient.

I don't encourage anyone to continue to allow a child to explore the block area every day without interruption while at the same time ignoring the fact that a child has not ever picked up a writing or drawing tool. I think our role is a bit more than this. We will all have stories about children who, once they have tried something new, develop confidence and a love of the new. We all know the children who have no knowledge of color names and never paint. We also know children who are not able to cope with change or being the center of attention or trying something new, rather who are crippled by this. Let's not rush too quickly, but try to bring the children across their own borders of comfort zone. It's about being conscious of the age and other development indicators of the children and having a vision of who they can be once they let themselves have experiences that encourage them to develop. So let's be respectful, but also let's encourage participation. Let's allow individual differences and at the same time encourage belonging to a group.

Image of the child

THE CHILD IS AN INDIVIDUAL

This can be quite a challenge, can't it? We have a *group* of children. Sometimes it seems like there are far too many children in the group, and perhaps this is the case despite regulations and accreditation. Some groups are different than other groups. The combination of different personalities, abilities and disabilities, interests and experiences means that every group of children is different and individual. We can't have complete chaos; there needs to be some routine (even if flexible), some structure to the day and rules of appropriate behavior. While we are doing all this, it is easy to adopt a one-size-fits-most approach to almost everything we do. It appears most often in the art and craft area unfortunately. We, the adults, invent the daily creation the children will later become involved in. So easily we invent mass-produced work that steals children's creative thoughts and exploration instead of providing materials ready to go in an assembly line.

There are other challenges for us, however, in all areas of the curriculum. When do we encourage a child to step out of his or her comfort zone and try something new or allow individual time frames? Our professional adult judgment may have to slip in here and there. It will dictate the way we do group times, use routines, and even how we operate indoor and outdoor environments. Of course safety issues, staffing numbers, reliability of children, clarity of vision and other situational considerations will need to be thought about, but do we use them as an excuse far too often?

I do recognize that some children thrive outdoors and some thrive indoors. While I believe all children will benefit from being in both environments, I am not so sure that every child needs to be in the same place at the same time. There must be ways we can treat children as individuals more often.

I like group times, and for most children it's an exciting and valuable experience, but not for all children and not for long periods of time. As children learn and develop, we expect they will attend and participate more readily and willingly; if not, perhaps we need to examine what is happening for the child. Is the child feeling too crowded, understanding the words we are using, hearing and seeing well enough? Be observant and thoughtful about what you observe. Don't jump to conclusions. Treat the child as an individual and see what's happening—try to see through the child's eyes.

Anne Stonehouse and others remind us in the NSW Curriculum Framework (2002, p. 53):

> The differences in children are no different than those that exist in adults, and yet there is a tendency to think in terms of a kind of ideal child and then to believe that any child can be molded into that ideal.

Reflections, challenges and wonderings

What are the challenges we face? Let's revisit a few of the ideas in this chapter. How can we encourage young children to develop more complex ways of being aware of who they are and who they might become, of the rights and feelings of others and of their place in the world? Let's begin with the self, with the senses and then with the ability to look inward, to reflect, consider and focus, to develop an inner calm and quietness, a safe place within ourselves from where we can look at the surrounding world. Games, songs, music, pictures, stories, conversations and experiences are the tools of the trade we often use.

Let's discover ways to encourage children to learn meditation, visualization and relaxation techniques. Being able to focus attention on something small, being able to see ourselves from the outside and observing our own behavior, are skills worth developing.

We can control our body. We can even control our heart rate and body temperature and achieve our own healing by harnessing the power of the mind. We can improve metacognition (thinking about thinking). We can improve the quality of our thinking and the imagination by learning intrapersonal techniques.

Let us find ways to help children learn the vocabulary associated with feelings, thoughts and the senses so they can describe and communicate what they are encountering.

Becoming mindful, being a witness to your own life and developing intrapersonal creativity, is about bringing together the functions of the frontal lobes as well as the neocortex of the brain (Gardner 1983). Some of the ideas we are experiencing today in the Western world have come from the Far East, from India and the Middle East, and we still have much to learn. What is your own personal journey, and how can you use your developing awareness to encourage young children on this path?

When we suggest that children paint or draw self-portraits, are we prepared to really look at what they know about themselves? Often it is much more than just the physical characteristics that are portrayed. I observed a child known for his erratic behaviors draw himself as a series of unconnected parts. Another who was often like a whirlwind drew himself like a dusty tornado. A shy child drew herself as very small, and a robust and boisterous child drew a large body and open mouth. I would encourage you to really look at the images they present. Perhaps young children are more knowledgeable about themselves than we give them credit for.

PUTTING IT TOGETHER

If you have been collecting bits and pieces for your educator's backpack throughout the journey of this book, you must have quite a full load by now. I hope that over the coming months and years you can slowly unpack, revisit and use some of the adventures and ideas I have brought to share with you. You are the key!

Connecting dimensions

Oliver Wendell Holmes (cited in Lazear 1999, p. 157) says:

> There are one-story intellects, two-story intellects, and three-story intellects with skylights.

> All fact collectors who have no aim beyond their facts are one-story men. Two-story men compare, reason, generalize, using the labor of fact collectors as their own. Three-story men idealize, imagine, predict—their best illumination comes from above the skylight.

When we ask children to describe and match, or recite, recall and retell a story, an event or an experience, we are asking them to use the ground floor of their intellect. When we suggest or challenge that they compare, classify, use their reason, solve a problem or explain, we move them to the next floor. When we open the skylights and we ask them to imagine, to judge or predict and speculate or estimate, we are involving the highest form of thinking. How often do you open the skylights?

Lachlan tells the group he is going fishing on one of the local lakes on the weekend. The children ask him about the boat. We encourage the children to find out how big, what color, where people sit, how to steer it, what the motor looks like (it has two, he tells us, one for trawling and one for going fast), how they keep safe, where the food goes, what happens to the fish they catch and any other question we can think of. Lachlan searches his memory for the words that will describe what he knows about the boat. The children draw their impressions of what they think it will look like, and Lachlan looks at their drawings. He can offer a few more ideas when he sees how his ideas are being interpreted. The following week his father brings the boat to the preschool. The children put a ladder over the side and climb up and into the boat. They ask questions, they examine, touch and look carefully, and they draw their new ideas. We compare what they predicted against what they now know. When we look at the photographs and the children's drawings later in the day, we notice one girl has written (from memory, later inside the classroom) the registration number on the side of her drawing. We have opened the skylights. We are reminded that we draw to learn more than we learn to draw.

Creating new experiences and ideas

A block building falls down. The adults ask the children what has happened to make it fall.

Some children have ideas about strong foundations and explain their ideas to the other builders; the children explore this and find it to be correct. An adult asks about plans for the building and shows them some house plans. The children look carefully at the lines and elevations and commence drawing plans for their own new buildings. Some children find the plans they have drawn are too complex and make alterations. Some find they have to build first and then draw the plans.

One child, when asked if he can draw his building, steps closer and removes some animals incorporated into the design. "Why did you do that?" the adult asks. "Because that would be too hard to draw," he smiles in reply. Fair enough.

Ashley designs a tower; first a foundation of blocks to create a circle, building from the connecting quarter-circle blocks in the center, spreading outward to the surrounding half-circle, then the larger quarter-circle surrounds. She places some archway blocks upright onto the circle, six in a row, and builds a tall tower of blocks across the flat surface. She perfects this building design over a few weeks; each time she solves a new problem. The adult draws her efforts or takes photographs and documents the child's learning. Eventually it becomes a lighthouse after a discussion about a local lighthouse, and Ashley is encouraged to share the design, step-by-step, with other children gathered around her. She shows them, talks with them about the problems and how she solved them: the things to watch for, getting the balance right, making sure that not too much hangs over on one side, etc. They take her ideas and create their own lighthouses and incorporate her basic techniques and ideas into new designs. They apply a principle, another example of three-story intellect.

Gerald and a few friends build the outline of a plane, a bomber. He sits on a chair at the controls, allocates a space to a gunner, and they set off over enemy territory. (It's the time of the first Gulf War.) David and a friend also build a plane and sit inside it to play, only they are not using the same context Gerald is working with. Suddenly some bombs in the form of small blocks start being lobbed on David and his crew. Of course there are calls of dismay. I overhear some conversations and realize that Gerald is playing the Gulf War. I put on a blue hat and sit between the planes. "What do you think you are doing?" asks Gerald. "I'm being the United Nations. I am here to make sure the big guys don't beat up the little guys." "Well, you can butt out," I am told unceremoniously. I call the warring parties together and ask for an explanation. The conversation goes like this:

"I am being the USA, and I am going to bomb the enemy in Iraq."

"I'm not the enemy," says David. "I am just flying a plane."

I wonder aloud, "Who is the enemy, Gerald?"

"All the people in Iraq."

I proceed, "Are the children in Iraq the enemy?"

"Well no, I suppose they can't be."

"Are all the mommies the enemy too? Are they baddies?"

"Well, no, they can't be either."

"And what about all the daddies—are they all baddies, are they all the enemy?"

"No, well, they couldn't be, could they? Just some of them."

"So, what are you going to do?" I ask Gerald.

"I think we should have some lunch and a cease-fire," he suggests, and that's what we do.

I asked Gerald to speculate, to imagine and to evaluate within the context of his knowledge. I opened the skylights.

Look for contexts and opportunities to engage children in the third-story intellect. Look for opportunities to challenge them and to encourage them to reflect on what they know in a new way, to be engaged with their thoughts, apply a principle or imagine a consequence. Encourage them to look within and find out who they are and what they believe to be true.

TAKING CARE OF YOURSELF

Knowing yourself well and how you react will help in whatever job you do and whatever relationship you find yourself in, but in particular when you are working for a committee, an owner, a local manager or even a group or team leader. Perhaps you are the director and have to handle everyone else's as well as your own emotions. It can be a challenge, can't it? Everyone is working hard, at the edge of his or her capabilities, with never enough time, enough space, enough quietness for imagination. We are pulled this way and that by government regulations and requirements of funding and licensing bodies. We can become extremely stressed without even stepping into a room full of children. You know yourself. What are your reactive buttons? How can you protect yourself from someone pushing those buttons? How can you react differently? How can you harness the nervousness you feel and the frustration or fear?

Looking philosophically and reflectively at who you are in the lives of the young child, what you believe based on what you know about child development theory and your own experience so far, is a great place to begin. You will find strength in the power of your convictions. Share your visions with trusted others, develop a supportive and caring network and find out ways to rid yourself of negative thoughts and feelings with physical exercise of some kind. Try yoga or tai chi, kick boxing, power walking, singing in a choir or with great gusto in the shower, pottery with a wheel, tennis, golf or horse riding—find an outlet and use it often.

It's very difficult to do, but try to surround yourself with positive people. Try to keep your personal life at home and not let it take over your entire life. Find your spiritual roots and explore this dimension more thoroughly. Take holidays, go for picnics, and wonder at the beauty of nature and your part in this experience called life. Use music and movement to alter your mood, praise yourself when you do well and allow yourself mistakes; they happen. Use your own intrapersonal dimensions to create a whole person. This is what draws everything together. It's the glue of life!

What children learn does not follow as an automatic result from what is taught. Rather, it is in large part due to the children's own doing as a consequence of their activities and our resources.

Loris Malaguzzi (1998b, p. 67)

9

PROGRAMMING, PLANNING, EVALUATION AND DOCUMENTATION

Ideas that work

Let's face it, we have a limited amount of time available in our daily work. Our priorities will always be the children and our relationships with them—listening, talking with, investigating, encouraging, and making sure they are safe and well, and so this more formal (recording and evaluating) part of our work needs to be slick, well-organized and efficient.

It is my intention in this final chapter to bring together some ideas gathered over many years and from a variety of sources. I have written on this topic extensively in another publication (Lubawy 2006), *From Observation to Reflection: A Practitioner's Guide to Programme Planning and Documentation*. I suggest that you read it in addition to this chapter.

I heard the comment made recently that early childhood educators have adapted and adopted so many new ideas in the last ten or so years that it's a little like looking at a series of slides on an overhead projector. Imagine, if you will, each new idea on a separate transparent sheet placed over the one before, layer upon layer until we have a kind of confusing mess. At some stage we have to start again, with a blank sheet, and develop our own diagram that is clear and makes sense. We can't just keep adding new ideas to old ones without removing some of the old. We can't possibly do everything all the time—it has become too complicated. This chapter will look at some of the old and much of the new and offer some suggestions for the blank sheet.

Before we begin, a reminder that it is important to inform new families that your center uses photographs to assist in the documentation of the program and that your intention is to use the first names of the children in the public and private narratives. Show the new families some old examples and explain that each new year brings insights into how the narrative can be told, so narratives may change slightly. The essential element of photographs and sensitive narrative will remain, however. Add an area to enrollment papers for parents to make comments and give permission for you to continue in this way. If you have families who are hesitant, give them some time to consider and make sure that their child's face or name does not appear in the journal without permission. Ask them again in a month or so when they see the reality. If you have a child who may not have his face shown for any number of reasons, make sure that you keep to the rules all year. It might be a little difficult, but I am sure you can make the most of the challenge.

Observation and then what?

There is no doubt that the foundation of everything we do is based on observation of the children. But what are we looking for and how are we gathering this information? Here is an observation.

I watch a child, about two, with her mother in the shopping center. They have shared a secret—the mother has whispered to the little girl and the child is smiling broadly with hands at the mouth. They go to the counter of the café and order and sit at a table nearby. The child lifts out the clasp of the safety belt on the shopping cart until her mother undoes it.

I am taken by the careful and respectful attitude of the parent as she lifts the child from the shopping cart and places her on the chair. Of course the child is not content with sitting on the chair until her surprise is delivered (a strawberry milk and an avocado sandwich). Instead, she stands on the chair and reaches across to pick up a packet of sugar. Then, finding that particularly uninteresting, she climbs down, one leg outstretched until it touches the floor. When balanced successfully on two feet, she explores the chairs. She notices that her own chair has a hole in the seat toward the back. She touches it, puts her finger into it and tells her parent, "There's a hole." She moves off to examine the three other chairs at her table and is delighted to find they all have holes in them. She tells her mother about her discovery.

The child looks to where I am sitting. She wiggles her fingers at me, and I reply in kind. She moves toward my table and examines just one chair for a hole. She is cautious in her approach, but when I smile she proceeds, and then when she looks up, I ask her, "Does it have a hole too?" She nods a yes to me and goes back to eat the food that has just arrived. She holds the carton of strawberry milk carefully on her lap and uses the straw her mother has provided, commenting after each sip about "the straw," pointing to and examining the hole in the end. She comments about the color of her mother's straw and her own; one is red and one blue. She takes a sandwich from the plate and enjoys a large bite. She is interested when the avocado squeezes onto her fingers and shows her mother the green on her little fingers and laughs.

The story is interesting, and when we look carefully we can iron out some developmental elements we might choose to comment on:

- the child understands the concept of secret or surprise;
- she has excellent hearing and understands body language;
- she sits well;
- she expresses delight easily with facial features and hands at the mouth;
- she understands how to undo the seat belt on the shopping cart but cannot undo it yet;
- she uses both hands cooperatively but does not cross the midline;
- she uses eye-hand coordination;
- she stands easily and can reach across a table;
- she can move herself from chair to floor successfully;
- she balances well on two feet;
- she can walk;
- she notices a feature on her chair and looks for a pattern;
- she understands that chairs belong to a "set";
- she communicates with a stranger using hand and facial gestures;
- she waits for a friendly reply;
- she ventures past her "own" area to test her hypothesis and make a generalization;
- she brings an object close to her body center for better control;
- she can suck through a straw;
- she understands the concept of "straw" and "hole";

- she is interested in and has knowledge of shape and color, naming red and blue;
- she notices cause and effect when she bites the sandwich and avocado squeezes out onto her finger; and
- she understands and uses humor.

There is a school of thought that suggests that we observe for developmental milestones and development. Yes, I agree, this is important, and it is essential for us to be familiar with what we would term the normal stages of development.

One short observation (such as the one above) is filled with detail, and with an experienced eye I would ascertain that her development and behavior are completely within normal limits. The story, however, makes it interesting. I could have simply listed the developmental tasks she completed with a hint at the context. I could also have told the story as above and checked off a series of items on a checklist and added the date.

Alternatively, I could have chosen to put the observation into an interesting shape like this:

I watch a child, about two, with her mother in the shopping center. They have shared a secret—the mother has whispered to the little girl and the child is smiling broadly with hands to mouth. They go to the counter of the café and order something and sit at a table nearby. The child lifts out the clasp of the safety belt on the shopping cart until her mother undoes it. I am taken by the careful and respectful attitude of the parent as she lifts the child from the shopping cart and places her on the chair. Of course the child is not content with sitting on the chair until her surprise is delivered (a strawberry milk and an avocado sandwich). Instead she stands on the chair and reaches across to pick up a packet of sugar. Then, finding that particularly uninteresting, she climbs down, one leg outstretched until it touches the floor. When balanced successfully on two feet, she explores the chairs. She notices that her own chair has a hole in the seat toward the back. She touches it, puts her finger into it and tells her parent, "There's a hole." She

(continued on next page)

The social child

The child "reads" the facial and hand gestures of others

She seeks relationship with mother and stranger

She is very capable of taking care of herself

She understands and uses humor

The communicating child

The child is a capable communicator, using words as well as hand and facial gestures

She understands a secret or surprise/treat

She shows pleasure in playing with language

She is using language to identify similarities and structures

The thinking, investigating, exploring, problem-solving child

The child shares an idea with her mother

She investigates a sugar packet and discards as uninteresting

She investigates the hole in her chair and gathers additional information

She forms a new concept about chairs with holes and tests her idea

She can use a straw

moves off to examine the three other chairs at her table and is delighted to find they all have holes in them. She tells her mother about her discovery. The child looks to where I am sitting. She twinkles her fingers at me, and I reply in turn. She moves toward my table and examines just one chair for a hole. She is cautious in her approach, but when I smile she proceeds, and then when she looks up, I ask her, "Does it have a hole too?" She nods a yes to me and goes back to eat the food that has just arrived. She holds the strawberry milk carefully on her lap and uses the straw her mother has provided, commenting after each sip about "the straw," examining the hole in the end. She takes a sandwich from the plate and enjoys a large bite. She is interested when the avocado squeezes onto her fingers and shows her mother the green on her little fingers and laughs.

The child's sense of self

The child sees herself as powerful and a valued member of her family

She sees herself as competent

She realizes she contributes to others' happiness

She is accepted as she is

The healthy, physical, active child

The child has a range of well-developed physical skills, such as sitting, standing, bending, walking, climbing

The child enjoys strawberry-flavored milk and avocado sandwiches

The creative child

The child feels safe and secure

She knows her mother will help her if needed

She invents a game of exploring holes in chairs

She delights in avocado on her finger

The feeling child

The child recognizes her own feelings

She expresses delight, mystery, excitement, friendship and humor

She is able to "read" others' feelings and situations

The spiritual and moral child

The child is interested in her surroundings

She understands about personal space

She can control her own behavior

We can also add details from a curriculum framework (as above) to support the observation. I would imagine though if we tried to do this with every observation we would soon run out of enthusiasm and time. It can mean that we are writing the same things over and over. Is it possible to keep it simple? The narrative tells the story. Do we have to clutter it with other ideas that prove we have done our job or know what we are looking at?

Instead, we can write our own version of the curriculum framework that covers a whole year and separates the various elements (feeling, social, creative and so on) and explores some of the ways that these will be nurtured during the year. THEN with that written we can simply write observations in story form and use these observations to plan further. When you have written such a document once, you can use it again and again, year to year, with changes resulting from your experiences. The framework, an overview of the year, is the structure the real events hang on. Yes, you can refer to the framework, or even add some words from it to your documentation now and then, but not every day and not with every observation! Being observant with our hearts and minds (especially for preverbal children), ears and eyes is the most important skill we bring to our work.

One observation can tell us so much. This observation is after a chance encounter in a shopping center. There are many ways (and I have isolated just a few) to present an observation. I chose to just tell the story as I saw and understood it. I might add a few reflections (*I am taken by the careful and respectful attitude of the parent as she lifts the child from the shopping cart and places her on the chair*) in the story or add them as additional items, such as:

I am taken by the careful and respectful attitude of the parent as she lifts the child from the shopping cart and places her on the chair.

Or with my "educator's hat" on, I might comment:

I am fascinated to see a small child making and testing a hypothesis about holes in chairs. This is the beginning of her understanding about classification, patterns and structures, so important to her developing mathematical knowledge.

If I had made the observation in a center and had the responsibility for planning the program, I would take the time to think about additions to the environment that might interest the child. It might end up looking like this:

Making connections
Yesterday I observed Amy exploring holes in the chairs at her lunch table. I wondered if she would be interested in holes in other equipment and items of furniture. I also wondered if she would enjoy making holes.

Provisions

The glue stick trays with holes

Playdough

Large beads and threads or pipe cleaners

Stacking puzzles and tubs

Cardboard cylinders

Cut-out small circle shapes to put on the window down low so she can look into the garden

Then I would watch to see what she did with the provisions.

Observation
Many of the children used the material provided today. Amy, however, was most interested in the large cardboard cylinders and chose to sit on the floor with one to her eye for some considerable time. Then she found a scarf and pushed it into one end of the cylinder and tried to get it out the other end. The cylinder was too long for this to be successful. She found other things to do instead.

Amy understands that something can be poked through a cylinder so it comes out the other end. She can hold a cylinder with one hand to look through but keeps both eyes open.

And this will lead to:

Projection and planning
We can either provide shorter cardboard cylinders or we can suspend several from the roof with string so they can be tipped to allow objects to roll through them. Perhaps she might be interested in trying both.

An invitation

We offered two environments today that might interest Amy.

The first basket contained a selection of round and circle items, some she could look through and others she could not.

The second environment consisted of several long cylinders of varying diameters hung on strings from the ceiling at Amy's height. The angles can easily be altered so either end of the cylinder will receive or expel an object. In a basket we added some small balls and some large beads. We also provided a very large dish to "catch" the falling objects.

We added both environments after morning snack time and made sure an adult was available to facilitate and interact verbally.

Both invitations were near the window so Amy could also choose to examine the garden through the objects if she wished.

Reflection
Is Amy responding to the circle shape or what she can do with one?
She can look through one, and she can put objects through one. Let's watch to see what develops.

And so the cycle progresses:

- observation;
- reflection;
- planning and projection;
- invitation;
- provision; and
- making connections.

Of course, what Amy might be most interested in is the taste and texture of avocado and we missed the point completely!

The labels can easily be altered to suit particular needs or ideas, but the cycle continues.

Eventually, the entire story is recorded with the photographs taken and any comments or gestures Amy makes noted so they can be brought together to make a new story about her journey of discovery, her project about holes. It could be called "Looking at holes from both sides now" or some such catchy title. This story can be made into a wall panel or into a book available for families to read or placed in the story corner for the children to read for themselves.

The "story" can also appear each day in installments in the classroom journal as it unfolds. Copies can be added to her portfolio with developmental comments (such as some from the checklist suggested earlier), and a copy of the "project" might be given to her family at some stage when she changes her investigation to something else.

We have undertaken a small journey (some of it imaginary in response to a chance encounter in the shopping center), but I hope you can see how such a small event can be used to develop an emergent curriculum. The "ideas" do not have to be huge, and they do not have to come from outside. They instead arise from our observation of a child and our imaginings of what the child might be interested in. We find ways then to bring out (emerge) not only the interest but also the curriculum in its many parts. You will note, I hope, that I have not said, "Amy cannot do this . . . or that . . . and therefore she needs. . . ." Instead I have attempted to bring forth her capabilities and interests and find ways to extend these.

When we know what most children are capable of around a particular age, we know what appears to be outside that range. I hesitate to use the word "normal" (for there is such a wide range of normal development), but it might be the best word in this circumstance. We quickly become aware that a particular child may be experiencing learning difficulties or is demonstrating behavior that sits outside the usual range. It is then that we need to seek additional guidance from an allied health professional. We can also reassure parents and offer suggestions when we have collected significant observations.

My suggestion is, however, that when we have several children of about the same age in a group, we can easily see if one child is not developing as well as we would hope. In fact, many of us will notice this within the first day or so of our contact with a new child. It helps, though, to have some documentary evidence as a focus for a conversation with a parent or to note in a referral to an allied health professional. Then I have to ask, do we need to collect developmental information for ALL the children or for only those children we are concerned about who appear to be outside what we can see is the normal range of development? This leads to the next consideration.

The other school of thought, and I lean more in this direction, is that we are not a medical or remedial service; rather, we are an educational and care service.

Carlina Rinaldi (2006, p. xix in *Insights*) defines this as being:

a relational place . . . It is a construction of relationships that are born of re-
ciprocal curiosity between the subject and the object . . .

Our focus is not so much on using the medical model (observe, diagnose and remediate) but more about observing and recognizing individual strengths and weaknesses
in the context of the whole child. If this is the case, then our observations will be more
about what children are wondering about, discovering, learning to do, investigating
and interested in and less about the skills they are demonstrating. My thought is that
when we document the learning story, the developmental story will be *included* in
what we are narrating rather than being the focus. Perhaps it is a subtle delineation,
but in practice it is quite different in appearance. Using an educational model, we
observe, provide, interact, make connections, predict and project, document and
then reflect and begin the cycle again. Yvonne Winer, in 1977, referred to our role
as being that of a catalyst and guide focusing on the creative and teachable moment,
and I still agree with her 30 years later.

Gunilla Dahlberg (1999, p. 3), in a keynote address in Sydney, challenged and
encouraged delegates with these words:

> We also agreed to work with observation and pedagogical documentation: In
> Sweden, these terms have traditionally been understood in relation to child
> development theories, i.e. using observations and documentation to assess and
> classify children against developmental norms. In the project we wanted to
> bordercross the power of the norm, by creating spaces for exchange of experi-
> ences, co-construction and reflection.

How then do we use our observations as the foundation from which we can bordercross the norm? (I love that collection of words; they just roll off the tongue and set
my imagination on fire: *bordercross the power of the norm*.) In making these bridges
so we can cross the borders and focus on the whole child, we tell the learning story
instead of using a developmentally focused checklist. These checklists are available in
a number of guises, from a plain and simple check-the-box variety (by far the quickest
and easiest to do) to a series of pages to photocopy and add a date, a small comment
and a photograph as evidence of the child having achieved the desired outcome (by
far the slowest and least satisfying from my point of view). There is a conformity and
sterility happening with this method that I find difficult to come to terms with.

Checklists infiltrate our minds, though, in a much subtler way, and we easily find
ourselves taking a photograph of an individual child in a moment in time to prove
something. However, unless we take a series of photographs, listen carefully and
watch (photographs do not replace observation; they only augment it), we do not tell
the whole story. If we are interested in the social construction of learning, then we
might tell the story of one child sharing a skill with another child and that might be
the focus. A substory might be that the child learning the new skill masters it easily in this context. We might have, therefore, several stories happening at the same
time. We can tease out elements from the story (as before) and plan accordingly. A
checklist is just a reminder to the adults of some developmental milestones that are
considered worth noticing. They are not the reason for the event, activity, environment or interaction that takes place. I will admit to planning my program in the

past so that I could check off a variety of skills and understandings or behaviors. I thought that was the only way. However, since encountering the ideas from Reggio Emilia, the NSW Curriculum Framework, *Te Whāriki* (from NZ) and other thoughts about the emergent curriculum, effective teaching and exploratory learning, I have discovered the excitement of taking a different approach. Don't, however, expect it all to fall into place in an instant. It will take a lifetime to explore some of the possibilities. You can be assured that each year will see you inventing new ways to document and program and then inventing anew the next year. That is what keeps us alive and motivated; we are constantly seeking to improve the quality of what we do.

Fundamentally, checklists are wonderful when we are students and learning about *established* child development theories. Remember, though, that they are theories, and the theorists may not have had the kind of intimate contact you will encounter over years. You can also be a theorist in your own educational laboratory (a classroom or playroom), but it takes a little time and some confidence as well as a supportive working environment, so be patient with yourself. Do not underestimate your knowledge of child development fact rather than theory! You do not have to assess and classify children against these norms for the rest of your career. They are a foundation that underpins our understanding. Our observations written as a learning story are more important and real than any item we find on a checklist.

When you think back over this book (assuming you have read from the beginning to the end) what do you remember most? The narratives? I expect and hope so; that's why they have been used so frequently. Narratives tell us more than just the story. They have a point we can reflect on and remember. A narrative is very powerful.

Carlina Rinaldi (2006, p. xix), writing in *Insights*, reminds us:

> Documentation is thus a narrative form. Its force of attraction lies in the wealth of questions, doubts and reflections that underlie the collection of data . . . They are three-dimensional writings, not aimed at giving the event objectivity but as expressing the meaning-making effort.

How then do we observe so that we can begin to tell the narrative? I found drawing my observations—a simple sketch with a few quickly written notes—a wonderful place to develop my observation skills. The children enjoyed having an adult draw what they were doing and often watched to see what I was looking at. My drawings began (before I had access to digital photography) as a way to record the incredible block building happening and developed into recording children hanging upside down on the Roman rings or making sand pies with their friends. When a building collapsed, the children used the drawings to rework it and solve the problem of making the building stronger and steadier. I found I could listen easily to the conversations and even jot some of the words down as the children became used to me being there in a friendly and nonthreatening role. It was a process more than a product. I didn't always wish to share my drawings with families, especially at first. I did, however, improve, as we do with daily practice, and finally I thought the drawings were more artistically acceptable.

As digital photography became a possibility, I found I could grab these images quickly, but along with this came the temptation to "click and run" without waiting to hear the whole story or notice the context. I found I had too many photographs and not enough knowledge. This was particularly the situation when work colleagues also took photographs! It became increasingly easy to take pretty pictures of children having a wonderful time but not tell the learning story in any depth.

Materials that support

Once we have observed—using our ears and eyes as well as our brains and hearts—we begin to dream about materials and experiences that will support, encourage, scaffold, enable, provoke and delight the children.

If our observations are of the "assess and classify" variety, then the materials and experiences we provide will have a clear focus, an outcome or an objective, and will remediate the situation we have observed. Let's face it: we sometimes do need to do this when we realize a child is having difficulties that are impacting his or her ability to cope within a group.

However, when our observations are about something a child has said, asked, commented on or is clearly interested in, the materials and experiences we provide will have a different, more open-ended and creative characteristic. How can we step forward into this direction? That's where we are going next.

Keeping clear of boxes

Boxes always look so neat; they are powerful, organized and rational. They can confine our creativity though: they often have a right and a wrong answer, they don't encourage open-ended discovery and expression and often they do not allow for individual differences. For some of us this is the only way we can contain our planning: we think in logical steps; we like to confine our ideas so we can see the links. But for the rest of us the boxes limit what we might otherwise be capable of. Work out what works best for you. This is not a question of either or; I am offering alternatives.

Ultimately, any label has the potential to become boxlike. Even a label like "creativity" can become just another box on the page unless we are careful. Dr. Julia Atkin (during a series of three-day workshops on teaching for effective learning, 1993) suggested that we could use softer shapes, open-ended shapes (there are some available in the autoshape area of Microsoft Word) or even hand-drawn shapes to encourage us to think more creatively.

The words used in the NSW Curriculum Framework or New Zealand's *Te Whāriki* offer useful suggestions for terms we can use to help shape our planning. For instance:

Making the connection

We noticed last week that Connor placed traffic cones around a deep hole he was excavating to provide for the safety of others. He added water from a hose but noticed that the hole never became full. We wondered how we could help him find a way to create a small lake.

Provision

A large sheet of thick plastic

Several buckets of large river stones

The hose and a tap close by

An adult to facilitate, supervise and interact

The focus might be a little different—same story!

Belonging
(focus on children working together)

We have noticed the exciting play that has been happening in the sandpit in the last few weeks as several children show leadership, playing an active role in the running of the program. Connor has been attempting to create a small lake, but the water keeps being absorbed by the sand. We have been wondering how we might provide materials and support so he and the group can investigate solutions.

Or, even more thoughtfully:

Reflection
There are a number of things interesting us at the moment: the way that some children are able to excite others creatively and positively, how children socially construct their learning and the ways in which children explore the possibilities of simple science—in this case how sand absorbs water.

There are other variations available, such as the construction of a mind map or concept web, a useful place to begin a journey of exploration with the children:

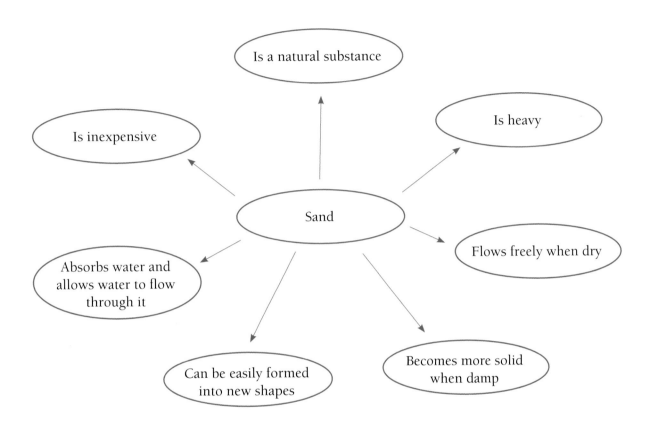

Experiment and find a way out of the boxes if you can. The narratives above do not easily fall into:

- the thinking, investigating, exploring and problem-solving child; or
- the communicating child; or even
- the social child.

Instead, the narrative contains parts of all these elements and more. To use Gunilla Dalhberg's words once again, can we bordercross not only the power of the norm but also the separations of curriculum and program development and *connect*?

Write it once

One of the significant challenges facing us is our efficient use of time and the need to document what is educationally important. For instance, when we set up a new environment for the first time, we can write *why* we chose to provide the materials. Was it in response to something we observed happening, for instance? We can add a photograph to record *how and where* it is set up. We can also list the materials being made available and some thoughts about how the area might be used, reflected against a background of what we know about child development theory. We can insert some of the statements we have made in our own version of the curriculum. When we take time to do this, it saves time later, for we can simply "cut and paste" from our own document.

Here is an example of how it works and might look:

February 6
Provision

We know that four-year-olds love using the sandpit. We also know that water (from a hose, a bucket, a water tray) adds to the enjoyment and possibilities of river sand.

We have added some other materials that might delight and interest the children:

- *A hose placed so the water flows over some rocks*
- *Some cuts of timber*
- *A couple of rubber tires*
- *Buckets and spades*
- *Some pieces of poly pipe in two diameters*
- *Shade*
- *Time to explore*
- *A container for shoes and socks, should they be taken off*
- *An adult to facilitate, supervise, encourage and interact with the children*

From the Curriculum Framework

This environment aims to encourage:

The child's sense of self

The child to feel powerful and competent

The child to make mistakes and learn from them

The child to have opportunities to work in relationship with others

The communicating child

The child to use verbal and nonverbal language to communicate ideas, solve problems and settle disputes

The thinking, investigating, exploring, problem-solving child

The child to solve problems with the flow of water

See the relationship between cause and effect

Delight in self-discovery and exploration

The healthy, physical, active child

Develop strong and healthy bodies

Development of gross-motor skills

The social child

An increasing orientation to others, ability to share, take turns and wait

The feeling child

Express feelings in appropriate ways

Learn to read other people's feelings and situations

The creative child

Innovate and express ideas using a range of media

The spiritual and moral child

Respect for and enjoyment of the natural environment

Observation
Sam dug a hole using the plastic spade and then filled the hole with water from a bucket. Despite having two hoses available, he preferred to fill the creek from a tap in the garden. He placed the pieces of timber over the hole and told us what he was making— a bridge.

Sam says, "It's a bridge."

Projection and planning
We are not sure yet what appeals to Sam.
• Is it being able to explore with freedom in the outdoors?
• Is it using something familiar?
• Is he thinking about the flow of water in a creek or river and the roadway above it (hence the bridge)?
• Is he wondering about the way the sand absorbs the water?
We'll provide experiences and materials next week to take into account some of these thoughts.

Reflection
Sand and water play is very important. It has a freedom to be creative, and it encourages play, real conversations and a lot of social skills. It also provides excellent science and math experiences; it's where children learn about evaporation and absorption, about mass and volume. Later they can attach "concepts" to these experiences.

We do not need to write in such detail about this environment every day. It is assumed it will be available for some time and we can plot the development of ideas as we go at random intervals. We will, however, document how this area is used by a variety of children over countless weeks. We will include narratives about children's exploration of the materials and how we have altered the environment as a result of our observations. We will document our thinking about where the children's wonderings might lead, what we know about the topic and how we can provide additional materials and experiences.

We don't need to keep our entire recording separate in different books. We don't have to write something for the classroom journal and then something else for posters and then quite separately something for individual portfolios. We don't even have to write additional material for professional documentation. When we try to do this, we just become defeated by the complexity and the amount of paper work. Let's see if we can invent a new way of operating.

It could look like this:

- First—The environment
  - How it is set up, where, why it is like it is and some ideas about how it might be used and its place within the curriculum.

- Then—The observation
  - Observe and collect the observation as a narrative; tell the story. Write comments suitable for a class journal. Remember to be sensitive in what you write so it can be read by anyone at this stage!

- Next . . .
  - Add a drawing or a photograph or series of photographs (if available) to enrich the narrative.

- And . . .
  - Record the cycle from observation to reflection—projection and planning, invitation, making connections, provisions.

- Then . . .
  - Select a narrative that illustrates one of the professional principles, date the copy, make suitable and short additional comments and file, ready for use at a later date.

- Then . . .
  - Make a copy of the narrative for a child's or for several children's individual portfolios (developmental records) and add short but important comments where necessary. These can be more personal than those found in the classroom (common) journal. (Still, take care with your comments. Keep them positive.)

- And possibly . . .
  - Collect a series of stories telling the history of a project that emerged and create a poster or book on the topic that can be displayed or added to the story-corner collection.

It works best to start with the environment and the story and then to make efficient use of your material. Some photographs might be useful when you bring the project together and tell the story from a new perspective. Some might not be used ever. You can take as many photographs as you need or would like, but you will only use some of them.

Sharing with parents

Kathy, a colleague, tells me excitedly about the renovations at her preschool. The office has been relocated near a new entry area, and there is a window between the entrance foyer and the office. This makes it possible for her to turn the computer monitor around so that it displays the photographs taken that day for parents to see as they enter the preschool.

She realizes she can't use all the photographs taken that day in her documentation—she simply does not have time to do that—but she can share the images gathered from the day and share them with the children and their families. She tells me the parents enter the foyer, and instead of coming into the room immediately, they pause and wait until the pictures have all scrolled through. This is the foundation level of documentation, a series of images.

A few other solutions are possible. One center has several monitors scattered throughout the building. One is for parents to view as they enter, and there are other monitors in each playroom so children can also see the pictures taken that day. Another center prints and pastes the pictures, without comment, into a scrapbook for parents to look at as they come and go. They then use some but not all of the pictures in the journal complete with narrative and other details. The staff tell me they often complete this after the children leave the center or in the evening if they have to and have the journal ready for the next day. This way it's not a rushed event; they can be more thoughtful. Ultimately it can be less stressful to devote some personal time rather than try to be all things to all people all the time.

Parents like to see what happens during the day and can see not only their own children but also other children participating in events either alone, in a small group or as part of a larger group. We cannot possibly document all these photographs thoughtfully, but we can share the images we have collected nonetheless.

I am troubled when an early childhood practitioner tells me she writes a comment about every child every day in her classroom journal. I can't see how anyone can do this with anything other than comments like "Hannah had a wonderful time playing in the doll's corner today" or "Sue spent ages with the puzzles today."

I am concerned because these comments are shallow. They don't tell us much at all. For instance, I would be interested to know if Sue often spends a lot of time with the puzzles or if this was the first time she ventured there. I would want to know which puzzles she was interested in and what techniques she used to solve them. Does she look at the shape of the pieces, using her fingers to trace the edges? Does she notice their size or concentrate on the clues of color and picture? Does she persevere when the puzzle is a little difficult, and does she ask for help? Does she offer assistance to other children when she sees they are experiencing difficulties? Does she leave the puzzle unfinished on the table or does she put it away so other children can enjoy it? Does she use her words to describe what she is doing? Is she adventurous and risk-taking, knowing that help is available if she needs it? There are so many questions I would want answered. I can't see how we can write one line about a child's day and leave it at that.

We can't write in detail about every child, and we can't do it every day! However, over a period of a few weeks we will have gathered some pictures and narratives that include all the children and give us a better idea of who they are and what makes them tick. This is worth recording in their portfolios over time. We can attempt to gather narratives about all children over a few weeks on average. The frequency will depend on the number of children using the center each week.

Some centers focus on certain children for a period of time as a way of making sure that all children are observed and planned for over a number of weeks. This seems to work well for some centers, and in others it is an artificial construct. If your center falls into the latter category, you can put a list of the children's names near where the pictures and narratives are added to portfolios. Over a few weeks, if you check the names as you place items in the records, you will see if anyone has been overlooked and make a point of observing what that child is doing and is interested in. My own experience is that over time it evens out naturally. We concentrate on a child or group of children exploring new skills or an idea, and for weeks these children will be the main focus of our documentation. But then a few weeks or a month later another child or group of children capture our attention. For me, a portfolio shows a child's development over time and highlights his or her own learning story. A portfolio doesn't finish at the end of every month, but continues over the year, and can continue as long as the child attends the center.

There are details about children's sleeping, toileting and eating patterns that we need to communicate to parents. I wonder if we can invent ways to make this as simple as possible. A check-the-box or short comment should suffice. I wonder if parents are really eager for this sort of trivia, or if they would rather know your ideas about their child. Perhaps they would like to know what makes their child a positive member of the group or about the particular talents you see emerging. We can spend a lot of time attending to trivia and miss the important things.

"I love the way you always have something positive to say about Adam," a parent comments. Well, yes, sometimes Adam can be a handful, but I love his investigating mind. He is a really scientific thinker, and he has some excellent understandings of literacy even though his words are not yet fully formed. I admire him and want to share my admiration. We have spoken about his delayed speech; I don't feel I need to keep coming back to the topic. His parents and the staff at the center are giving him plenty to talk about and encouraging his efforts. A speech pathologist sees him once a week, so let's leave it at that, and in the meantime I love to share the positive highlights of his day!

The children: How can they be part of this?

John attends preschool on Tuesday, and his best friend, Lachlan, attends on Monday and Tuesday. One Monday Lachlan creates an interesting pattern with red, yellow, green and blue magnetic shapes on a whiteboard. I take a photograph, as I am interested in the knowledge and appreciation of symmetry he displays as well as the way he has classified the colors and shapes so obviously in his design. The following day I notice John creating a pattern with red, yellow, green and blue magnetic shapes on the whiteboard. I comment that his friend made a pattern very similar to his the day before. He comments, "I know. I saw it in the journal this morning."

The journal can be a very useful educational tool. First, it shows the children what kinds of things interest you and what you value. It must be a rewarding experience to have your learning story documented in the journal. Second, we can use the journal to share a child's wondering, exploration or discovery from a previous week or the day before with the other children. The child in question can tell what they were doing, how they went about it. They can also give lessons to other children or offer to invite them into a group to explore the possibilities. The journal helps spread good ideas. It validates, it informs and it encourages as well as records. The children can make suggestions about what they would like added to the journal—perhaps not every day but sometimes. For instance, they can make comments about an event from the day, or you can write down their comments about "the best part of today." You can invite the children to draw about an experience, a visiting performer or story from the day, and their drawings (photocopied at 50 percent original size) can be added to the journal along with the photographs so that the event has an additional richness. The journal shows everyone that the contributions made by children and their families to the program are valued, and this will encourage more participation.

Knowing more about each child

It is difficult when we see a child only once a week to build a strong bond and to develop knowledge about her. It is much easier to do when we see that child more often, or when we have been with her over a couple of years. It does not mean, however, that we don't give it our best shot. Instead, we try to learn about each child, even if just a little. It takes time; observations and interactions happen over months. At the end of the year when finalizing the details in a portfolio, I often get a "feel" for who this child has been. With 80 to 90 children in a sessional preschool, it might almost take that long for the wholeness of the child to become evident. We do what we can.

I am hopeful, though, that we can make progress. That each adult member of the team can know more about some of the children and be prepared to share her insights with the rest of the team. It matters that we have more than one adult in a room of children. Our individual talents, interests and personality will make each one of us special to some of the children in very different ways, and they to us. Let's build on this and not give up.

Journals and portfolios

For me, a journal, a class or group journal, is a catchall of everything I can collect. It has observations with photographs or drawings from some of the events of the day that attracted me (or one of my work colleagues). It contains a narrative about the event, identifies a link with previous narratives, documents the materials or experiences either planned in advance or spontaneously added that day and provides some thoughts about what happened and where ideas might progress.

It might document a special event, a story read (in connection with an ongoing discussion that has been happening), and it might include some of the music, dance or drama experiences for the day. It usually has some of the children's work we have observed either in the art and craft area or in the sandpit, on the swings or under the bushes. It might document, in a series of pictures taken over time, the way a child has focused on a particular problem worth solving or played heartedly about. It contains the planning for the next week, the curriculum design for the year, my (and others') reflective considerations and things we want to share with families.

I try to make it more than a "court report" that contains "we did this, and then we did that" type of comments. I try to tell the children's story as much as possible. "Oh, I see," a visiting teacher said after spending some hours reading the classroom journal. "This is about what the children are doing, not about what you are doing." I was delighted—she had described the outcome I was aiming for but was never sure if it was as clear as I would have liked it to be.

The portfolio on the other hand belongs to the child. It's his record of the year. It contains his work, gathered here and there, sometimes offered by the child, sometimes photocopied and added that way. The portfolios are as individual as the children. They don't follow a prescribed pattern or format, and they just emerge like the curriculum. The portfolio also contains copies of the narratives from the journal, one printed for each child involved in that experience or endeavor. It shows friendships with other children, and yes, it includes their faces and first names as well. The children are social beings. We often say this in our philosophical statements, so let the portfolio reflect it. If I have a family who has a particular reason why their child may not be included in the photographs of other children, THEN I deal with it at the time. I don't like to see portfolios of lonely children, always working alone or on adult-inspired projects. Instead, I want the portfolio to tell their own individual stories while recognizing the importance of socially constructed learning. Many families refer to the portfolios as "the million dollar books" and tell me how their children look again and again to the books in the coming years, refreshing memories of experiences and friendships.

Image of the child

Janet Robertson (2006 in *Insights*) reminds us that what we expect to see is in fact what we do see. If we expect to see vulnerable and helpless or troubled children, then that is what we will see, and that is the image we will present to the world in our journals, portfolios, wall panels and newsletters. However, if our image is of children being capable and competent, strong, interesting, powerful and individual, then this is what we will observe happening and what we will present to others. If our image and our documentation do not match, then we are going to undergo enormous stress from cognitive dissonance. Let's do and document what we believe.

One of my big concerns is the way children are portrayed in the public arena. For instance, I saw a child in the shopping center just before Easter wearing a mass-produced set of bunny ears in cardboard cutout and decorated with cotton wool. This may have been something we have come to expect; it feels almost normal, but is it the best way to portray children? Is this all they are capable of being and doing? I wonder what this says to members of the community. How can we expect recognition for the valuable contribution early childhood educators and young children make to the community when we undervalue the children's achievements and abilities? When we send home creativity reducing adult products (CRAP, for short), we do ourselves as well as the children a disservice. This might not be one of your hang-ups, but I feel really strongly about it. Yes, it happens in schools, but is that a good enough reason?

Anne Stonehouse and others, writing in the NSW Curriculum Framework (2002), remind us that we can choose to be cute or authentic with children. It will reflect our image of childhood and it will influence our practice. Let's remind ourselves that children are interesting, informed, capable and changing, but when we consider them as being cute, we seriously underestimate them and our role in the center. Let's be real. Let's be authentic with children.

A colleague shows me a huge, colorful and very expensive piece of climbing equipment in the corner of the garden. Then she shows me an inexpensive set of thin irrigation pipes placed under the ground with a myriad of joints and small plastic taps that, when attached to the garden hose and turned on, create an amazing scientific adventure playground of mud and water. She comments that anyone driving past sees the expensive and colorful climbing equipment and thinks, "That's what children do; they run around and climb all day"; the real action, however, the scientific problem-solving and creative play, is happening on a piece of equipment worth about $50. "The children play on the climbing equipment for the first few weeks of the year," she tells me, "and then they use the rest of the garden, especially this mud and water patch. They play endless hours here, digging, moving the pipes, turning taps on and off, controlling the water, and all for $50. Anyone driving past just doesn't see what they are doing for the rest of the year." There is a political reality in the art and craftwork we send home, in the newsletters we write and in the language we use, and in the way we document the children's learning.

I have written more detailed thoughts about the image of the child in *From Observation to Reflection: A Practitioner's Guide to Programme Planning and Documentation.* If you are interested, I suggest you get a copy and read further. A companion book, *Pancakes and Red Buckets: Creating an Emergent Curriculum with Children Aged Birth to Five* Years (Lubawy 2007), may also assist you in your journey. You can find out more about my current work with my husband and business partner, Peter Law, on our Web site, www.jnpconsulting.com.au.

Cultural richness

> *A child sits in the sand. He has excavated a hole and occupies it fully. The other children shovel sand on top of him. He is sitting, so I am not concerned about him being smothered; I can relax and watch what is happening. Suddenly he stands up, the sand falling away in a shower. He comments, "It's cold under there."*

The educational possibilities are very broad at this stage, and I wonder, where might this be heading and how can we use it? Let's think of a few possibilities, the scientific questions of why sand is colder underneath and warmer on top, about the effects of sunlight and shade, night and day, wetness and dryness. We could measure the temperature and graph the observations or rely on our awareness of heat as experienced with our hands or feet. Which would work the best in this situation? A little biology might be happening, and some math thrown in for good measure.

We could also wander down the path of investigating houses of people who live in very cold or very hot areas. How do they deal with extremes of climate? Before air-conditioning, what did people do for shelter, and how did they construct houses? The subject area then becomes social studies, with a scientific and historical twist.

We can also combine all these ideas and create provocations, experiences and environments that lead the children toward discovering the way people live in different situations, but with the relevance of what we can experience in the here and now of our own center garden! These are invitations to encounter cultural richness in ways that children can relate to. It's about seeing the everyday situation and then finding out what happens here or there. What are the contexts of the human experience? (*To see the world in a grain of sand*, as William Blake wrote.) The only limitations are our own unwillingness to embark on the adventure or our own lack of knowledge. Both can be remedied.

Being inclusive

When I reflect on almost 30 years in the classroom, my memories are of many wonderful children: the really clever children who inspired us all and asked the difficult questions; those who disrupted but were involved and interested; and the children who struggled with learning or getting around. Children at both ends of the educational and ability spectrum inspired and interested me, and I learned a lot about development, learning and education because of them.

My own first experience with including children with disabilities in the preschool environment was with my first preschool appointment. I had been working in a school for specific purposes, and all the children in my class had had additional needs. When I moved to the new center, a couple of my pupils came with me! What a delightful journey it has been to include these and other children in the program. I learned early that it isn't about "remediation" or "therapy." It is about "including" and recognizing the ability of individual children in individual ways.

We have not always been successful, and I have had to admit that the preschool environment is not the best situation for every child. But these children have been in the absolute minority—in fact, there have been only two in 30 years! We are not always able to achieve the impossible. We just get very close to it most of the time.

The individual has always been the key element. If we concentrate on creating environments where children can succeed, where their contributions are valued and used, where they are acknowledged as being capable and competent in their own way instead of being measured against a set of scales, then we are able to address each situation uniquely. Inclusion is much more than integration. It's about making all aspects of the program available to all the children, not removing them for specialized experiences but allowing them to work and play alongside other children. It's more about addressing the situation right now, right here, rather than focusing our intentions on "getting ready for big school." You win some, and you lose some—and this applies to all children, not just the children with additional needs.

An overview

Our observations of children today shape the provisions we make for tomorrow. The ways children respond cause us to reflect and plan ahead, to project where the ideas might lead. It sounds quite ad-hoc, but in fact it does not need to be. We can create an overview for the year, a curriculum overview and plan that brings together the key learning areas from curriculum documents, as well as our knowledge of the topics that children are often interested in. Think broadly, think about the year and then use this as your own structure. Then you will be free to explore and meander with the children. Whenever you wonder if you are meeting the elements of the curriculum, take another look at it and check off the areas already covered. Then you will discover you have achieved much more than you thought possible, but without dictating or controlling the children's learning. Instead, you have acted as a catalyst, a scaffolder, a guide and a provider. These may be the only few years in the child's life when this can happen. Let's not rob children of the experience.

Young Andrew is one of those children who fits in well, but nothing in particular seems to enchant him. I feel I have missed seeing the real Andrew somehow. It concerns me, but no matter what I do, there is not the spark I have hoped for.

One day when some black-winged birds fly overhead announcing their arrival for the winter, I comment, "Winter must be coming. The currawongs are here," and I promise to bring a song about just this topic the next day. Slim Dusty sings the song in question, a song included on a compilation CD put out by ABC Records some years ago.

I play the song as promised:

When the Currawongs come down from the mountains
To the warmer valley country down below
When the Currawongs come down from the timber
It's a sign of rough weather, rain and snow!

I notice a glazed look of pleasure come across Andrew's face.

"I just love Slim Dusty," he tells me with a big sigh of pleasure.

"Yes, I do too," I reply. "Peter and I are going to his concert in a few weeks' time."

"So am I. My poppy is taking me. He loves Slim Dusty too," Andrew adds.

We don't realize then of course that shortly after the concert Slim would pass away, but what an experience for us all. However, the comment that rings in my ears is Andrew talking to his mother on the way out of the room that afternoon. "I had a good idea and she went with it."

The light starts to shine. I have touched his interest, and the rest of the year is a delight as he goes from strength to strength and enthusiasm to enthusiasm. A connection has been made.

Taking care of yourself. Time management

If there is a direct correlation between the imagination and creativity of the adult and that of the children as Ian Broinowski (2002) states in his research, then the way we manage stress and our workload matters, not just to us but also to the children. We owe it to ourselves and to the children to take good care of ourselves by managing time well. In each chapter I have addressed this issue, but here is an opportunity to remind you just how important it is.

A few ideas come to mind:

- You are paid for a fair day's work! Not a fair night and weekend as well. I admit that, at times, we need to put in a bit of additional time, to visit the center on a weekend, to rearrange an environment, or to sit down and write details into a journal—but not every day! When we are faced with this situation, we can sit and complain about it, we can put if off or we can just get on with it. Once the task is finished we are free to get on with our lives, so don't procrastinate—get it done. It pays well in terms of feeling more relaxed and enthusiastic.

- Take time off when you are sick. We are given sick leave for when we are indeed sick. It's not for "taking a sick day," but it can be used as a preventive when we are feeling burnt out. One day can make a big difference to our ability to recover from a cold quickly, and we should not be spreading our viruses around more than we need to.

- Praise yourself. We are often quick to put ourselves down, and believe me, there are plenty of people to do that already, so why should you do that to yourself? Be honest about your abilities, but give yourself some pats on the back for the good job you are doing. A journal about yourself that recognizes your accomplishments will encourage you further.

- Develop a sense of humor. Dr. Shayne Yates and Patricia Cameron-Hill (2001, p. 12) write lightheartedly but earnestly:

  Stress saps stamina and stress steals sleep.
  Stress makes you miserable and prone to weep.
  Stress causes tension and stress makes you sick.
  Ulcers, heart disease and a floppy . . . (I will leave you to complete the poem).

- Be physically active. Shayne and Patricia add (p. 210):

  Walking is possibly the most underrated form of exercise in the world, yet it is so convenient. We can do it anytime, we don't need special clothes or equipment and we can do it on our own, it is easy on the joints and it's free! . . . just 30 minutes daily . . . can reduce the risk of premature death by 65%.

- They also advise us to:
  —get enough sleep;
  —eat well, drink water;
  —watch alcohol consumption;
  —stop smoking and limit the intake of caffeine—take care of yourself; only then can you take care of others.

- Get help when you need it. If you are experiencing power struggles at work, ask someone to assist you in tracking it down and dealing with it. Don't ignore it and hope it will go away; problems such as this tend to just keep growing. Be a leader when you are required to be—there are times to be a friend and there are times to be a leader. Communicate but don't appease. I once had a strange comment from a parent about the emphasis placed on creativity and play when we could be doing a lot more "formal" work in preparation for school. I knew the topic was addressed in the Curriculum Framework. I found the quote and popped it into the next newsletter. She spoke to me later. "I got the message in the newsletter. I had never thought of that before." I didn't have to attack the problem head-on (which makes me really uncomfortable). I had hoped that I could use subtler methods. Of course, sometimes you just have to go head-on and get it over with! Your call!

Using technology

A common comment as we travel around talking to people at workshops is, "I'm not very good on the computer." Well, the computer age is here. We are on the information superhighway, like it or not. I heard the singer Judy Small one evening tell her audience that she felt like a "*piece of roadkill on the information superhighway.*" Don't join her. Go for lessons, ask someone to show you new ideas, read and test out new skills, get faster and more efficient, but do it! Hiding your head in the sand is not the answer. Learn to use the computer, printer, Internet, CD player, DVD player, digital camera—use them often, play with them, have fun, but get to know them. I know how frustrating it can be; I know I still have a few pockets of resistance left that bite me from time to time. Move forward. Don't be crippled by technology. An older friend of mine (she is nearing 80) has a laptop. She goes to Internet cafés when traveling, she uses a cash card, does her banking on the Internet, and pays her bills online. Of course, she gets into a bit of a bother here and there, but it's not usually her fault. It's usually the equipment not working properly. She asks for help when she needs it, and she is never refused. If she can do it, so can you! No excuses.

A computer with spell-check (warning: don't add misspelled words to the dictionary and don't rely 100 percent on the spell-check tool) and grammar programs can save you a lot of embarrassment when you are writing newsletters. Make newsletters as interesting and professional as you can. Take care to make them well and create graphics that attract attention. A good newsletter reflects your professionalism and the quality of the center. Keep equipment up to date and in good repair.

Ethics and privacy

Our words should never cause harm, so be careful what you write in your journal. You may be aware that Ken's mother has a problem with alcohol; she has spoken to you about it and is trying hard to overcome the addiction. This means that Ken is often late arriving. You **don't** write:

Because Ken was late this morning (his mother has trouble getting herself started some mornings; she has a drinking problem), we didn't see the beautiful leaf he brought for us to share until morning snack!

Instead, you write:

Ken and his mother delighted us with a beautiful leaf they found as they walked to preschool this morning. The other children looked at it under the magnifying glass, identifying the colors and inventing new words to describe the exact shades and later took it to the light table to see how light travels through it and how it alters the perception of color. Thanks, Ken. Great idea.

Of course I am being extreme here, but we can easily harm if we are not thinking about the reader. Families delight in the stories of the day, but we don't need to include photographs that humiliate; in fact, let's hope we don't take these pictures even accidentally. Children are not "cute," so don't portray them as being so in your photographs, and please don't go down the "cute things the children said today" pathway; it diminishes them, you and your center. Be respectful with your comments and your photographs.

If you are respectful and aware, then you should not have to consider ethics and privacy issues—you are already covering those issues. Avoid using the surnames of the children in your journal, but I don't see any reason why first names shouldn't be used. It's what you add as comments that makes the difference. Respectful stories expressing the marvelous events and discoveries from the day are not a privacy issue for me; the attitude is what makes the difference. You may disagree with me if you like, but that's where I am coming from. More of an issue is the use of full names on sign-in sheets, or a list of addresses and phone numbers displayed so that anyone can read them. Also, it's the words we use in our ordinary conversations that are the real threat to privacy. (*Oh yes, we often have trouble with him. He comes from a violent family, you know.*") A common comment heard is, "*I don't think she is ready for school yet,*" in a conversation over a meal when staff have time to celebrate a birthday at a public venue after work hours. Keep your conversations in check, please. I am also aware that medical information about allergies or medication can be a source of privacy concern when displayed in a public area. Keep these comments and pieces of information in staff only areas.

Record what?

Let's take one more look at this aspect. It matters what photographs we take, focusing on the work the children are doing rather than on their smiling faces. These photographs are for documentation, not to brighten up the journal with happy snaps. It matters what we write about the photographs. Use thoughtful comments about learning, investigating, exploring, wondering, questioning, thinking and talking rather than the ambiguous and generic, "We had a wonderful time blowing bubbles today." Why did you blow bubbles today? What led up to this event, what questions, comments, and conversations created the opportunity? What did the children say when they were blowing the bubbles? What happened when they sucked in instead of breathed out? How far did the bubbles travel, what made the biggest ones and did anyone discover how to catch them without bursting them? Where might this extend to tomorrow or next week? What are the children learning when they blow bubbles?

So many different and wonderful things happen each and every day; we can't possibly document every question, comment and adventure. Consider documenting things that matter, are of interest and show children developing and learning; tell the learning stories.

Reflections, challenges and considerations

Here are a few research-based challenges from Ian Broinowski (2002, pp. 101–2) that are worth considering.

He concludes that indicators of high-quality care are:

- staff showing genuine interest in helping the children express and explore ideas, while at the same time respecting the needs of other children's personal space;
- staff consistently modifying their approach in response to a child's temperament, cultural background and competence;
- staff relating in a warm and friendly way to the children and to their families;
- staff making sure siblings at the center have opportunities to interact with one another;
- staff being aware of what children find amusing and interesting; and
- staff supporting and encouraging children's pretend play.

Feel free to add your own indicators.

FINALLY

If you have read this book from cover to cover, front to back, then you are now at the end of this particular journey, and so am I! It has been an adventure for me, remembering stories, reflecting on implications, investigating what others have written, reading and talking with people and considering my own in-classroom research. I hope you have learned a lot, because I have. I hope this book at least encourages you so that you feel enthusiastic and competent and that it challenges you to grow in your chosen profession.

At the start of my career, Yvonne Winer spoke about the importance of creativity above all else. She told a story of a child having lunch, biting into a sandwich and discovering the remaining shape made an excellent gun. She cherished the image of a center where this expression of an idea was possible and challenged us to create similar centers of our own. Her words changed me for the better; her encouragement along the way has sustained me in my adventures with young children. I hope that through my words, her message (and the message of her own teachers and mentors and their teachers and mentors through the last 100 or so years) will sustain, challenge and encourage you in your continuing professional journey.

Now I am able to travel, talk with groups, visit centers and read and think about the issues that face those of us who touch the future—the early childhood professionals, teachers, assistants, workers, educators (or whatever term you think we can use). Peter and I have crisscrossed the globe, driving and flying huge distances. It is my hope that for the next years we can continue to do this, staying in touch and bringing the message of respect and enthusiasm to anyone who will listen. Remember to say hello!

References

Ainsworth MDS, Blehar MC, Waters E and Wall S (Eds), 1978, *Patterns of Attachment: A Psychological Study of the Strange Situation*, Erlbaum, Hillsdale, NJ, cited by Dolby R, 2005, in 'Overview of attachment theory and consequences for emotional development', Paper presented at Child Abuse Prevention: Everybody's Business conference.

Angelou M, 2003, *Thriving is Elegant: Words of Inspiration from Maya Angelo*, HMK.LIC.

Ashton-Warner S, 1963, *Teacher*, Penguin, England.

Atkin J, 1993, *Teaching for Effective Learning*, notes from workshop at Griffith and Narrandera NSW.

Banani S, 1987, 'Life's Rainbow', in Martz, Sandra Haleman (Ed), *When I am an Old Woman I Shall Wear Purple*, Papier-Mache Press, Watsonville, USA.

Blake W, 1803, 'Auguries of innocence', in Bronowski J (Ed), *William Blake*, 1958, Penguin Books Ltd, England.

Bowby J, 1958, 'The nature of the child's tie to his mother', International Journal of Psycho- Analysis, XXXIX, pp 1–23.

Bowlby J, 1969, *Attachment and Loss, Vol. 1: Attachment*, Basic Books, New York.

Bowlby J, 1973, *Attachment and Loss, Vol 2: Separation*, Penguin, Harmondswroth, Middlesex.

Bradley L and Bryant PE, 1983, 'Categorizing sounds and learning to read—a causal connection', *Nature*, vol 301, pp 419–21.

Broinowski I, 2002, *Toward Creativity in Early Childhood Education: A study of enchantment, imagination and creativity of an early childhood educator*, self-published sections from PhD Thesis.

Cameron-Hill P and Yates S, 2000, *You Won't Die Laughing!: How to Have Less Stress in Your Life and More Fun*, Argyle Publications, Australia.

Campbell D, 1983, *Introduction to the Musical Brain*, Magnamusic-Baton, Richardson, Texas.

Carson R, 1962, *Silent Spring*, Houghton Mifflin, USA.

Child Care Information Exchange, 2006, *Importance of Outdoor Play*, Exchange Everyday, 17 April.

Child Care Information Exchange, 2006, *Music Promotes Motor Skills*, Exchange Everyday, 19 April.

Child Care Information Exchange, 2007, *Fostering a Love of Nature*, Exchange Everyday, 2 January.

Clay M, 1985, 'Engaging with the School System: A study of interactions in new entrant classrooms', *New Zealand Journal of Educational Studies*, vol 20, no 1, pp 20–38.

Comune di Reggio Emilia, 1996, *Catalogue della mostra*. I Ceno Linguaggi dei Bambini, Reggio Children, Reggio Emilia Italy.

Cunxin Li, 2003, *Mao's Last Dancer*, Penguin, Australia.

Curtis D and Carter M, 2000, *The Art of Awareness: How Observation Can Transform Your Teaching*, St. Paul MN, Redleaf Press.

Curtis D and Carter M, 2003, *Designs for Living and Learning: Transforming Early Childhood Environments*, St. Paul MN, Redleaf Press.

Dahlberg G, 1999, "Early Childhood Pedagogy in a Changing World—A practice-oriented research project troubling dominant discourses within the field of early childhood education," *Unpacking Observation and Documentation: Experiences from Italy, Sweden and Australia* conference papers, Macquarie University 24–25th September.

Davis D (Ed), 1998, *Do's and Don'ts of Inclusive Language*, Media Task Force, Honolulu County Committee on the Status of Women, reprinted (Online) Available <http://honolulu.hawaii.edu/intranet/committees/FacDevCom/guidebk/teachtip/inclusiv.htm> (accessed on 23 January 2008).

de Bono E, 1992, *Six Thinking Hats for Schools (Books 1–4) Resource Book*, Hawker Brownlow, Cheltenham, Victoria.

de Bono E, 2005, *The Six Value Medals: The Essential Tools for Success in the 21st century*, Random House, Sydney.

Dolby R, 2005, 'Overview of attachment theory and consequences for emotional development', Paper presented at Child Abuse Prevention: Everybody's Business conference.

Dowrick S, 1997, *Forgiveness and Other Acts of Love*, Penguin Books, Australia.

Edwards C, Gandini L and Forman G, 1998, *The Hundred Languages of Children*, Ablex Publishing, USA.

Edwards J, 2000, 'The things we steal from children', Paper presented at Early Years in Education Society conference, Perth.

Egan K, 1992, *Imagination in Teaching and Learning*, Routledge, London.

Eisner E, 1985, 'Curriculum ideals for children under eight', 17th National Triennial AECA Conference, September, Brisbane, Australia.

Elliott S (Ed), 2007, *The Outdoor Playspace Naturally: For Children Birth to Five Years*, Pademelon Press, Castle Hill, NSW.

Fleet A, 2001, 'Diversity silenced', in *Unpacking Interpretation: De-constructions from Australia, America and Reggio Emilia*, conference papers from the 6th Unpacking Conference, UNSW. 16–17th July.

Fleet A, Patterson C, Robertson J (Eds), 2006, *Insights: Behind Early Childhood Pedagogical Documentation*, Pademelon Press, Castle Hill, NSW.

Gardner H, 1983, *Frames of Mind: The Theory of Multiple Intelligences*, Harper and Row, New York.

Gardner H, 1991, *The Unschooled Mind*, Basic Books, New York.

Gardner H, 1993, 'A Conversation with Howard Gardner', in *Educational Leadership*, vol 50, no 7, April.

Gardner H, 1996, *Are There Additional Intelligences?*, Harvard Graduate School of Education, Cambridge, Mass.

Greenman J, 1998, *Places for Childhoods: Making Quality Happen in the Real World*, Child Care Information Exchange, Redmond Washington USA.

Greenman J, 2005, *Caring Spaces, Learning Places: Children's Environments That Work*, Child Care Information Exchange, Redmond Washington USA.

Hart B and Risley T, 1995, 'Meaningful differences in the everyday experience of young American children', Paul H. Brookes Publishing Co. cited in Talaris Research

Institute, 2005, *Look at the Big Bubbles!*, Available <http://www.talaris.org/spotlight_bubbles.htm> (accessed 23 January 2008).

Hoff E and Naigles L, 2002, 'How children use input to acquire a lexicon', *Child Development*, 73, 418–33 cited in Talaris Research Institute, 2005, *Look at the Big Bubbles!*, Available <http://www.talaris.org/spotlight_bubbles.htm> (accessed 23 January 2008).

Johnson D, Johnson R and Holubec EJ, 1988, *Cooperation in the Classroom*, Interaction Book Company, Edina, USA.

Katz L, 1998, 'What can we learn from Reggio Emilia?' In Edwards C, Gandini L and Forman G, 1998, *The Hundred Languages of Children: The Reggio Emilia Approach Advanced Reflections*, Ablex Publishing, USA.

King ML, 1963, 'I have a dream', speech delivered in Washing DC, accessed <http://www.americanrhetoric.com/speeches/mlkihaveadream.htm>.

Kolbe U, 2001, *Rapunzel's Supermarket*, Peppinot Press, Byron Bay.

Kolbe U, 2005, *It's Not a Bird Yet: The Drama of Drawing*, Peppinot Press, Byron Bay.

Lazear D, 1999, *Eight Ways of Knowing: Teaching for Multiple Intelligences*, Hawker Brownlow Education, Australia.

Lovelock J, 1979, *Gaia: A New Look at Life on Earth*, Oxford University Press, Oxford.

Lowrie T, 1999, *Lego Loss Reignites Traditional vs Electronic Toy*, available <http://news.csu.edu.au/director/latestnews/science.cfm?itemID=A9BA7FCAD2BBF627CA29A794E25DDD69&printtemplate=release> (accessed 23 January 2008).

Lubawy J and Jarratt B, 1999, *Building Walls of Wombats: Constructing Knowledge with Young Children*, Pademelon Press, Castle Hill, New South Wales.

Lubawy J, 2006, *From Observation to Reflection: A Practitioner's Guide to Programme Planning and Documentation*, Joy and Pete Consulting, Wagga Wagga.

Lubawy J, 2007, *Pancakes and Red Buckets: Creating an Emergent Curriculum with Children Aged Birth to Five Years*, Joy and Pete Consulting, Wagga Wagga.

Malaguzzi L, 1998a, 'No way. The Hundred is There', in Edwards C, Gandini L and Forman G, 1998, *The Hundred Languages of Children*, Ablex Publishing, USA.

Malaguzzi L, 1998b, 'History, Ideas, and Basic Philosophy: An Interview with Lella Gandini' in Edwards C, Gandini L and Forman G, 1998, *The Hundred Languages of Children*, Ablex Publishing, USA.

Maslow AH, 1943, 'A theory of human motivation', *Psychological Review* 50, pp 370–96.

Miller K, 1985, *Ages and Stages: Developmental Descriptions & Activities Birth Through Eight Years*, TelShare Publishing Co. Inc, USA.

Miller K, 1990, *More Things to Do with Toddlers and Twos*, TelShare Publishing Co. Inc, USA.

Miller K, 1994, *Learning Environments for Young Children*, Workshop, Wagga Wagga.

Miller, K. 1984, *Things to Do with Toddlers and Twos*. TelShare Publishing Co. Inc, USA.

Montessori M, 1973, *The Absorbent Mind*, Kalakshetra, Madras, India.

Mulligan J, 2007, *Promoting Structural Thinking in the Early Mathematics Curriculum*, available <http://cmslive.curriculum.edu.au/leader/default.asp?id=15604>, (accessed 23 January 2008).

Mulligan JT, Mitchelmore MC and Prescott A, 2006, 'Integrating concepts and processes in early mathematics: The Australian Pattern and Structure Mathematics Awareness Project (PASMAP)', *Proceedings of the 30th annual conference of the International Group for the Psychology of Mathematics Education*, Prague, July 2006, cited in Mulligan, J. 2007 *Promoting Structural Thinking in the Early Mathematics*

Curriculum, Curriculum Leadership, Vol 5, Issue 40, available <http://cmslive. curriculum.edu.au/leader/default.asp?id=15604> (accessed 23 January 2008).

Mulligan JT, Prescott A, Papic M and Mitchelmore MC, 2006, *Improving Early Numeracy Through a Pattern and Structure Mathematics Awareness Program (PASMAP)*, Proceedings of the 29th annual conference of the Mathematics Education Research Group of Australasia, Canberra, MERGA, cited in Mulligan J, 2007, *Promoting Structural Thinking in the Early Mathematics Curriculum*, Curriculum Leadership, Vol 5, Issue 40, available <http://cmslive.curriculum.edu.au/leader/default.asp?id=15604>, (accessed 23 January 2008).

Myers-Walls JA (Ed), 2008, Talking With Children When the Talking Gets Tough, available <http://supportofficer.org/children/talkingchildren.htm> (accessed 23 January 2008).

Nicholson S, 1974, 'How not to cheat children: The theory of loose part', in Coates G (Ed), *Alternate Learning Environments*, Dowden, Hutchinson and Ross, Stroudsberg, USA cited in Greenman J, 2005, *Caring Spaces, Learning Places: Children's Environments That Work*, Child Care Information Exchange, Redmond Washington, USA.

Orff C, 1978, *The Schoolwork*, Translated by Murray M, SchottMusic Corporation, New York cited in Lazear D, 1999, *Teaching for Multiple Intelligences*, Hawker Brownlow Education, Australia.

Pelo A, 2007, *The Language of Art: Inquiry-Based Studio Practices in Early Childhood Settings*, Redleaf Press, St Paul, MN.

Platt J quoted in Ferguson M, 1980, *The Aquarian Conspiracy: Personal and Social Transformation in the 1980's*, JP Tarcher, Los Angeles.

Rinaldi C, 1998, 'Projected curriculum constructed through documentation—Progettazione: An interview with Lella Gandini' in Edwards C,Gandini L and Forman G, 1998, *The Hundred Languages of Children*, Ablex Publishing, USA.

Rinaldi C, 2001, 'Documentation and assessment: What is the relationship?' in Giudici C, Rinaldi C and Krechevsky M (Eds), *Making Learning Visible: Children as Individual and Group Learners*, Reggio Children, Reggio Emilia, Italy, pp 78–89.

Robertson J, 2006, 'Reconsidering our images of children: What shapes our educational thinking?' in Fleet A, Patterson C and Robertson J, 2006, *Insights: Behind Early Childhood Pedagogical Documentation*, Pademelon Press, Castle Hill, NSW, pp 37–54.

Rockwell R, Sherwood E and Williams R, 1983, *Hug a Tree*, Gryphon House, USA.

Rockwell R, Williams R and Sherwood E, 1992, *Everybody Has a Body*, Gryphon House, Maryland USA.

Russell P, 1983, *The Global Brain: Speculations on the Evolutionary Leap to Planetary Consciousness*, JP Tarcher, Los Angeles.

Russell S and Edwards J, 2006, *The Things We Steal From Children*, available <http://www.idec2006.org/pdf/edwards_steal.pdf> (Accessed 23 January 2008).

Shafer A, 2001, Keynote Address, An International Festival of Learning: Fremantle, personal reflection.

Schiller P, 1999, *Start Smart!*, Gryphon House, Maryland USA.

Schiller P, 2001, *Creating Readers*, Gryphon House, Maryland USA.

Sherwood E, Williams R and Rockwell R, 1990, *More Mudpies to Magnets*, Gryphon House, Maryland USA.

Silberg J and Schiller P, 2002, *The Complete Book of Rhymes, Songs, Poems, Fingerplays and Chants*, Gryphon House, Maryland USA.

Silberg J, 2005, *Reading Games for Young Children*, Gryphon House, Maryland USA.

Smith D and Goldhaber J, 2004, *Poking, Pinching & Pretending*, Redleaf Press, St Paul, USA.

Stevenson C and Kolbe U, 1999, *Living and Learning Creatively*, workshop at Macquarie University NSW, (personal reflection).

Stonehouse A et.al, 2002, *NSW Curriculum Framework: The Practice of Relationships*, NSW Department of Community Services.

Suzuki D, 2003, *A David Suzuki Collection: A Lifetime of Ideas*, Greystone Books, Vancouver.

Talaris Research Institute, 2005, *Look at the Big Bubbles!*, available<http://www.talaris.org/spotlight_bubbles.htm> (accessed 23 January 2008).

Te Whāriki: He Whāriki Mātauranga mōngā Mokopuna o Aotearoa, New Zealand Early Childhood Curriculum.

Thomas N, Mulligan JT and Goldin GA, 2002, 'Children's representations and cognitive structural development of the counting sequence 1–100', *Journal of Mathematical Behavior*, 21, 117–133.

University of Maine Cooperative Extension Bulletin #4077, 2007, *Winning Ways to Talk with Young Children*, available<http://www.umext.maine.edu/onlinepubs/htmpubs/4077.htm> (accessed 23 January 2008).

Williams R, Cunningham D and Lubawy J, 2005, *Preschool Math*, Gryphon House, USA.

Winer Y, 2005, *Stories for Telling*, Pademelon Press, Castle Hill, New South Wales.

Winer Y, 2006, *Dance Shaba Dance! and Other Puppet Stories*, The Beaded Frog Books, Toowoomba, Australia.

Yates S and Cameron-Hill P, 2001, *You Won't Die Laughing! How to Have Less Stress in Your Life and More Fun*, Argyle Publications, Australia.

Zollo L, 2006, 'Co-constructing competent babies and mothers'. *The Challenge*, vol 9, no 4, February, Reggio Emilia Information Exchange, Hawthorn Australia.

Picture books

Allen P, 1982, *Who Sank the Boat?*, Thomas Nelson, Melbourne, Australia.

Browne E, 1994, *Handa's Surprise*, Walker Books, London.

Carle E, 1991, *The Tiny Seed and the Giant Flower*, Simon and Schuster Children's Publishing, USA.

Dodd L, 1993, *Hairy Maclary from Donaldson's Dairy*, Puffin Books, England.

Dugan M and Power M, 1994, *Daisy Drew an Elephant*, Moondrake, Victoria.

Fox M, 1986, *Hattie and the Fox*, Scholastic Press, Lindfield NSW.

Fox M, 1989, *Night Noises*, Omnibus Books, Adelaide.

Germein K, 1999, *Big Rain Coming*, Clarion Books, New York.

Gurney N, 1986, *The King, the Mice and the Cheese*, HarperCollins, USA.

Gurney N and Gurney E, 1989, *The King, the Mice and the Cheese*, Random House, USA.

Hunt N, 1982, *Whistle up the Chimney*, William Collins, Australia.

Joose B, 1991, *Mama, Do You Love Me?*, Chronicle Books, San Francisco.

Joose B, 2005, *Papa, Do You Love Me?*, Chronicle Books, San Francisco.

Pak, S. 1999, *dear juno*, Puffin Books, New York.

Scott A, 1992, *On Mother's Lap*, Clarion Books, New York.

Wagner J, 1975, *Aranea, A Story About a Spider*, Kestral Books, Australia.

Winer Y, 1985, *Mr Brown's Magnificent Apple Tree*, Ashton Scholastic, Gosford, Australia.

Winer Y, 2005, 'Brolga's Dance' in *Stories for Telling*, Pademelon Press, Castle Hill, NSW.

Music CDs

Dusty Slim. 1988. "When Currawongs Come Down," on Ian McNamara's *Australia All Over Two*. ABC Records, Australia.

Ecker Haylie, Eos Chater, Tania Davis, and Gay-Yee Westerhoff. 2000. *Bond Born*. Decca.

Jewish Traditional et al., 1997. *Jewish Favorites*. Centaur.

The Baby Einstein Music Box Orchestra. 2000. *Baby Mozart*. The Baby Einstein Music Company LLC.

Index